D0911453

A REASON FOR THE HOPE WITHIN

JOHN HENRY NEWMAN

A REASON FOR THE HOPE WITHIN

Sermons on The Theory of Religious Belief

Dimension Books
Denville, New Jersey 07834

First America Printing 1985
for
Dimension Books, Inc.
P.O. Box 811
Denville, N.J. 07834

ISBN 0-87193-219-9

ADVERTISEMENT.

Of the following Sermons, the First and Fifth were preached by the Author in Vice-Chancellor's Preaching Turns; the Second in his own; the Third, Fourth, Sixth, Seventh, and Eighth, in his turns as Select Preacher.

The Six which close the Volume, since 1832, were preached on such casual opportunities as the kindness of private friends has afforded him.

Though he has employed himself for the most part in discussing portions of one and the same subject, yet he need scarcely say, that his Volume has not the method, completeness, or scientific exactness in the use of language, which are necessary for a formal Treatise upon it; nor, indeed, was such an undertaking compatible with the nature and circumstances of the composition.

Littlemore, Feb. 4, 1843.

CONTENTS.

SERMON I.

THE PHILOSOPHICAL TEMPER, FIRST ENJOINED BY THE GOSPEL.

Preached July 2, 1826, Act Sunday.

JOHN viii. 12.

SERMON II.

THE INFLUENCE OF NATURAL AND REVEALED RELIGION RESPECTIVELY.

Preached on Easter Tuesday, April 13, 1830.

1 JOHN i. 1—3.

SERMON III.

THE USURPATIONS OF REASON.

Preached December 11, 1831.

MATT. xi. 19.

SERMON IV.

PERSONAL INFLUENCE, THE MEANS OF PROPAGATING THE TRUTH.

Preached January 22, 1832.

HEB. xi. 34.

SERMON V.

ON JUSTICE, AS A PRINCIPLE OF DIVINE GOVERNANCE.

Preached April 8, 1832.

JER. viii. 11.

SERMON VI.

CONTEST BETWEEN FAITH AND SIGHT.

Preached May 27, 1832.

1 JOHN v. 4.

SERMON VII.

HUMAN RESPONSIBILITY, AS INDEPENDENT OF CIRCUMSTANCES.

Preached November 4, 1832.

GEN. iii. 13.

SERMON XII.

EXPLICIT AND IMPLICIT REASON.

Preached on St. Peter's Day, 1840.

1 PET. iii. 15.

SERMON XIII.

WISDOM, AS CONTRASTED WITH FAITH AND WITH BIGOTRY.

Preached on Whit-Tuesday, June 1, 1841.

1 COR. ii. 15.

SERMON XIV.

THE THEORY OF DEVELOPMENTS IN RELIGIOUS DOCTRINE.

Preached on the Purification, 1843.

LUKE ii. 19.

SERMON I.

THE PHILOSOPHICAL TEMPER, FIRST ENJOINED BY THE GOSPEL.

Preached July 2, 1826, Act Sunday.

JOHN viii. 12.

" Then spake Jesus again unto them, saying, I am the Light of the world."

FEW charges have been more frequently urged by unbelievers against Revealed Religion, than that it is hostile to the advance of philosophy and science. That it has discouraged the cultivation of literature can never with any plausibility be maintained, since it is evident that the studies connected with the history and interpretation of the Scriptures have, more than any others, led to inquiries into the languages, writings, and events of ancient times. Christianity has always been a learned religion; it came into the world as the offspring of an elder system, to which it was indebted for much which it contained, and which its professors were obliged continually to consult.

B

The Pagan philosopher, on enrolling himself a member of the Christian Church, was invited, nay, required, to betake himself to a line of study almost unknown to the schools of Greece. The Jewish books were even written in a language which he did not understand, and opened to his view an account of manners and customs very different from those with which he was familiar. The writings of the ancients were to be collected, and their opinions examined ; and thus those studies which are peculiarly called learned would form the principal employment of one who wished to be the champion of the Christian faith. The philosopher might speculate, but the theologian must submit to learn.

It cannot, then, be maintained that Christianity has proved unfavourable to literary pursuits; yet, from the very encouragement it gives to these, an opposite objection has been drawn, as if on that very account it impeded the advancement of philosophical and scientific knowledge. It has been urged, with considerable plausibility, that the attachment which it has produced to the writings of the ancients has been prejudicial to the discovery of new truths, by creating a jealousy and dislike of whatever was contrary to received opinions. And thus Christianity has been represented as a system which stands in the way of improvement, whether in politics, education, or science; as if it were adapted to the state of knowledge, and conducive to the happiness, of the age in which it was introduced, but a positive evil

in more enlightened times; because, from its claim
to infallibility, it cannot itself change, and therefore
must ever be endeavouring to bend opinion to its own
antiquated views.   Not to mention the multitude of
half-educated men who are avowedly hostile to Revealed Religion, and who watch every new discovery
or theory in science, in hope that something to its dis-
advantage may thence be derived, it is to be lamented
that many even of the present respectable advocates
of improvements in the condition of society, and
patrons of general knowledge, seem to consider the
interests of the human race quite irreconcileable with
those of the Christian Church; and though they
think it indecorous or unfeeling to attack religion
openly, yet appear confidently to expect that the
progress of discovery and general cultivation of the
human mind must terminate in the fall of Christianity.

It must be confessed that the conduct of Christians has sometimes given countenance to these erroneous views respecting the nature and tendency of
Revealed Religion.   Too much deference has been
paid to ancient literature.   Admiration of the genius
displayed in its writings, an imagination excited
by the consideration of its very antiquity, not unfrequently the pride of knowledge and a desire of
appearing to be possessed of a treasure which the
many do not enjoy, have led men to exalt the sentiments of former ages to the disparagement of
modern ideas.   With a view, moreover, to in-

crease (as they have supposed) the value and dignity of the sacred volume, others have been induced
to set it forth as a depository of all truth, philosophical as well as religious ; although St. Paul seems
to limit its utility to profitableness for doctrine, re-
proof, correction, and instruction in righteousness.
Others, again, have been too diligent and too hasty
in answering every frivolous and isolated objection to
the words of Scripture, which has been urged,—nay,
which they fancied might possibly be urged,—from
successive discoveries in science ; too diligent, because
their minute solicitude has occasioned them to lose
sight of the Christian evidence as a whole, and to
magnify the objection, as if (though it were unanswer-
able) it could really weigh against the mass of argument producible on the other side ; and too hasty
because, had they been patient, succeeding discoveries would perhaps of themselves have solved for
them the objection, without the interference of a
controversialist. The ill consequences of such a procedure are obvious : the objection has been recognized as important, while the solution offered has too
often been inadequate or unsound. To feel jealous
and appear timid, on witnessing the enlargement of
scientific knowledge, is almost to acknowledge that
there may be some contrariety between it and Revelation.

Our Saviour, in the text, calls Himself the Light
of the world ; as David had already said, in words

which especially belong to this place and this day, "The Lord is my Light;" and though He so speaks of Himself as bringing religious knowledge to an ignorant and apostate race, yet we have no reason to suppose that He forbids lawful knowledge of any kind, and we cannot imagine that He would promulgate, by His inspired servants, doctrines which contradict previous truths which He has written on the face of nature.

The objection to Christianity, to which the foregoing remarks relate, may be variously answered.

First, by referring to the fact that the greatest Philosophers of modern times—the founders of the new school of discovery, and those who have most extended the boundaries of our knowledge—have been forced to submit their reason to the Gospel; a circumstance which, independent of the argument for the strength of the Christian evidence which the conviction of such men affords, at least shows that Revealed Religion cannot be very unfavourable to scientific inquiries, when those who sincerely acknowledged the former still distinguished themselves above others in the latter.

Again, much might be said on the coincidence which exists between the general principles which the evidence for Revelation presupposes, and those on which inquiries into nature proceed. Science and Revelation agree in supposing that nature is governed by uniform and settled laws. Scripture, properly understood, is decisive in removing all those irregular agents which are supposed to interrupt, at their own pleasure, the order of nature. Almost every religion but that of the Bible and those derived from it, has supposed the existence of an indefinite number of beings, to a certain extent independent of each other, able to interfere in the affairs of life, and whose interference (supposing it to exist) being reducible to no law, took away all hope of obtaining any real information concerning the actual system of the universe. On the other hand, the inspired writers are express in tracing all miraculous occurrences to the direct interposition, or at least the permission of the Deity ; and since they also imply that miracles are displayed, not at random, but with a purpose, their declarations in this respect entirely agree with the deductions which scientific observation has made concerning the general operation of established laws, and the absence of any arbitrary interference with them on the part of beings exterior to the present course of things. The supposition, then, of a system of established laws, on which all philosophical investigation is conducted, is also the very foundation on which the evidence for Revealed Religion rests. It is the more necessary to insist upon this, because some writers have wished to confuse the Jewish and Christian faiths with those other religions and those popular superstitions, which are framed on no principle, and supported by no pretence of reasoning.

Without enlarging, however, on arguments of this

nature, it is proposed now to direct attention to the moral character which both the Jewish and Christian religions hold up as the excellence and perfection of human nature; for we shall find that some of those habits of mind which are throughout the Bible represented as alone pleasing in the sight of God, are the very habits which are necessary for success in scientific investigation, and without which it is quite impossible to extend the sphere of our knowledge. If this be so, then the fact is accounted for without difficulty, why the most profound philosophers have acknowledged the claims of Christianity upon them. And further, considering that the character which Scripture draws of the virtuous man as a whole is (what may be called) an original character,—only the scattered traces of it being found in authors unacquainted with the Bible,—an argument will almost be established in favour of Christianity, as having conferred an intellectual as well as a spiritual benefit on the world.

For instance, it is obvious that to be in earnest in seeking the truth is an indispensable requisite for finding it. Indeed, it would not be necessary to notice so evident a proposition, had it not been for the strange conduct of the ancient philosophers in their theories concerning nature and man. There seems to have been but one or two of them who were serious and sincere in their inquiries and teaching. Most of them considered speculations on philosophical subjects rather in the light of an amusement than of a grave employment,—as an exercise for ingenuity, or an indulgence of fancy,—to display their powers, to collect followers, or for the sake of gain.   Indeed, it seems incredible that any men, who were really in earnest in their search after truth, should have begun with theorizing, or have imagined that a system which they were conscious they had invented almost without data, should happen, when applied to the actual state of things, to harmonize with the numberless and diversified phenomena of the world. Yet, though it seems to be so obvious a position when stated, that in forming any serious theory concerning nature, we must begin with investigation, to the exclusion of fanciful speculation or deference to human authority, it was not generally recognized or received as such, till a Christian philosopher forced it upon the attention of the world.   And surely he was supported by the uniform language of the whole Bible, which tells us that truth is too sacred and religious a thing to be sacrificed to the mere gratification of the fancy, or amusement of the mind, or party spirit, or the prejudices of education, or attachment (however amiable) to the opinions of human teachers, or any of those other feelings which the ancient philosophers suffered to influence them in their professedly grave and serious discussions.

Again : modesty, patience, and caution, are dispositions of mind quite as requisite in philosophical inquiries as seriousness and earnestness, though not so obviously requisite. Rashness of assertion, hastiness in drawing conclusions, unhesitating reliance on our own acuteness and powers of reasoning, are inconsistent with the homage which nature exacts of those who would know her hidden wonders. She refuses to reveal her mysteries to those who come otherwise than in the humble and reverential spirit of learners and disciples. So, again, that love of paradox which would impose upon her a language different from that which she really speaks, is as unphilosophical as it is unchristian. Again, indulgence of the imagination, though a more specious fault, is equally hostile to the spirit of true philosophy, and has misled the noblest among the ancient theorists, who seemed to think they could not go wrong while following the natural impulses and suggestions of their own minds ; and were conscious to themselves of no low and unworthy motive influencing them in their speculations.

Here, too, may be mentioned the harm which has been done to the interests of science by excessive attachment to system. The love of order and regularity, and that perception of beauty which is most keen in highly gifted minds, has too often led men astray in their scientific researches. From seeing but detached parts of the system of nature, they have been carried on, without data, to arrange, supply, and complete. They have been impatient of knowing but in part, and of waiting for future dis-

coveries; they have inferred much from slender premises, and conjectured when they could not prove.
It is by a tedious discipline that the mind is taught
to overcome those baser principles which impede it
in philosophical investigation, and to moderate those
nobler faculties and feelings which are prejudicial when
in excess. To be dispassionate and cautious, to be fair
in discussion, to give to each phenomenon which
nature successively presents its due weight, can-
didly to admit those which militate against our own
theory, to be willing to be ignorant for a time, to
submit to difficulties, and patiently and meekly proceed, waiting for further light, is a temper (whether
difficult or not at this day) little known to the
heathen world; yet it is the only temper in which we
can hope to become interpreters of nature, and it is
the very temper which Christianity sets forth as the
perfection of our moral character.

Still further, we hear much said in praise of the
union of scientific men, of that spirit of brotherhood
which should join together natives of different countries as labourers in a common cause. But were the
philosophers of ancient times influenced by this
spirit? In vain shall we look among them for the
absence of rivalry; and much less can we hope to
find that generosity of mind, which in its desire of
promoting the cause of science, considers it a slight
thing to be deprived of the credit of a discovery
which is really its due. They were notoriously jealous
of each other, and anxious for their personal conse-

quence, and treasured up their supposed discoveries with miserable precaution, allowing none but a chosen few to be partakers of their knowledge. On the contrary, it was Christianity which first brought into play on the field of the world the principles of charity, generosity, disregard of self and country, in the prospect of the universal good; and which suggested the idea of a far-spreading combination, peaceful yet secure.

It cannot be denied, however, that the true philosophical spirit did not begin to prevail till many ages after the preaching of Christianity, nay, till times comparatively of recent date; and it has, in consequence, been maintained that our own superiority over the ancients in general knowledge, is not owing to the presence of the Christian religion among us, but to the natural progress of improvement in the world. And doubtless it may be true, that though a divine philosophy had never been given us from above, we might still have had a considerable advantage over the ancients in the method and extent of our scientific acquirements. Still, admitting this, it is also true that Scripture was, in matter of fact, the first to describe and inculcate that single-minded, modest, cautious, and generous spirit, which was, after a long time, found so necessary for success in the prosecution of philosophical researches. And though the interval between the propagation of Christianity and the rise of modern science is certainly very long, yet it may be fairly maintained that the philosophy of the Gospel had no opportunity to extend itself in the province of matter till modern times. It is not surprising if the primitive Christians, amid their difficulties and persecutions, and being for the most part individuals in the less educated ranks of life, should have given birth to no new school for investigating nature ; and the learned men who from time to time joined them were naturally scholars in the defective philosophies of Greece, and followed their masters in their physical speculations ; and having more important matters in hand, took for granted what they had no means of ascertaining. Nor is it wonderful, considering how various is the subject-matter, and how multiform have been the developments of Christianity at successive eras, that the true principles of scientific research were not elicited in the long subsequent period. Perhaps the trials and errors through which the Church has passed in the times which have preceded us, are to be its experience in ages to come.

It may be asked how it comes to pass, if a true philosophical temper is so allied to that which the Scriptures inculcate as the temper of a Christian, that any men should be found distinguished for discoveries in science, who yet are ill-disposed towards those doctrines which Revelation enjoins upon our belief. The reason may be this : the humility and teachableness which the Scripture precepts inculcate are connected with principles more solemn and doctrines more awful than those which are necessary for the temper of mind in which scientific investigation must be conducted ; and though the Christian spirit is admirably fitted to produce the tone of thought and inquiry which leads to the discovery of truth, yet a slighter and less profound humility will do the same. The philosopher has only to confess that he is liable to be deceived by false appearances and reasonings, to be biassed by prejudice, and led astray by a warm fancy; he is humble because sensible he is ignorant, cautious because he knows himself to be fallible, docile because he really desires to learn. But Christianity, in addition to this confession, re-quires him to acknowledge himself to be a rebel in the sight of God, and a breaker of that fair and goodly order of things which the Creator once estab-lished. The philosopher confesses himself to be im-perfect ; the Christian feels himself to be sinful and corrupt. The infirmity of which the philosopher must be conscious is but a relative infirmity—imper-fection as opposed to perfection, of which there are infinite degrees. Thus he believes himself placed in a certain point of the scale of beings, and that there are beings nearer to perfection than he is, others farther removed from it. But the Christian acknowledges that he has fallen away from that rank in creation which he originally held; that he has passed a line, and is in consequence not merely im-perfect, but weighed down with positive, actual evil. Now there is little to lower a man in his own opinion, in his believing that he holds a certain definite sta-

tion in an immense series of creatures, and is in
consequence removed, by many steps, from perfection; but there is much very revolting to the minds
of many, much that is contrary to their ideas of harmony and order, and the completeness of the system
of nature, and much at variance with those feelings
of esteem with which they are desirous of regarding
themselves, in the doctrine that man is disgraced and
degraded from his natural and original rank; that
he has, by sinning, introduced a blemish into the
work of God; that he is guilty in the court of
heaven, and is continually doing things odious in
the sight of the Divine holiness. And as the whole
system of the Christian faith depends upon this doctrine, since it was to redeem man from deserved
punishment that Christ suffered on the cross, and in
order to strengthen him in his endeavours to cleanse
himself from sin, and prepare for heaven, that the
Holy Spirit has come to rule the Church, it is not
wonderful that men are found, admirable for their
philosophical temper and their success in investigating nature, and yet unworthy disciples in the school
of the Gospel.

Such men often regard Christianity as a slavish
system, which is prejudicial to the freedom of thought,
the aspirations of genius, and the speculations of enterprise; an unnatural system, which sets out with
supposing that the human mind is out of order, and
consequently bends all its efforts to overthrow the
constitution of feeling and belief with which man

is born, and to make him a being for which nature never intended him; and a pernicious system, which unfits men for this life by fixing their thoughts on another, and which, wherever consistently acted upon, infallibly leads (as it often has led) to the encouragement of the monastic spirit, and the extravagances of fanaticism.

Although, then, Christianity seems to have been the first to give to the world the pattern of the true spirit of philosophical investigation, yet, as the principles of science are, in process of time, more fully developed, and become more independent of the religious system, there is much danger lest the philosophical school should be found to separate from the Christian Church, and at length disown the parent to whom it has been so greatly indebted. And this evil has in a measure befallen us; that it does not increase, we must look to that early religious training, to which there can be no doubt all persons—those in the higher as well as in the poorer classes of the community—should be submitted.

To conclude. The ignorance of the first preachers of Christianity has been often insisted on, particularly by the celebrated historian of the Roman Empire, as a presumption or proof of their hostility to all enlightened and liberal philosophy. If, however, as has been contended, from the precepts they delivered, the best canons may be drawn up for scientific investigation, the fact will only tend to prove that *they* could not, unassisted, have originated or selected precepts so enlarged and so profound; and thus will contribute something to the strength of those accumulated probabilities, which on other grounds are so overpowering, that they spoke not of themselves, but as they were moved by the inspiration of God Himself.

SERMON II.

THE INFLUENCE OF NATURAL AND REVEALED
RELIGION RESPECTIVELY.

Preached on Easter Tuesday, April 13, 1830.

1 John i. 1—3.

" That which was from the beginning, which we have heard,
which we have seen with our eyes, which we have looked
upon, and our hands have handled, of the Word of life; (For
the Life was manifested, and we have seen It, and bear witness, and show unto you that Eternal Life, which was with the
Father, and was manifested unto us;) That which we have seen
and heard declare we unto you, that ye also may have fellowship with us."

THE main purpose of our Saviour's incarnation, as
far as we are permitted to know it, was that of re-
conciling us to God, and purchasing for us eternal
life by His sufferings and death. This purpose was
accomplished when He said, " It is finished," and gave
up the ghost.

But on His rising from the dead, He extended to
us two additional acts of grace, as preparatory to the
future blessing, and of which, as well as of our resur-

rection, that miracle itself was made the evidence. "Go ye, teach all nations, baptizing them in the name of the Father, and of the Son, and of the Holy Ghost." In this commission to His disciples was intimated, on the one hand, His merciful design of " gathering together in one the children of God that were scattered abroad," by the gracious operation of the Holy Spirit ; and on the other hand His intended grant of a system of religious truth, grounded on that mysterious economy of Divine Providence, in which His own incarnation occupies the principal place.

It is proposed, in the following discourse, to treat of a subject connected with the latter of these two great Christian blessings—viz. to attempt to determine the relation which this revealed system of doctrine and precept bears to that of Natural Religion, and to compare the two together in point of practical efficacy.   Those other and still greater mercies of the Christian covenant have been mentioned only, lest, in discussing the subject of religious knowledge, any disregard should be implied of those fundamental doctrines of our faith, the atonement, and the abiding presence of the Holy Spirit in the Church.

Now, in investigating the connexion between Natural and Revealed Religion, it is necessary to explain in what sense religious doctrines of any kind can with propriety be called natural.   For from the abuse of the term " Natural Religion," many persons will not allow the use of it at all.

When, then, religion of some sort is said to be *natural*, it is not here meant that any religious system has been actually traced out by unaided Reason. We know of no such system, because we know of no time or country in which human Reason *was* unaided. Scripture informs us that revelations were granted to the first fathers of our race, concerning the nature of God and man's duty to Him ; and scarcely a people can be named, among whom there are not traditions, not only of the existence of powers exterior to this visible world, but also of their actual interference with the course of nature, followed up by religious communications to mankind from them. The Creator has never left Himself without such witness as might anticipate the conclusions of Reason, and support a wavering conscience and perplexed faith. No people (to speak in general terms) has been denied a revelation from God, though but a portion of the world has enjoyed an authenticated revelation.

Admitting this fully, let us speak of *the fact ;* of the actual state of religious belief of pious men in the heathen world, as attested by their writings still extant ; and let us call this attainable creed Natural Religion.

Now in the first place, it is obvious that Conscience is the essential principle and sanction of Religion in the mind. Conscience implies a relation between the soul and a something exterior, and that moreover superior, to itself; a relation to an excellence which it does not possess, and to a tribunal over which it has

no power. And since the more closely this inward
monitor is respected and followed, the clearer, the
more exalted, and the more varied its dictates become, and the standard of excellence is ever outstrip-
ping, while it guides, our obedience, a moral conviction is thus at length obtained of the unapproachable nature as well as the supreme authority of That,
whatever it is, which is the object of the mind's contemplation.   Here, then, at once, we have the elements of a religious system ; for what is Religion but
the system of relations existing between us and a
Supreme Power, claiming our habitual obedience :
"the blessed and only Potentate, who only hath immortality, dwelling in light unapproachable, whom no
man hath seen or can see ?"

Further, Conscience implies a difference in the
nature of actions, the power of acting in this way
or that as we please, and an obligation of acting
in one particular way in preference to all others ; and
since the more our moral nature is improved, the
greater inward power of improvement it seems to
possess, a view is laid open to us both of the capa-
bilities and prospects of man, and the awful importance of that work which the law of his being lays
upon him.   And thus the presentiment of a future
life, and of a judgment to be passed upon present conduct, with rewards and punishments annexed, forms
an article, more or less distinct, in the creed of Natural Religion.

Moreover, since the inward law of Conscience

brings with it no proof of its truth, and commands attention to it on its own authority, all obedience to it is of the nature of Faith; and habitual obedience implies the direct exercise of a clear and vigorous faith in the truth of its suggestions, triumphing over opposition both from within and without; quieting the murmurs of Reason, perplexed with the disorders of the present scheme of things, and subduing the appetites, clamorous for goods which promise an immediate and keen gratification.

While Conscience is thus ever the sanction of Natural Religion, it is, when improved, the rule of Morals also. But here is a difference : it is, as such, essentially religious ; but in Morals it is not necessarily a guide, only in proportion as it happens to be refined and strengthened in individuals. And here is a solution of objections which have been made to the existence of the moral sense, on the ground of the discordancy which exists among men as to the excellence or demerit of particular actions. These objections only go to prove the uncertain character (if so be) of the inward law of right and wrong ; but are not, even in their form, directed against the certainty of that general religious sense, which is implied in the remorse and vague apprehension of evil which the transgression of Conscience occasions.

Still, unformed and incomplete as is this law by nature, it is quite certain that obedience to it is attended by a continually growing expertness in the science of Morals. A mind, habitually and honestly conforming itself to its own full sense of duty, will at length enjoin or forbid with an authority second only to an inspired oracle. Moreover, in a heathen country, it will be able to discriminate with precision between the right and wrong in traditionary superstitions, and will thus elicit confirmation of its faith even out of corruptions of the truth. And further, it will of course realize in its degree those peculiar rewards of virtue which appetite cannot comprehend; and will detect in this world's events, which are but perplexities to mere unaided Reason, a general connexion existing between right moral conduct and happiness, in corroboration of those convictions which the experience of its own private history has created.

Such is the large and practical religious creed attainable (as appears from the extant works of heathen writers) by a vigorous mind which rightly works upon itself, under (what may be called) the Dispensation of Paganism. It may be even questioned whether there be any essential character of Scripture doctrine which is without its place in this moral revelation. For here is the belief in a principle exterior to the mind to which it is instinctively drawn, infinitely exalted, perfect, incomprehensible; here is the surmise of a judgment to come; the knowledge of unbounded benevolence, wisdom, and power, as traced in the visible creation, and of moral laws unlimited in their operation; further, there is something of hope respecting the availableness of repentance, so far (that is) as suffices for religious support;

lastly, there is an insight into the rule of duty, increasing with the earnestness with which obedience to that rule is cultivated.

This sketch of the religious knowledge not impossible to Heathen Philosophy, will be borne out by its writings, yet will be only obtained by a selection of the best portions of them. Hence we derive two conclusions: that the knowledge was *attainable*—for what one man may attain is open to another; on the other hand, that, in general, it was not *actually attained*—for else there would be no need of so confined a selection of them. And thus we are carried on to the inquiry already proposed — viz. *where* it was that Natural Religion failed in practical effect, and how Revealed Religion supplies the deficiency. Out of the many answers which might be given to this question, let us confine ourselves to that which is suggested by the text.

Natural Religion teaches, it is true, the infinite power and majesty, the wisdom and goodness, the presence, the moral governance, and, in one sense, the unity of the Deity; but it gives little or no information respecting what may be called His *Personality*. It followed that, though Heathen Philosophy knew so much of the moral system of the world, as to see the duties and prospects of man in the same direction in which Revelation places them, this knowledge did not preclude a belief in fatalism, which might, of course, consist in unchangeable moral laws, as well as physical. And though Philosophy acknowledged an intelligent, wise, and beneficent Principle of nature, still this too was, in fact, only equivalent to the belief in a pervading Soul of the Universe, which consulted for its own good, and directed its own movements, by instincts similar to those by which the animal world is guided; but which, strictly speaking, was not an object of worship, inasmuch as each intelligent being was, in a certain sense, himself a portion of it. Much less would a conviction of the Infinitude and Eternity of the Divine Nature lead to any just idea of His *Personality*, since there can be no circumscribing lineaments nor configuration of the Immeasurable, no external condition or fortune to that Being who is all in all. Lastly, though Conscience seemed to point in a certain direction as a witness for the real moral locality (so to speak) of the unseen God, yet, as it cannot prove its own authority, it afforded no argument for a Governor and Judge, distinct from the moral system itself, to those who disputed its informations.

While, then, Natural Religion was not without provision for all the deepest and truest religious feelings, yet presenting no tangible history of the Deity, no points of His personal character [1] (if we may so speak without irreverence); it wanted that most efficient incentive to all action, a starting or rallying point,

---

[1] The author was not acquainted, at the time this was written, with Mr. Coleridge's Works, and a remarkable passage in his Biographia Literaria, in which several portions of this Sermon are anticipated. It has been pointed out to him since by the kindness of a friend.—Vide Biogr. Lit. vol. i. p. 199.

—an object on which the affections could be placed, and the energies concentrated. Common experience in life shows how the most popular and interesting cause languishes, if its head be removed; and how political power is often vested in individuals, merely for the sake of the definiteness of the practical impression which a personal presence produces. How, then, should the beauty of virtue move the heart, while it was an abstraction? " Forma quidem honestatis, si *oculis cerneretur*, admirabiles amores excitaret sapientiæ ;" but, till " seen and heard and handled," it did but witness against those who disobeyed, while they acknowledged it; and who, seemingly conscious where their need lay, made every effort to embody it in the attributes of individuality, embellishing their " Logos," as they spoke, with figurative actions, and worshipping it as the personal development of the Infinite Unknown.

But, it may be asked, was Heathen religion of no service here? It testified, without supplying the need; it bore testimony to it, by attempting to attribute a personal character and a history to the Divinity; but it failed, as degrading His invisible majesty by unworthy, multiplied and inconsistent images, and as shattering the moral scheme of the world into partial and discordant systems, in which appetite and expedience received the sanction due only to virtue. And thus refined philosophy and rude natural feeling each attempted separately to enforce obedience to a religious rule, and each failed on its own side. The

God of philosophy was infinitely great, but an abstraction; the God of paganism was intelligible, but degraded by human conceptions. Science and nature could produce no joint-work; it was left for an express revelation to propose the Object in which they should both be reconciled, and to satisfy the desires of both in a real and manifested incarnation of the Deity.

When St. Paul came to Athens, and found the altar dedicated to the Unknown God, he professed his purpose of declaring to the Heathen world, Him " whom they ignorantly worshipped." He proceeded to condemn their polytheistic and anthropomorphic errors, to disengage the notion of a Deity from the base earthly attributes in which Heathen religion had enveloped it, and to appeal to their own literature in behalf of the true nature of Him in whom " we live, and move, and have our being." But, after thus acknowledging the abstract correctness of the philosophical system, as far as it went, he preaches unto them Jesus and the Resurrection; i. e. he embodies the moral character of the Deity in those historical notices of it, which have been made the medium of theChristian manifestation of His attributes.

It is hardly necessary to enter into any formal proof that this is one principal object, as of all revelation, so especially of the Christian; viz. to relate some course of action, some conduct, a life (to speak in human terms) of the One Supreme God. Indeed, so evidently is this the case, that one very common, though superficial objection to the Scriptures, is founded on their continually ascribing to Almighty God human passions, words, and actions. The first chapter of the book of Job is one instance which may suggest many more; and those marks of character are especially prominent in Scripture, which imply an extreme opposition to an eternal and fated system, inherent freedom of will, power of change, long-suffering, placability, repentance, delight in the praises and thanksgivings of His creatures, failure of purpose, and the prerogative of dispensing His mercies according to His good pleasure. Above all, in the New Testament, the Divine character is exhibited to us, not merely as love, or mercy, or holiness (attributes which have a vagueness in our conceptions of them from their immensity), but these and others as seen in an act of *self-denial* — a mysterious quality when ascribed to Him, who is all things in Himself, but especially calculated (from the mere meaning of the term) to impress upon our minds the personal character of the Object of our worship. " God so loved the world," that He *gave up* His only Son ; and the Son of God " *pleased not Himself.*" In His life we are allowed to discern the attributes of the Invisible God, drawn out into action in accommodation to our weakness. The passages are too many to quote, in which this object of His incarnation is openly declared. " In Him dwelleth all the fulness of the Godhead bodily." " He that hath

seen Him, hath seen the Father." He is a second
Creator of the world, condescending (as it were) to
repeat for our contemplation, in human form, that distinct personal work, which made " the morning stars
sing together, and all the sons of God shout for joy."
In a word, the impression upon the religious mind
thence made is appositely illustrated in the words of
the text, " That which was from the beginning,
which we have heard, which we have seen with our
eyes, which we have looked upon, and our hands
have handled, of the Word of Life ; (For the Life was
manifested, and we have seen It, and bear witness,
and show unto you that Eternal Life, which was with
the Father, and was manifested unto us ;) That which
we have seen and heard declare we unto you, that ye
also may have fellowship with us."

No thought is more likely to come across, and
haunt the mind, and slacken its efforts under Natural
Religion, than that after all we may be following a
vain shadow, and disquieting ourselves without cause,
while we are giving up our hearts to the noblest instincts and aspirations of our nature. The Roman
Stoic, as he committed suicide, complained he had
worshipped virtue, and found it but an empty name.
It is even now the way of the world to look upon the
religious principle as a mere peculiarity of temper, a
weakness, or an enthusiasm, or refined feeling (as the
case may be), characteristic of a timid and narrow, or of
an heated or a highly-gifted mind. Here, then, Revela-

tion meets us with simple and distinct *facts* and *actions*, not with painful inductions from existing phenomena, not with generalized laws or metaphysical conjectures, but with *Jesus and the Resurrection;* and " *if Christ be* not risen" (it confesses plainly), "then is our preaching vain, and your faith is also vain." Facts such as this are not simply evidence of the truth of the revelation, but the media of its impressiveness. The life of Christ brings together and concentrates truths concerning the chief good and the laws of our being, which wander idle and forlorn over the surface of the moral world, and often appear to diverge from each other. It collects the scattered rays of light, which, in the first days of creation, were poured over the whole face of nature, into certain intelligible centres, in the firmament of the heaven, to rule over the day and over the night, and to divide the light from the darkness. Our Saviour has all those abstract titles of moral excellence bestowed upon Him which philosophers have invented. He is the Word, the Light, the Life, the Truth, Wisdom, the Divine Glory. St. John announces in the text, " The Life was manifested, and we *have seen* It."

And hence will follow an important difference in the moral character formed in the Christian school, from that which Natural Religion has a tendency to create. The philosopher aspires towards a divine *principle;* the Christian, towards a Divine *Agent.* Now, dedication of our energies to the service of a person is the occasion of the highest and most noble

virtues,—disinterested attachment, self-devotion, loyalty; habitual humility, moreover, from the knowledge that there must ever be one that is above us.
On the other hand, in whatever degree we approximate towards a mere standard of excellence, we do
not really advance towards it, but bring it to us;
the excellence we venerate becomes part of ourselves
—we become a god to ourselves. This was one
especial consequence of the pantheistic system of the
Stoics, the later Pythagoreans, and other philosophers; in proportion as they drank into the spirit of
eternal purity, they became divine in their own estimation; they contrasted themselves with those who
were below them, knowing no being above them by
whom they could measure their proficiency. Thus
they began by being humble, and, as they advanced,
humility and faith wore away from their character.
This is strikingly illustrated in Aristotle's description
of a perfectly virtuous man. An incidental and un-
studied greatness of mind is described as marking
the highest moral excellence, and truly; but the genuine nobleness of the virtuous mind, as shown in a
superiority to common temptations, forbearance, generosity, self-respect, calm high-minded composure, is
deformed by an arrogant contempt of others, a disregard of their feelings, and a harshness and repul-
siveness of external manner. That is, the philosopher saw clearly the tendencies of the moral system,
the constitution of the human soul, and the ways
leading to the perfection of our nature; but when

he attempted to delineate the ultimate complete consistent image of the virtuous man, how could he be expected to do this great thing, who had never seen Angel or Prophet, much less the Son of God manifested in the flesh?

At such pains is Scripture, on the other hand, to repress the proud self-complacency just spoken of, that not only is all moral excellence expressly referred to the Supreme God, but even the principle of good, when implanted and progressively realized in our hearts, is still continually revealed to us as a Person, as if to mark strongly that it is not our own, and must lead us to no preposterous self-adoration. For instance, we read of Christ being formed in us—dwelling in the heart—of the Holy Spirit making us His temple; particularly remarkable is our Saviour's own promise: "If a man love Me, he will keep My words; and My Father will love him, and We will *come unto him, and make our abode with* him."

It may be observed, that this method of personation (so to call it) is carried throughout the revealed system. The doctrine of the Personality of the Holy Spirit has just been referred to. Again, the doctrine of original sin is centred in the person of Adam, and in this way is made impressive and intelligible to the mass of mankind. The Evil Principle is revealed to us in the person of its author, Satan. Nay, not only thus, in the case of really existing beings, as the first man and the Evil Spirit, but even when a figure must be used, is the same system continued. The body of faithful men, or Church, considered as the dwelling-place of the One Holy Spirit, is invested with a metaphorical personality, and is bound to act as one, in order to those practical ends of influencing and directing human conduct in which the entire system may be considered as originating. And, again, for the same purpose of concentrating the energies of the Christian body, and binding its members into close union, it was found expedient, even in Apostolic times, to consign each particular church to the care of one pastor, or bishop, who was thus made a personal type of Christ mystical, the new and spiritual man; a centre of action and a living witness against all heretical or disorderly proceedings.

Such, then, is the Revealed system compared with the Natural—teaching religious truths historically, not by investigation; revealing the Divine nature, not in works, but in action; not in His moral laws, but in His spoken commands; training us to be subjects of a kingdom, not citizens of a Stoic republic; and enforcing obedience, not on Reason so much as on Faith.

And now that we are in possession of this great gift of God, Natural Religion has an use and importance which it before could hardly possess. For as Revealed Religion enforces doctrine, so Natural Religion recommends it. It is hardly necessary to observe, that the whole revealed scheme rests on nature for the validity of its evidence. The claim of miraculous power or knowledge assumes the existence of a Being capable of exerting it; and the matter of the revelation itself is evidenced and interpreted by those awful, far-reaching analogies of mediation and vicarious suffering, which we discern in the visible course of the world. There is, perhaps, no greater satisfaction to the Christian than that which arises from his perceiving that the Revealed system is rooted deep in the natural course of things, of which it is merely the result and completion; that his Saviour has interpreted for him the faint or broken accents of Nature; and that in them, so interpreted, he has, as if in some old prophecy, at once the evidence and the lasting memorial of the truths of the Gospel.

It remains to suggest some of the conclusions which follow from this view, thus taken, of the relation of Revealed to Natural Religion.

1. First, much might be said on the evidence thence deducible for the truth of the Christian system. It is one point of evidence that the two systems coincide in declaring the same substantial doctrines: viz., as being two independent witnesses in one and the same question; an argument contained by implication, though not formally drawn out, in Bishop Butler's Analogy. It is a further point of evidence to find that Scripture completes the very deficiency of nature; and, while its doctrines of Atonement and Mediation are paralleled by phenomena in the visible course of things, to discern in it one solitary doctrine, which from

its nature has no parallel in this world, an Incarnation of the Divine Essence, an intrinsic evidence of its truth in the benefit thus conferred on religion.

2. Next, light is thus thrown upon the vast practical importance of the doctrines of the Divinity of our Lord, and of the Personality of the Holy Spirit. It is the impiety, indeed, involved in the denial of these, which is the great guilt of anti-Trinitarians; but, over and above this, such persons go far to destroy the very advantages which the Revealed system possesses over the Natural; and throw back the science of morals and of human happiness into that state of vagueness and inefficiency from which Christianity has extricated it. On the other hand, we learn besides, the shallowness of the objection to the doctrine of the Holy Trinity, grounded on its involving a plurality of Persons in the Godhead; since, if it be inconceivable, as it surely is, how Personality can in any way be an attribute of the infinite, incommunicable Essence of the Deity, or in what particular sense it is ascribed to Him, Unitarians, so called (to be consistent), should find a difficulty in the doctrine of an Unity of Person, as well as of a Trinity; and, having ceased to be Athanasians, should not stop till they become Pantheists.

3. Further, the same view suggests to us the peculiar perverseness of schism, which tends to undo the very arrangement which our Lord has made, for arresting the attention of mankind, and leading them to seek their true moral good; and which (if followed to

its legitimate results) would reduce the world to the very state in which it existed in the age of the heathen moralist familiar to us in this place, who, in opening his treatise, bears witness to the importance of a visible Church, by consulting the opinions of mankind as to the means of obtaining happiness; and not 'till disappointed in sage and statesman, the many and the educated, undertakes himself an examination of man's nature, as if the only remaining means of satisfying the inquiry.

4. And hence, at the same time, may be learned the real religious position of the heathen, who, we have reason to trust, are not in danger of perishing, except so far as all are in such danger, whether in heathen or Christian country, who do not follow the secret voice of conscience, leading them on by Faith to their true though unseen good. For the prerogative of Christians consists in the possession, not of exclusive knowledge and spiritual aid, but of gifts high and peculiar; and though the manifestation of the Divine character in the Incarnation is a singular and inestimable benefit, yet its absence is supplied in a degree, not only in the inspired record of Moses, but even, with more or less strength, as the case may be, in those various traditions concerning divine providences and dispensations which are scattered through the heathen mythologies.

5. Lastly, a comment is hence afforded us on the meaning of a phrase perplexed by controversy—that

of " preaching Christ."   By which is properly meant,
not the putting Natural Religion out of sight, nor the
separating one doctrine of the Gospel from the rest,
as having an exclusive claim to the name of Gospel;
but the displaying *all* that Nature and Scripture
teaċh concerning Divine Providence (for they teach
the same great truths), whether of His majesty, or His
love, or His mercy, or His holiness, or His fearful anger,
through the medium of the life and death of His Son,
Jesus Christ.   A mere moral strain of teaching duty
and enforcing obedience fails in persuading to practice, not because it appeals to conscience, and commands and threatens, (as is sometimes supposed,) but
because it does not urge and illustrate virtue in the
Name and by the example of our blessed Lord.   It
is not that natural teaching gives merely the Law,
and Christian teaching gives the tidings of pardon,
and that a command chills or formalizes the mind,
and that a free forgiveness converts it; (for nature
speaks of God's goodness as well as of His severity,
and Christ surely of His severity as well as of His
goodness;) but that in the Christian scheme we find
all the Divine Attributes (not mercy only, though
mercy pre-eminently) brought out and urged upon
us, which were but latent in the visible course of
things.   Hence it appears that the Gospels are the
great instruments (under God's blessing) of fixing
and instructing our minds in a religious course, the
Epistles being rather comments on them than in-

tended to supersede them, as is sometimes maintained. Surely it argues a temper of mind but partially moulded to the worship and love of Christ, to make this distinction between His teaching and that of His Apostles, when the very promised office of the Comforter in His absence was, not to make a new revelation, but expressly "to bring all things to their remembrance" which "*He* had said to them;" *not* to " speak of Himself," but " to receive of Christ's, and show it unto them." The Holy Spirit came " to glorify Christ," to declare openly to all the world that *He* had come on earth, suffered, and died, who was also the Creator and Governor of the world, the Saviour, the final Judge of men. It is the Incarnation of the Son of God rather than any doctrine drawn from a partial view of Scripture (however true and momentous it may be) which is the article of a standing or a falling Church. " Every spirit that confesseth not that Jesus Christ is come *in the flesh*, is not of God; . . . this is that spirit of anti-Christ;" for, not to mention other more direct considerations, it reverses, as far as in it lies, all that the revealed character of Christ has done for our faith and virtue. And hence the Apostles' speeches in the book of Acts and the primitive creeds insist almost exclusively upon the history, not the doctrines, of Christianity; it being designed that by means of our Lord's Economy the great doctrines of theology are to be taught, the facts of that Economy giving its peculiarity and force to the Revelation.

May it ever be our aim thus profitably to use that last and complete manifestation of the Divine Attributes and Will contained in the New Testament, setting the pattern of the Son of God ever before us, and studying so to act as if He were sensibly present, by look, voice, and gesture, to approve or blame us in all our private thoughts and all our intercourse with the world!

SERMON III.

THE USURPATIONS OF REASON.

Preached December 11, 1831.

MATT. xi. 19.

" Wisdom is justified of her children."

SUCH is our Lord's comment upon the perverse conduct of His countrymen, who refused to be satisfied
either with St. John's reserve or His own condescen-
sion.   John the Baptist retired from the world, and
when men came to seek him, spoke sternly to them.
Christ, the greater Prophet, took the more lowly
place, and freely mixed with sinners.   The course of
God's dealings with them was varied to the utmost
extent which the essential truth and unchangeable-
ness of His moral government permitted; but in
neither extreme of austereness or of grace did it persuade.   Having exposed this remarkable fact in the
history of mankind, the Divine Speaker utters the
solemn words of the text, the truth which they con-

vey being the refuge of disappointed mercy, as well
as a warning addressed to all whom they might con-
cern. " Wisdom is justified of her children :" as if He
said, " There is no act on God's part, no truth of religion, to which a captious Reason may not find objections; and in truth the evidence and matter of
Revelation are not addressed to the mere unstable
Reason of man, nor can hope for any certain or adequate reception with it.   Divine Wisdom speaks not
to the world, but to her own children, or those who
have been already under her teaching, and who,
knowing her voice, understand her words, and are
suitable judges of them.   These justify her."

In the text, then, a truth is expressed in the form
of a proverb, which is implied all through Scripture as
a basis on which its doctrine rests—viz. that there is
no necessary connexion between the intellectual and
moral principles of our nature ; that on religious subjects we may prove anything or overthrow anything,
and can arrive at truth but accidentally, if we merely
investigate by what is commonly called Reason, which
is in such matters but the instrument at best, in the
hands of the legitimate judge, spiritual discernment.
When we consider how common it is in the world at
large to consider the intellect as the characteristic
part of our nature, the silence of Scripture in regard
to it (not to mention its positive disparagement of it)
is very striking.   In the Old Testament scarcely any
mention is made of the existence of the Reason as
a distinct and chief attribute of mind; the sacred

language affording no definite and proper terms expressive either of the general gift or of separate faculties in which it exhibits itself. And as to the New Testament, need we but betake ourselves to the description given us of Him who is the Only-begotten Son and Express Image of God, to learn how inferior a station in the idea of the perfection of man's nature is held by the mere Reason? While there is no profaneness in attaching to Christ those moral attributes of goodness, truth, and holiness, which we apply to man, there would be an obvious irreverence in measuring the powers of His mind by any standard of intellectual endowments, the very names of which sound mean and impertinent when ascribed to Him. St. Luke's declaration of His growth " in *wisdom* and stature," with no other specified advancement, is abundantly illustrated in St. John's Gospel, in which we find the Almighty Teacher rejecting with apparent disdain all intellectual display, and confining Himself to the enunciation of deep truths, intelligible to the children of wisdom, but conveyed in language altogether destitute both of argumentative skill, and what is commonly considered eloquence.

To account for this silence of Scripture concerning intellectual excellence, by affirming that the Jews were not distinguished in that respect, is hardly to the point ; for surely a lesson is conveyed to us in the very circumstance of such a people being chosen as the medium of a moral gift. If it be further

objected, that to speak concerning intellectual endowments fell beyond the range of inspiration, which
was limited by its professed object, this is no objection, but the very position here maintained. No one
can deny to the intellect its own excellence, nor deprive it of its due honours; the question is merely this,
whether it be not limited in its turn, as regards its
range, so as not without intrusion to exercise itself
as an independent authority in the field of morals
and religion.

Such surely is the case ; and the silence of Scripture concerning intellectual gifts need not further
be insisted on, either in relation to the fact itself,
or the implication contained in it. Were a being
unacquainted with mankind to receive information
concerning human nature from the Bible, would he
ever conjecture its actual state, as developed in society
in all the various productions and exhibitions of
what is called talent ? And, next viewing the world
as it is, and the Bible in connexion with it, what
would he see in the actual history of Revelation,
but the triumph of the moral powers of man over
the intellectual, of holiness over ability, far more
than of mind over brute force ? Great as was
the power of the lion and the bear, the leopard,
and that fourth nameless beast, dreadful and terrible
and strong exceedingly, God had weapons of their
own kind to bruise and tame them. The miracles of
the Church displayed more physical power than the
hosts of Pharaoh and Sennacherib. Power, not mind,

was opposed to power; yet to the refined Pagan intellect, the rivalry of intellect was not granted. The
foolish things of the world confounded the wise, far
more completely than the weak the mighty.   Human
philosophy was beaten from its usurped province, but
not by any counter-philosophy; and unlearned Faith,
establishing itself by its own inherent strength, ruled
the Reason as far as its own interests were concerned,
and from that time has employed it in the Church,
first as a captive, then as a servant; not as an equal,
and in nowise (far from it) as a patron.

I propose now to make some remarks upon the
place which Reason holds in relation to Religion, the
light in which we should view it, and certain en-
croachments of which it is sometimes guilty; and I
think that, without a distinct definition of the word,
which would carry us too far from our subject[1], I can
make it plain what I take it to mean.   Sometimes,
indeed, it stands for all in which man differs from
the brutes, and so includes in its signification the
faculty of distinguishing between right and wrong,
and the directing principle in conduct.   In this sense
I certainly do not here use it, but in a narrower signification, which it usually bears, as representing or
synonymous with the intellectual powers, and as
opposed as such to the moral qualities, and to Faith.

This opposition between Faith and Reason takes
place in two ways, when either of the two encroaches

---

[1] For an explanation of the word, *vide infra*, Discourses ix. and x.

upon the province of the other. It would be an absurdity to attempt to find out mathematical truths by the purity and acuteness of the moral sense. It is a form of this mistake which has led men to apply such Scripture communications as are intended for religious purposes to the determination of physical questions. This error is perfectly understood in these days by all thinking men. This was the usurpation of the schools of theology in former ages, to issue their decrees to the subjects of the Senses and the Intellect. No wonder Reason and Faith were at variance. The other cause of disagreement takes place when Reason is the aggressor, and encroaches on the province of Religion, attempting to judge of those truths which are subjected to another part of our nature, the moral sense. For instance, suppose an acute man, who had never conformed his life to the precepts of Scripture, attempted to decide on the degree and kind of intercourse which a Christian should have with the world, or on the measure of guilt involved in the use of light and profane words, or which of the Christian doctrines were generally necessary to salvation, or to judge of the wisdom or use of consecrating places of worship, or to determine what kind and extent of reverence should be paid to the Lord's Day, or what portion of our possessions set apart for religious purposes; questions these which are addressed to the cultivated moral perception, or, what is sometimes improperly termed, " *feeling ;*" improperly, because feeling comes and goes, and, having no root in our nature, speaks with no divine authority; but the moral perception, though varying in the mass of men, is fixed in each individual, and is an original element within us. Hume, in his Essay on Miracles, has well propounded a doctrine, which at the same time he misapplies. He speaks of " those dangerous friends or disguised enemies to the Christian Religion, who have undertaken to defend it by the principles of human Reason." " Our most holy Religion," he proceeds, " is founded on *Faith*, not on Reason." This is said in irony; but it is true as far as every important question in Revelation is concerned, and to forget this is the error which is at present under consideration.

That it is a common error is evident from the anxiety generally felt to detach the names of men of ability from the infidel party. Why should we be desirous to disguise the fact, if it be such, that men distinguished, some for depth and originality of mind, others for acuteness, others for prudence and good sense in practical matters, yet have been indifferent to Revealed Religion,—why, unless we have some misconceived notion concerning the connexion between the intellect and the moral principle? Yet, is it not a fact, for the proof or disproof of which we need not go to history or philosophy, when the humblest village may show us that those persons who turn out badly, as it is called,—who break the laws first of society, then of their country,—are commonly the very men who have received more than the ordinary share of intellectual gifts? Without turning aside to explain or account for this, thus much it seems to show us, that the powers of the intellect (in that degree, at least, in which, in matter of fact, they are found among us) do not necessarily lead us in the direction of our moral instincts, or confirm them; but if the agreement between the two be but matter of accident, what testimony do we gain from the mere Reason to the truths of Religion?

Why should we be surprised that one faculty of our compound nature should not be able to do that which is the work of another? It is as little strange that the mind, which has only exercised itself on matters of literature or science, and never submitted itself to the influence of Divine perceptions, should be unequal to the contemplation of a moral revelation, as that it should not perform the office of the senses. There is a strong analogy between the two cases. Our Reason assists the senses in various ways, directing the application of them, and arranging the evidence they supply; it makes use of the facts subjected to them, and to an unlimited extent deduces conclusions from them, foretels facts which are to be ascertained, and confirms doubtful ones; but the man who neglected experiments and trusted to his vigour of talent, would be called a theorist; and the blind man who seriously professed to lecture on light and colours could scarcely hope to gain an audience. Or suppose his lecture proceeded, what might be expected from him? Starting from the terms of science which would be the foundation and materials of his system, instead of apprehended facts, his acuteness and prompt imagination might carry him freely forward into the open field of the science; he might discourse with ease and fluency, till we almost forgot his lamentable deprivation; at length, on a sudden, he would lose himself in some great and inexpressible mistake, betrayed in the midst of his career by some treacherous word, which he incautiously explained too fully or dwelt too much upon; and we should find that he had been using words without corresponding ideas: on witnessing his failure, we should view it indulgently, qualifying our criticism by the remark, that the exhibition was singularly good for a blind man.

Such would be the fate of the officious Reason, busying itself without warrant in the province of sense. In its due subordinate place there, it acts but as an instrument; it but assists and expedites, saving the senses the time and trouble of working. Give a man a hundred eyes and hands for natural science, and you materially loosen his dependence on the ministry of Reason.

This illustration, be it observed, is no adequate parallel of the truth which led to it; for the subject of light and colours is at least within the grasp of scientific definitions, and therefore cognisable by the intellect far better than morals. Yet apply it, such as it is, to the matter in hand, not, of course, with the extravagant object of denying the use of the Reason in religious inquiries, but in order to ascertain what is its real place in the conduct of them. And in explanation of it I would make two additional observations:—first, we must put aside the indirect support afforded to Revelation by the countenance of the intellectually gifted portion of mankind; I mean, in the way of *influence*. Reputation for talent, learning, or scientific knowledge, has natural and just claims on our respect, and recommends a cause to our notice. So does power; and in this way power, as well as intellectual endowments, is necessary to the maintenance of religion, in order to secure from mankind a hearing for an unpleasant subject; but power, when it has done so much, attempts no more; or if it does, it loses its position, and is involved in the fallacy of persecution. Here the parallel holds good—it is as absurd to argue men, as to torture them, into believing.

But in matter of fact (it will be said) Reason *can* go further; for we can reason about Religion, and we frame its Evidences. Here, then, secondly, I observe, we must deduct from the real use of the Reason in religious inquiries, whatever is the mere setting right of its own mistakes. The blind man who reasoned himself into errors in optics might possibly reason himself out of them; yet this would be no proof that extreme acuteness was necessary or useful in the science itself. It was but necessary for a blind man; that is, supposing he was bent on attempting to do what from the first he ought not to have attempted; and, after all, with the uncertainty whether he would gain or lose in his search after scientific truth, by his experiment. Now, so numerous and so serious have been the errors of theorists on religious subjects (that is, of those who have speculated without caring to act on their sense of right; or have rested their cause on mere arguments, instead of attempting a direct contemplation of its subject-matter), that the correction of them has required the most vigorous and subtle exercise of the Reason, and has almost engrossed its efforts. Unhappily the blind teacher in morals can ensure himself a blind audience, to whom he may safely address his paradoxes, which are sometimes admitted even by religious men, on the ground of those happy conjectures which his acute reason now and then makes, and which they verify. What an indescribable confusion hence arises between truth and falsehood, in systems, parties, and persons ! What a superhuman talent is demanded to unravel the checkered and tangled web; and what gratitude is due to the gifted individual who by his learning or philosophy in part achieves the task ! yet not gratitude in such a case to the Reason as a principle of research, which is merely undoing its own mischief, and poorly and tardily redressing its intrusion into a province not its own; but to the man, the moral being, who has subjected it in his own person to the higher principles of his nature.

To take an instance. What an extreme exercise of intellect is shown in the theological teaching of the Church! Yet how was it necessary? chiefly, from the previous errors of heretical reasonings, on subjects addressed to the moral perception. For while Faith was engaged in that exact and well-instructed devotion to Christ which no words can suitably describe, the forward Reason stepped in upon the yet uninclosed ground of doctrine, and attempted to describe there, from its own resources, an image of the Invisible. Henceforth the Church was obliged, in self-defence, to employ the gifts of the intellect in the cause of God, to trace out (as near as might be) the faithful shadow of those truths, which unlearned piety admits and acts upon, without the medium of intellectual representation.

This obviously holds good as regards the Evidences also, great part of which are rather answers to objections than direct arguments for Revelation; and even the direct arguments are far more effective in the confutation of captious opponents, than in the conviction of inquirers. Doubtless the degree in which we depend on argument in religious subjects varies with each individual, so that no strict line can be drawn: still, let it be inquired whether these Evidences are not rather to be viewed as splendid philosophical investigations than practical arguments; at best bulwarks intended for overawing the enemy by their strength and number, rather than for actual use in the war. In matter of fact, *how* many men do we suppose, in a century, out of the whole body of Christians, have been primarily brought to belief, or retained in it, by an intimate and lively perception of the force of what are technically called the Evidences? And why are there so few? Because to the mind already familiar with the truths of Natural Religion, enough of evidence is at once afforded by the mere fact of the present existence of Christianity; which, viewed in its connexion with its principles and upholders and effects, bears on the face of it the signs of a divine ordinance in the very same way in which the visible world attests to us its own divine origin;—a more accurate investigation, in which superior talents are brought into play, merely bringing to light an innumerable alternation of arguments, for and against it, which forms indeed an ever-increasing series in its behalf, but still does not get beyond the first suggestion of plain sense and religiously-trained reason; and in fact, perhaps, never comes to a termination. Nay, so alert is the instinctive power of an educated conscience, that by some secret faculty, and without any intelligible reasoning process, it seems to detect moral truth wherever it lies hid, and feels a conviction of its own accuracy which bystanders cannot account for; and this especially in the case of Revealed Religion, which is one comprehensive moral fact,—according to the saying which is parallel to the text, " I know My sheep and am known of Mine[2]."

From considerations such as the foregoing, it

[2] John x. 14.

appears that exercises of Reason are either external,
or at least only ministrative to religious inquiry and
knowledge: accidental to them, not of their essence;
useful in their place, but not necessary.   But in order
to obtain further illustrations, and a view of the importance, of the doctrine which I would advocate,
let us proceed to apply it to the circumstances of
the present times.   Here, first, in finding fault with
the times, it is right to disclaim all intention of com-
plaining of them.   To murmur and rail at the state
of things under which we find ourselves, and to prefer a former state, is not merely indecorous, it is absolutely unmeaning.   We are ourselves necessary
parts of the existing system, out of which we have individually grown into being, into our actual position
in society.   Depending, therefore, on the times as
a condition of existence, in wishing for other times
we are, in fact, wishing we had never been born.
Moreover, it is ungrateful to a state of society, from
which we daily enjoy so many benefits, to rail against
it.   Yet there is nothing unbecoming, unmeaning, or
ungrateful in pointing out its faults and wishing them
away.

   In this day, then, we see a very extensive development of an usurpation which has been preparing,
with more or less of open avowal, for some centuries,--
the usurpation of Reason in morals and religion.   In
the first years of its growth it professed to respect
the bounds of justice and sobriety: it was little in
its own eyes; but getting strength, it was lifted up;

and casting down all that is called God, or worshipped, it took its seat in the temple of God, as His representative. Such, at least, is the consummation at which the Oppressor is aiming;—which he will reach, unless He who rids His Church of tyrants in their hour of pride, look down from the pillar of the cloud, and trouble his host.

Now, in speaking of an usurpation of the Reason at the present day, stretching over the province of religion, and in fact over the Christian Church, no admission is made concerning the degree of cultivation which the Reason has at present reached in the territory which it has unjustly entered. A tyrant need not be strong; he keeps his ground by prescription and through fear. It is not the profound thinkers who intrude with their discussions and criticisms within the sacred limits of moral truth. A really philosophical mind, if unhappily it has ruined its own religious perceptions, will be silent; it will understand that religion does not lie in its way: it may disbelieve its truths, it may account belief in them a weakness, or, on the other hand, a happy dream, a delightful error, which it cannot itself enjoy;—any how, it will not usurp. But men who know but a little, are for that very reason most under the power of the imagination, which fills up for them at pleasure those departments of knowledge to which they are strangers; and as the ignorance of abject minds shrinks from the spectres which it frames there, the

ignorance of the self-confident is petulant and pre-
suming.

The usurpations of the Reason may be dated from
the Reformation. Then, together with the tyranny,
the legitimate authority of the ecclesiastical power
was more or less overthrown; and in some places its
ultimate basis also, the moral sense. One school of
men resisted the Church; another went further, and
rejected the supreme authority of the law of Conscience. Accordingly, Revealed Religion was in a
great measure stripped of its proof; for the existence
of the Church had been its external evidence, and its
internal had been supplied by the moral sense.
Reason now undertook to repair the demolition it
had made, and to render the proof of Christianity
independent both of the Church and of the law of
nature. From that time (if we take a general view
of its operations) it has been engaged first in making
difficulties by the mouth of unbelievers, and then
claiming power in the Church as a reward for having,
by the mouth of apologists, partially removed them.

The following instances are in point, in citing
which let no disrespect be imagined towards such
really eminent men as were at various times concerned in them. Wrong Reason could not be met
when miracle and inspiration were suspended, except
by rightly-directed Reason.

1. As to the proof of the authority of Scripture.
This had hitherto rested on the testimony borne to it

by the existing Church.   Reason volunteered proof, not different, however, in kind, but more subtle and complicated in its form,—took the evidence of past ages, instead of the present, and committed its keeping (as was necessary) to the oligarchy of learning: at the same time, it boasted of the service thus rendered to the cause of Revelation, that service really consisting in the external homage thus paid to it by learning and talent, not in any great direct practical benefit, where men honestly wish to find and to do God's will, to act for the best, and to prefer what is safe and pious, to what shows well in argument.

2. Again, the Evidences themselves have been elaborately expanded; thus satisfying, indeed, the liberal curiosity of the mind, and giving scope for a devotional temper to admire the manifold wisdom of God, but doing comparatively little towards keeping men from infidelity, or turning them to a religious life. The same remark applies to such works on Natural Theology as treat of the marks of design in the creation, which are beautiful and interesting to the believer in a God ; but, where men have not already recognized God's voice within them, ineffective, and this moreover possibly from some unsoundness in the intellectual basis of the argument.

3. A still bolder encroachment was contemplated by the Reason, when it attempted to deprive the moral law of its intrinsic authority, and to rest it upon a theory of present expediency.   Thus, it constituted

itself the court of ultimate appeal in religious dis-
putes, under pretence of affording a clearer and
more scientifically-arranged code than is to be collected from the obscure precedents and mutilated
enactments of the Conscience.

4. A further error, connected with the assumption
just noticed, has been that of making intellectually-
gifted men arbiters of religious questions, in the place
of the children of wisdom.   As far as the argument
for Revelation is concerned, it is only necessary to
show that Christianity has had disciples among men
of the highest ability; whereas a solicitude already
alluded to has been shown to establish the orthodoxy
of some great names in philosophy and science, as if
truly it were a great gain to religion, and not to them,
if they *were* believers.   Much more unworthy has
been the practice of boasting of the admission of infidels concerning the beauty or utility of the Christian
system, as if it were a great thing for a Divine gift
to obtain praise for human excellence from proud or
immoral men.   Far different is the spirit of our own
Church, which, rejoicing, as she does, to find her children walking in truth, never forgets the dignity and
preciousness of the gifts she offers; as appears, for
instance, in the warnings prefacing the Communion
Service, and in the Commination,—above all, in the
Athanasian Creed, in which she but follows the
example of the early Church, which first withdrew
her mysteries from the many; then, when contro-

versy exposed them, guarded them with an anathema,
—in each case, lest curious reason might rashly gaze
and perish.

5. Lastly,—Another dangerous artifice of the
usurping Reason has been, the establishment of
societies, in which literature or science has been the
essential bond of union, to the exclusion of religious
profession.   These bodies, many of them founded
with no bad intention, have gradually led to an undue
exaltation of the Reason, and have formed an uncon-
stitutional power, advising and controlling the legitimate authorities of the soul.   In troubled times, such
as the present, associations, the most inoffensive in
themselves, and the most praiseworthy in their object, hardly escape this blame.   Of this nature have
been the literary meetings and societies of the last
two centuries, not to mention recently-established
bodies of a less innocent character.

And, further, let it be a question, whether the
theories on Government, which exclude Religion from
the essential elements of the State, are not also offshoots of the same usurpation.

And now, what remains but to express a confidence, which cannot deceive itself, that, whatever be
the destined course of the usurpations of the Reason
in the scheme of Divine Providence, its fall must at
last come, as that of other proud aspirants before it?
" Fret not thyself," says David, " because of evil
doers, neither be thou envious against the workers of

iniquity; for they shall soon be cut down like the grass, and wither as the green herb;" perishing as that high-minded Power, which the Prophet speaks of, who sat in the seat of God, as if wiser than Daniel, and acquainted with all secrets, till at length he was cast out from the holy place as profane, in God's good time[3] Our plain business, in the meantime, is to ascertain and hold fast our appointed station in the troubled scene, and then to rid ourselves of all dread of the future; to be careful, while we freely cultivate the Reason in all its noble functions, to keep it in its subordinate place in our nature : while we employ it industriously in the service of Religion, not to imagine that, in this service, we are doing any great thing, or directly advancing its influence over the heart; and, while we promote the education of others in all useful knowledge, to beware of admitting any principle of union, or standard of reward, which may practically disparage the supreme authority of Christian fellowship. Our great danger is, lest we should not understand our own principles, and should weakly surrender customs and institutions, which go far to constitute the Church what she is, the pillar and ground of moral truth,—lest, from a wish to make religion acceptable to the world in general, more free from objections than any moral system can be made, more immediately and visibly beneficial to the temporal interests of the community than God's com-

---

[3] Ezek. xxviii. 3. 16.

prehensive appointments condescend to be, we betray it to its enemies; lest we rashly take the Scriptures from the Church's custody, and commit them to the world, that is, to what is called public opinion; which men boast, indeed, will ever be right on the whole, but which, in fact, being the opinion of men, who, as a body, have not cultivated the internal moral sense, and have externally no immutable rules to bind them, is, in religious questions, only by accident right, or only on very broad questions, and to-morrow will betray interests which to-day it affects to uphold.

However, what are the essentials of our system, both in doctrine and discipline; what we may safely give up, and what we must firmly uphold; such practical points are to be determined by a more mature wisdom than can be expected in a discussion like the present, or indeed can be conveyed in any formal treatise. It is a plainer and a sufficiently important object, to contribute to the agitation of the general subject, and to ask questions which others are to answer.

SERMON IV.

PERSONAL INFLUENCE, THE MEANS OF
PROPAGATING THE TRUTH.

Preached January 22, 1832.

HEBR. xi. 34.

" Out of weakness were made strong."

THE history of the Old Testament Saints, conveyed in
these few words, is paralleled or surpassed in its
peculiar character by the lives of those who first
proclaimed the Christian dispensation. " Behold, I
send you forth as lambs among wolves," was the
warning given them of their position in the world,
on becoming Evangelists in its behalf. Their miraculous powers gained their cause a hearing, but did
not protect themselves. St. Paul records the fulfilment of our Lord's prophecy, as it contrasts the
Apostles and mankind at large, when he declares,
" Being reviled, we bless; being persecuted, we suffer
it; being defamed, we intreat; we are made as the
filth of the world, and are the offscouring of all

things unto this day [1]."   Nay, these words apply not
only to the unbelieving world; the Apostle had
reason to be suspicious of his Christian brethren, and
even to expostulate, on that score, with his own
converts, his " beloved sons."   He counted it a
great gain, such as afterwards might be dwelt upon
with satisfaction, that the Galatians did not despise
nor reject him on account of the infirmity which
was in his flesh; and, in the passage already referred
to, he mourns over the fickleness and coldness of the
Corinthians, who thought themselves wise, strong,
and honourable, and esteemed the Apostles as fools,
weak, and despised.

Whence, then, was it, that in spite of all these impediments to their success, still they succeeded?   How
did they gain that lodgment in the world, which they
hold down to this day, enabling them to perpetuate
principles distasteful to the majority even of those
who profess to receive them?   What is that hidden
attribute of the Truth, and how does it act, prevailing, as it does, single-handed, over the many and
multiform errors, by which it is simultaneously and
incessantly attacked?

Here, of course, we might at once refer its success
to the will and blessing of Him who revealed it, and
who distinctly promised that He would be present
with it, and with its preachers, " alway, even unto
the end."   And, of course, by realizing this in our

---

[1] 1 Cor. iv. 12, 13.

minds, we learn dependence upon His grace in our own endeavours to recommend the Truth, and encouragement to persevere. But it is also useful to inquire into the human means by which His Providence acts in the world, in order to take a practical view of events as they successively come before us in the course of human affairs, and to understand our duty in particulars; and, with reference to these means, it is now proposed to consider the question. Here, first of all,—

It is plain that we cannot rightly ascribe the influence of moral truth in the world to the gift of miracles, which was entrusted to the persons who promulgated it in that last and perfect form, in which we have been vouchsafed it; that gift having been withdrawn with the first preaching of it. Nor, again, can it be satisfactorily maintained that the visible Church, which the miracles formed, has taken their place in the course of Divine Providence, as the basis, strictly speaking, on which the Truth rests; though doubtless it is the appointed instrument, in even a fuller sense than the miracles before it, by which that Truth is conveyed to the world: for, though it is certain that a community of men, who, as individuals, were but imperfectly virtuous, would, in the course of years, gain the ascendancy over vice and error, however well prepared for the contest, yet no one pretends that the visible Church is thus blest; the Epistle to the Corinthians sufficiently showing, that, in all ages, true Christians, though contained in it, and forming its life and strength, are scattered and hidden in the multitude, and, but partially recognizing each other, have no means of combining and co-operating.   On the other hand, if we view the Church simply as a political institution, and refer the triumph of the Truth, which is committed to it, merely to its power thence resulting,—then, the question recurs, first, how is it that this mixed and heterogeneous body, called the Church, has, through so many centuries, on the whole, been true to the principles on which it was first established; and then, how, thus preserving its principles, it has, over and above this, gained on its side, in so many countries and times, the countenance and support of the civil authorities.   Here, it would be sufficient to consider the three first centuries of its existence, and to inquire by what means, in spite of unearthly principles, it grew and strengthened in the world; and how, again, corrupt body as it was then as now, still it preserved, all the while, with such remarkable fidelity those same unearthly principles which had been once delivered to it.

Others there are who attempt to account for this prevalence of the Truth, in spite of its enemies, by imagining, that, though at first opposed, yet it is, after a time, on mature reflection, admitted by the world in general, from a real understanding and conviction of its excellence; that it is in its nature level to the comprehension of men, considered merely as rational beings, without reference to their moral cha-

2

racter, whether good or bad; and that, in matter of
fact, it is recognized and upheld by the mass of men,
taken as individuals, not merely approved by them,
taken as a mass, in which some have influence over
others,—not merely submitted to with a blind, but
true instinct, such as is said to oppress inferior animals in the presence of man, but literally advocated
from an enlightened capacity for criticising it; and,
in consequence of this notion, some men go so far as
to advise, that the cause of Truth should be frankly
committed to the multitude as the legitimate judges
and guardians of it.

Something may occur to expose the fallacy of this
notion, in the course of the following remarks, on
what I conceive to be the real method by which the
influence of spiritual principles is maintained in this
carnal world. But here, it is expedient at once to
appeal to Scripture against a theory, which, whether
plausible or not, is scarcely Christian. The following
texts will suggest a multitude of others, as well as of
Scripture representations, hostile to the idea that
moral truth is easily or generally discerned. " The
natural man receiveth not the things of the Spirit of
God[2]." " The light shineth in darkness, and the darkness comprehended it not[3]." " Whosoever hath, to
him shall be given[4]." " Wisdom is justified by her
children[5]."

On the other hand, that its real influence consists

[2] 1 Cor. ii. 14.   [3] John i. 5.   [4] Matt. xiii. 12.   [5] Ibid. xi. 19.

directly in some inherent moral power, in virtue in some shape or other, not in any evidence or criterion level to the undisciplined reason of the multitude, high or low, learned or ignorant, is implied in texts, such as those referred to just now:—" I send you forth as sheep in the midst of wolves; *be ye, therefore*, wise as serpents, and harmless as doves."

This being the state of the question, it is proposed to consider, whether the influence of Truth in the world at large does not arise from *the personal influence*, direct and indirect, of those who are commissioned to teach it.

In order to explain the sense in which this is asserted, it will be best to begin by tracing the mode in which the moral character of such an organ of the Truth is formed ; and, in a large subject, I must beg permission to be somewhat longer (should it be necessary) than the custom of this place allows.

We will suppose this Teacher of the Truth so circumstanced as one alone among the sons of Adam has ever been, such a one as has never transgressed his sense of duty, but from his early childhood upwards has been only engaged in increasing and perfecting the light originally given him. In him the knowledge and power of acting rightly have kept pace with the enlargement of his duties, and his inward convictions of Truth with the successive temptations opening upon him from without to wander from it. Other men are surprised and overset by the sudden weight of circumstances against which they have not provided ; or, losing step, they strain and discompose their faculties in the effort, even though successful, to recover themselves ; or they attempt to discriminate for themselves between little and great breaches of the law of conscience, and allow themselves in what they consider the former; thus falling down precipices (as I may say) when they meant to descend an easy step, recoverable the next moment. Hence it is that, in a short time, those who started on one line make such different progress, and diverge in so many directions. Their conscience still speaks, but having been trifled with, it does not tell truly; it equivocates, or is irregular. Whereas in him who is faithful to his own divinely implanted nature, the faint light of Truth dawns continually brighter; the shadows which at first troubled it, the unreal shapes created by its own twilight-state, vanish; what was as uncertain as mere feeling, and could not be distinguished from a fancy except by the commanding urgency of its voice, becomes fixed and definite, and strengthening into principle, it at the same time developes into habit. As fresh and fresh duties arise, or fresh and fresh faculties are brought into action, they are at once absorbed into the existing inward system, and take their appropriate place in it. Doubtless beings, disobedient as most of us, from our youth up, cannot comprehend even the early attainments of one who thus grows in wisdom as truly as he grows in stature; who has no antagonist principles unsettling each other—no errors to unlearn ; though something is suggested to our imagination by that passage in the history of our blessed Lord, when at twelve years old He went up with His parents to the temple. And still less able are we to understand the state of such a mind, when it had passed through the temptations peculiar to youth and manhood, and had driven Satan from him in very despair.

Concerning the body of opinions formed under these circumstances,—not accidental and superficial, the mere reflection of what goes on in the world, but the natural and almost spontaneous result of the formed and finished character within,—two remarks may be offered. 1. That every part of what may be called this moral creed will be equally true and necessary; and if, as we may reasonably suppose, the science of morals extends indefinitely into the details of thought and conduct, numberless particulars, which we are accustomed to account indifferent, may be in fact indifferent in no truer sense, than in physics there is really any such agent as chance; our ignorance being the sole cause of the seeming variableness on the one hand in the action of nature, on the other in the standard of faith and morals. This is practically important to remember, even while it is granted that no exemplar of holiness has been exhibited to us, at once faultless yet minute; and, again, that in all existing patterns, besides actual defects, there are also the infirmities and varieties of disposition, taste, and talents, nay of bodily organization, to modify the dictates of that inward light

which is itself divine and unerring. It is important,
I say, as restraining us from judging hastily of opinions and practices of good men into which we ourselves cannot enter; but which, for what we know,
may be as necessary parts of the Truth, though too
subtle for our dull perceptions, as those great and
distinguishing features of it which we, in common
with the majority of sincere men, admit. And particularly will it preserve us from rash censures of the
Primitive Church, which, in spite of the corruptions
which disfigured it from the first, still in its collective
holiness may be considered to make as near an approach to the pattern of Christ as fallen man ever will
attain; being, in fact, a revelation in some sort of that
Blessed Spirit in a bodily shape, who was promised
to us as a second Teacher of Truth after Christ's de-
parture, and became such upon a subject-matter far
more diversified than that on which our Lord had revealed Himself before Him. For instance, for what we
know, the Episcopal principle, or the practice of Infant Baptism, which are traceable to Apostolic times,
though not clearly proved by the Scripture records,
may be as necessary in the scheme of Christian truth
as the doctrine of the Divine Unity, or man's responsibility, which in the artificial system are naturally
placed as the basis of religion, as being first in order
of succession and time. And this, be it observed,
will account for the omission in Scripture of express
sanctions of these and similar principles and observances; provided, that is, the object of the written

word be, not to unfold a system for our intellectual
contemplation, but to secure the formation of a certain character.

2. And in the second place, it is plain, that the
gifted individual whom we have imagined, will of all
men be least able (as such) to defend his own views,
inasmuch as he takes no external survey of himself.
Things which are the most familiar to us, and easy
in practice, require the most study, and give the most
trouble in explaining; as, for instance, the number,
combination, and succession of muscular movements
by which we balance ourselves in walking, or utter
our separate words; and this quite independently of
the existence or non-existence of language suitable
for describing them. The longer any one has perse-
vered in the practice of virtue, the less likely is he
to recollect how he began it; what were his difficulties
on starting, and how surmounted; by what process
one truth led to another; and to elicit justly what
are the real reasons latent in his mind for particular
observances or opinions. He holds the whole assemblage of moral notions almost as so many collateral
and self-evident facts. Hence it is that some of the
most deeply-exercised and variously gifted Christians,
when they proceed to write or speak upon religion,
either fail altogether, or cannot be understood except
on an attentive study; and after all, perhaps, are
illogical and unsystematic, assuming what their readers require proved, and seeming to mistake connexion or antecedence for causation, probability for

evidence. And over such as these it is, that the minute
intellect of inferior men has its moment of triumph,
men who excel in a mere shortsighted perspicacity;
not understanding that, even in the case of intellectual excellence, it is considered the highest of gifts
to possess an intuitive knowledge of the beautiful in
art, or the effective in action, without reasoning or
investigating; that this, in fact, is *genius*; and that
they who have a corresponding insight into moral
truth (as far as they have it) have reached that especial perfection in the spiritual part of their nature,
which is so rarely found, and so greatly prized among
the intellectual endowments of the soul.

Nay, may we not further venture to assert, not only
that moral Truth will be least skilfully defended by
those, as such, who are the genuine depositories of
it, but that it cannot be adequately explained and
defended in words at all? Its views and human
language are incommensurable.   For, after all, what
is language but an artificial system adapted for particular purposes, which have been determined by our
wants? And here, even at first sight, can we imagine
that it has been framed with a view to ideas so refined, so foreign to the whole course of the world, as
those which (as Scripture expresses it) "no man can
learn," but the select remnant who are "redeemed
from the earth," and in whose mouth "is found no
guile[6]?"   Nor is it this heavenly language alone

[6] Rev. xiv. 3, 5.

which is without its intellectual counterpart. Moral character in itself, whether good or bad, as exhibited in thought and conduct, surely cannot be duly represented in words. We may, indeed, by an effort, reduce it in a certain degree to this arbitrary medium ; but in its combined dimensions it is as impossible to write and read a man (so to express it), as to give literal depth to a painted tablet.

With these remarks on the nature of moral Truth, as viewed externally, let us conduct our secluded teacher, who is the embodied specimen of it, after his thirty years' preparation for his office, into the noise and tumult of the world ; and in order to set him fairly on the course, let us suppose him recommended by some external gift, whether ordinary or extraordinary, the power of miracles, the countenance of rulers, or a reputation for learning, such as may secure a hearing for him from the multitude of men. This must be supposed, in consequence of the very constitution of the present world. Amid its incessant din, nothing will attract attention but what cries aloud and spares not. It is an old proverb, that men profess a sincere respect for virtue, and then let her starve; for they have at the bottom of their hearts an evil feeling, in spite of better thoughts, that to be bound to certain laws and principles is a superstition and a slavery, and that freedom consists in the actual exercise of the will in evil as well as in good ; and they witness (what cannot be denied) that a man who throws off the yoke of strict conscientiousness, indefinitely increases his producible talent for the time, and his immediate power of attaining his ends. At best they will but admire the religious man, and treat him with deference; but in his absence they are compelled (as they say) to confess that a being so amiable and gentle is not suited to play his part in the scene of life; that he is too good for this world; that he is framed for a more primitive and purer age, and born out of due time. Μακαρίσαντες ὑμῶν τὸ ἀπειρόκακον, says the scoffing politician in the history, οὐ ζηλοῦμεν τὸ ἄφρον; would not the great majority of men, high and low, thus speak of St. John the Apostle, were he now living?

Therefore, we must invest our Teacher with a certain gift of power, that he may be feared. But even then, how hopeless does his task seem to be at first sight! how improbable that he should be able to proceed one step farther than his external recommendation carries him forward! so that it is a marvel how the Truth has ever been spread and maintained among men. For, recollect, it is not a mere set of opinions that he has to promulgate, which may lodge on the surface of the mind; but he is to be an instrument in changing (as Scripture speaks) the heart, and modelling all men after one exemplar; making them like himself, or rather One above himself, who is the beginning of a new creation. Having (as has been said) no sufficient eloquence—nay, not language at his command—what instruments can he be said to possess? Thus he is, from the nature of the case,

thrown upon his personal resources, whether greater
or less; for it is plain he cannot commit his charge
to others as his representatives, and be translated
(as it were) and circulated through the world, till he
has made others like himself.

Turn to the history of Truth, and these anticipations are fulfilled.   Some hearers of it had their
conscience stirred for a while, and many were affected by the awful simplicity of the Great Teacher;
but the proud and sensual were irritated into opposition;   the philosophic considered His doctrines
strange and chimerical; the multitude followed for
a time in senseless wonder, and then suddenly abandoned an apparently falling cause.   For, in truth,
what was the task of an Apostle, but to raise the
dead? and what trifling would it appear, even to the
most benevolent and candid men of the world, when
such a one persisted to chafe and stimulate the limbs
of the inanimate corpse, as if his own life could be
communicated to it, or motion would continue one
moment after the external effort was withdrawn! in
the poet's words,

> θράσος ἀκούσιον
> ἀνδράσι θνήσκουσι κομίζων.

Truly such a one must expect, at best, to be accounted but a babbler, or one deranged by his "much
learning"—a visionary and an enthusiast,—

> κἄρτ' ἀπομούσως ἦσθα γεγραμμένος,

fit for the wilderness or the temple; a jest at the

Areopagus, and but a gladiatorial show at Ephesus, ἐπιθανάτιος, an actor in an exhibition which would finish in his own death.

Yet (blessed be God!) the power of Truth actually did, by some means or other, overcome these vast obstacles to its propagation; and what those means were, we shall best understand by contemplating it, as it now shows itself when established and generally professed; an ordinary sanction having taken the place of miracles, and infidelity being the assailant instead of the assailed party.

It will not require many words to make it evident how impetuous and (for the time) how triumphant an attack the rebellious Reason will conduct against the long-established, over-secure, and but silently-working system of which Truth is the vital principle.

1. First, every part of the Truth is novel to its opponent; and, seen detached from the whole, becomes an objection. It is only necessary for Reason to ask many questions ; and, while the other party is investigating the real answer to each in detail, to claim the victory, which spectators will not be slow to award, fancying (as is the manner of men) that clear and ready speech is the test of Truth. And it can choose its questions, selecting what appears most objectionable in the tenets and practices of the received system ; and it will (in all probability) even unintentionally, fall upon the most difficult parts ; what is on the surface being at once most conspicuous, and also furthest removed from the centre on which

it depends. On the other hand, its objections will be complete in themselves from their very minuteness. Thus, for instance, men attack the ceremonies and discipline of the Church, appealing to common sense, as they call it; which really means, appealing to some proposition which, though true in its own province, is nothing to the purpose in theology; or appealing to the logical accuracy of the argument, when every thing turns on the real meaning of the terms employed, which can only be understood by the religious mind.

2. Next, men who investigate in this merely intellectual way, without sufficient basis and guidance in their personal virtue, are bound by no fears or delicacy. Not only from dulness, but by preference, they select ground for the contest, which a reverent Faith wishes to keep sacred; and, while the latter is looking to its stepping, lest it commit sacrilege, they have the unembarrassed use of their eyes for the combat, and overcome, by skill and agility, one stronger than themselves.

3. Further, the warfare between Error and Truth is necessarily advantageous to the former, from its very nature, as being conducted by set speech or treatise; and this, not only for a reason already assigned, the deficiency of Truth in the power of eloquence, and even of words, but moreover from the very neatness and definiteness thereby required in the handling of the argument. Truth is vast and far-stretching, viewed as a system; and, viewed in

2

its separate doctrines, it depends on the combination of a number of various, delicate, and scattered evidences : hence it can scarcely be exhibited in a given number of sentences. If it be attempted, its advocate, unable to exhibit more than a fragment of the whole, must round off its rugged extremities, and unite its straggling lines, by much the same process by which an historical narrative is converted into a tale. This, indeed, is the very *art* of composition, which, accordingly, is only with extreme trouble preserved clear of exaggeration and artifice; and who does not see that all this is favourable to the cause of error,—to that party which has not faith enough to be patient of doubt, and has just talent enough to consider perspicuity the chief excellence of a writer? To illustrate this, we may contrast the works of Bishop Butler with those of that popular infidel writer at the end of the last century, who professed to be the harbinger of an Age of Reason.

4. Moreover, this great, though dangerous faculty which evil employs as its instrument in its warfare against the Truth, may simulate all kinds of virtue, and become the rival of the true saints of God, whom it is opposing. It may draw fine pictures of virtue, or trace out the course of sacred feelings or of serious reflections. Nothing is so easy as to be religious on paper; and thus the arms of Truth are turned, as far as may be found necessary, against itself.

5. It must be further observed, that the exhibitions of Reason, being complete in themselves, and

having nothing of a personal nature, are capable almost of an omnipresence by an indefinite multiplication and circulation, through the medium of composition: here, even the orator has greatly the advantage over the religious man; words may be heard by thousands at once,—a good deed will be witnessed and estimated at most by but a few.

6. To put an end to these remarks on the advantages accruing to Error in its stru gle with Truth, the exhibitions of the Reason, being in their operation separable from the person exerting them, possess little or no responsibility. To be anonymous is almost their characteristic, and with it all the evils attendant on the unchecked opportunity for injustice and falsehood.

Such, then, are the difficulties which beset the propagation of the Truth: its want of instruments, as an assailant of the world's opinions; the keenness and vigour of the weapons producible against it when itself in turn is to be attacked. How, then, after all, has it maintained its ground among men, and subjected to its dominion unwilling minds, some even bound to the external profession of obedience, others at least in a sullen neutrality, and the inaction of despair?

I answer, that it has been upheld in the world, not as a system, not by books, not by argument, nor by temporal power, but by the personal influence of such men as have already been described, who are at once the teachers and the patterns of it; and, with some suggestions in behalf of this statement, I shall conclude.

1. Here, first, is to be taken into account the natural beauty and majesty of virtue, which is more or less felt by all but the most abandoned. I do not say virtue in the abstract,—virtue in a book. Men persuade themselves, with little difficulty, to scoff at principles, to ridicule books, to make sport of the names of good men; but they cannot bear their presence: it is holiness, embodied in personal form, which they cannot steadily confront and bear down: so that the silent conduct of a conscientious man secures for him from beholders a feeling different in kind from any which is created by the mere versatile and garrulous Reason.

2. Next, consider the extreme rarity, in any great perfection and purity, of simple-minded, honest devotion to God; and another instrument of influence is discovered for the cause of Truth. Men naturally prize what is novel and scarce; and, considering the low views of the multitude on points of social and religious duty, their ignorance of those precepts of generosity, self-denial, and high-minded patience, which religion enforces, nay, their scepticism (whether known to themselves or not) of the existence in the world of severe holiness and truth, no wonder they are amazed when accident gives them a sight of these excellences in another, as though they beheld a miracle; and they watch it with a mixture of curiosity and awe.

3. Besides, the conduct of a religious man is quite above them. They cannot imitate him, if they try. It may be easy for the educated among them to make speeches, or to write books; but high moral excellence is the attribute of a school to which they are almost strangers, having scarcely learned, and that painfully, the first elements of the heavenly science. One little deed, done against natural inclination for God's sake, though in itself of a conceding or passive character, (to brook an insult, to face a danger, or to resign an advantage,) has in it a power outbalancing all the dust and chaff of mere profession; the profession whether of enlightened benevolence and candour, or, on the other hand, of high religious faith and of fervent zeal.

4. And men feel, moreover, that the object of their contemplation is beyond their reach—not open to the common temptations which influence men, and grounded on a foundation which they cannot explain. And nothing is more effectual, first in irritating, then in humbling the pride of men, than the sight of a superior altogether independent of themselves.

5. The consistency of virtue is another gift, which gradually checks the rudeness of the world, and tames it into obedience to itself. The changes of human affairs, which first excited and interested, at length disgust the mind, which then begins to look out for something on which it can rely, for peace and rest; and what can then be found immutable and sure, but God's word and promises, illustrated and conveyed to

the inquirer in the person of His faithful servants?
Every day shows us how much depends on firmness
for obtaining influence in practical matters; and
what are all kinds of firmness, as exhibited in the
world, but likenesses and offshoots of that true stability of heart which is stayed in the grace, and in the
contemplation of Almighty God?

6. Such especially will be the thoughts of those
countless multitudes, who, in the course of their trial,
are from time to time weighed down by affliction, or
distressed by bodily pain.   This will be, in their case,
the strong hour of Truth, which, though unheard and
unseen by men as a body, approaches each one of
that body in his own turn, though at a different time.
Then it is that the powers of the world, its counsels,
and its efforts (vigorous as they seemed to be in the
race), lose ground, and slow-paced Truth overtakes
them; and thus it comes to pass, that, while the outward course of things seems ever hastening onwards
to open infidelity and sin, there are ten thousand
secret obstacles, graciously sent from God, cumbering
its chariot-wheels, so that they drive heavily, and
saving it from utter ruin.

Even with these few considerations before us, we
shall find it difficult to estimate the moral power
which a single individual, trained to practise what he
teaches, may acquire in his own circle, in the course
of years.   While the Scriptures are thrown upon the
world, as if the common property of any who choose
to appropriate them, he is, in fact, the legitimate in-

terpreter of them, and none other; the Inspired Word being but a dead letter, (ordinarily considered,) except as transmitted from one mind to another. While he is unknown to the world, yet, within the range of those who see him, he will become the object of feelings different in kind from those which mere intellectual excellence excites. The men commonly held in popular estimation are greatest at a distance; they become small as they are approached; but the attraction, exerted by unconscious holiness, is of an urgent and irresistible nature; it persuades the weak, the timid, the wavering, and the inquiring; it draws forth the affection and loyalty of all who are in a measure like-minded; and over the thoughtless or perverse multitude it exercises a sovereign compulsory sway, bidding them fear and keep silence, on the ground of its own right Divine to rule them; its hereditary claim on their obedience, though they understand not the principles or counsels of that spirit, which is " born, not of blood, nor of the will of the flesh, nor of the will of man, but of God."

And if such be the personal influence excited by the Teacher of Truth over the mixed crowd of men whom he encounters, what (think we) will be his power over that select number, just referred to, who have already, in a measure, disciplined their hearts after the law of holiness, and feel themselves, as it were, individually addressed by the invitation of his example? These are they whom our Lord especially calls His " elect," and came to " gather together in

one," for they are worthy. And these, too, are they
who are ordained in God's Providence to be the salt
of the earth,—to continue, in their turn, the succession of His witnesses, that heirs may never be
wanting to the royal line, though death sweeps away
each successive generation of them to their rest and
their reward. These, perhaps, by chance fell in with
their destined father in the Truth, not at once discerning his real greatness. At first, perhaps, they
thought his teaching fanciful, and parts of his conduct extravagant or weak. Years might pass away
before such prejudices were entirely removed from
their minds; but by degrees they would discern more
and more the traces of unearthly majesty about him ;
they would witness, from time to time, his trial under
the various events of life, and would still find, whether
they looked above or below, that he rose higher, and
was based deeper, than they could ascertain by
measurement. Then, at length, with astonishment
and fear, they would become aware that Christ's
presence was before them ; and, in the words of
Scripture, would glorify God in His servant [7]; and
all this while they themselves would be changing into
that glorious Image which they gazed upon, and be
in training to succeed him in its dissemination.

Will it be said, This is a fancy, which no experience
confirms ? First, no irreligious man can know anything concerning the hidden saints. Next, no one,

---

[7] Gal. i. 24.

religious or not, can detect them without attentive study of them. But, after all, say they are few, such high Christians; and what follows? They are enough to carry on God's noiseless work. The Apostles were such men; others might be named, in their several generations, as successors to their holiness. These communicate their light to a number of lesser luminaries, by whom, in its turn, it is distributed through the world; the first sources of illumination being all the while unseen, even by the majority of sincere Christians,—unseen as is that Supreme Author of Light and Truth, from whom all good primarily proceeds. A few highly-endowed men will rescue the world for centuries to come. Before now even one man[8] has impressed an image on the Church, which, through God's mercy, shall not be effaced while time lasts. Such men, like the Prophet, are placed upon their watch-tower, and light their beacons on the heights. Each receives and transmits the sacred flame, trimming it in rivalry of his predecessor, and fully purposed to send it on as bright as it has reached him; and thus the self-same fire, once kindled on Moriah, though seeming at intervals to fail, has at length reached us in safety, and will in like manner, as we trust, be carried forward even to the end.

To conclude. Such views of the nature and history of Divine Truth are calculated to make us con-

---

[8] Athanasius.

tented and resigned in our generation, whatever be
the peculiar character or the power of the errors of
our own times.   For Christ never will reign visibly
upon earth ; but in each age, as it comes, we shall
read of tumult and heresy, and hear the complaint
of good men marvelling at what they conceive to be
the especial wickedness of their own times.

Moreover, such considerations lead us to be satisfied with the humblest and most obscure lot; by
showing us, not only that we may be the instruments
of much good in it, but that (strictly speaking) we
could scarcely in any situation be direct instruments
of good to any besides those who personally know
us, who ever must form a small circle ; and as to
the indirect good we may do in a more exalted station (which is by no means to be lightly esteemed),
still we are not absolutely precluded from it in a
lower place in the Church.   Nay, it has happened
before now, that comparatively retired posts have
been filled by those who have exerted the most extensive influences over the destinies of religion in the
times following them ; as in the arts and pursuits of
this world, the great benefactors of mankind are frequently unknown.

Let all those, then, who acknowledge the voice of
God speaking within them, and urging them heaven-
ward, wait patiently for the end, exercising themselves, and diligently working, with a view to that day
when the books shall be opened, and all the disorder
of human affairs reviewed and set right ; when " the

last shall be first, and the first last;" when " all things that offend, and they which do iniquity," shall be gathered out and removed; when "the righteous shall shine forth as the sun," and Faith shall see her God; when " they that be wise shall shine as the brightness of the firmament, and they that turn many to righteousness as the stars, for ever and ever."

SERMON V.

ON JUSTICE, AS A PRINCIPLE OF DIVINE
GOVERNANCE.

Preached April 8, 1832.

JER. viii. 11.

" They have healed the hurt of the daughter of my people
slightly, saying, Peace, peace, when there is no peace."

THERE will ever be persons who take a favourable
view of human nature, as it actually is found in the
world, and of the spiritual condition and the prospects of mankind. And certainly the face of things
is so fair, and contains so much that is interesting
and lofty, that the spectator may be pardoned if, on
the first sight, he is disposed to believe them to be
as cheerful and as happy as they appear,—the evils of
life as light and transitory, and its issue as satisfactory. Such easy confidence is natural in youth ; nay,
it is even commendable at a time of life in which
suspicion and incredulity are unbecoming ; that is,
it *would* be commendable, did not Scripture acquaint
us from the very first (by way of warning, previous

to our actual experience) with the deceitfulness of the world's promises and teaching; telling us of the opposition between Sight and Faith, of that strait gate and that narrow way, the thought of which is to calm us in youth, that it may enliven and invigorate us in old age.

Yet, on the other hand, it cannot be denied that even the information of Scripture results in a cheerful view of human affairs, and condemns gloom and sadness as a sin, as well as a mistake; and thus, in fact, altogether sanctions the conclusions gathered from the first sight of the course of the world. But here is an instance, such as not unfrequently is found, of an opinion being abstractedly true, and yet the person who holds it wrong in his *mode* of holding it; so that while the terms in which he conveys it approach indefinitely near to those in which the true view is contained, neverthless men who maintain the very reverse may be nearer the truth than he is. It often happens that, in pursuing the successive stages of an investigation, the mind continually reverses its judgment to and fro, according as the weight of argument passes over and back again from the one alternative of the question to the other; and in such a case the ultimate utility of the inquiry does not consist in the conclusion finally adopted, which may be no other than that with which the inquiry was commenced; but in the position in which we have learned to view it, and the circumstances with which we have associated it. It is plain, too, that the man who has

gone through many of these progressive alterna-
tions of opinion, but has for some cause or other
stopped short of the true view legitimately termi-
nating the inquiry, would be further from it in the
mere enunciation of his sentiments, but in the state
of his mind far nearer to it, than he who has not examined the subject at all, and is right by accident.
Thus it happens, men are cheerful and secure from
ignorance of the evils of life; and they are secure,
again, from seeing the remedy of the evils ; and, on
the other hand, they are desponding from seeing the
evils without the remedy : so that we must never say
that an individual is right, merely on the ground of
his holding an opinion which happens to be true, unless he holds it in a particular manner ; that is, under
those conditions, and with that particular association
of thought and feeling, which in fact is the interpretation of it.

That superficial judgment, which happens to be
right without deserving to be so, is condemned in the
text.   The error of the prophets and priests there
spoken of consisted, not in promising a *cure* for the
wounded soul, but in healing the hurt of the daughter
of God's people *slightly*, saying, Peace, peace, before
they had ascertained either the evil or the remedy.
The Gospel is in its very name a message of peace,
but it must never be separated from the bad tidings
of our fallen nature, which it reverses ; and he who
speaks of the state of the world in a sanguine way,
may indeed be an advanced Christian, but he may

also be much less even than a proselyte of the gate;
and if his security and peace of mind be merely the
calm of ignorance, surely the men whom he looks
down upon as narrow-minded and superstitious, whose
religion consists in fear not in love, shall go into the
kingdom of heaven before him. We are reminded
of this important truth by the order of our ecclesiastical year. Easter Day, our chief Festival, is preceded by the forty days of Lent, to show us that
they, and they only, who sow in tears, shall reap in
joy.

Remarks such as these are scarcely necessary, as
far as we of this place are concerned, who, through
God's blessing, are teachers of His truth, and " by
reason of use have our senses exercised to discern
both good and evil." Yet it is impossible not to observe, and it is useful to bear in mind, that mankind
at large is not wiser or better than heretofore ; rather,
that it is an especial fault of the present day, to mistake the false security of the man of the world for
the composure, cheerfulness, and benevolence of the
true Christian ; while all the shades of character between these two, though indefinitely more deserving
of our respect than the former of them, I mean the
superstitious, the bigot, the intolerant, and the fa-
natic, are thrust out of the way as inhuman and
offensive, merely because their knowledge of themselves is more exact than their apprehension of the
Gospel, and their zeal for God's honour more energetic than their love of mankind.

This in fact is the fault incident to times of political peace and safety, when the world keeps well together, no motions stirring beneath it, to disturb the continuity of its surface, which for the time presents to us a consistent and finished picture. When the laws of a country are upheld and obeyed, and property secure, the world appears to realize that vision of constancy and permanence which it presented to our youthful imagination. Human nature appears more amiable than it really is, because it is not tried with disappointments; more just, because it is then its interest to respect the rights of others; more benevolent, because it can be so without self-denial. The warnings contained in the historical Scriptures, concerning the original baseness and corruption of the heart, are, in the course of time, neglected; or rather these very representations are adduced as a proof how much better the world now is than it was once; how much more enlightened, refined, intellectual, manly; and this, not without some secret feeling of disrespect towards the writers of the plain facts recorded in the Bible, as if, even were the case so bad as they make it' appear, it had been more judicious and humane to have said nothing about it.

But, fairly as this superficial view of human nature answers in peaceable times; speciously as it may argue, innocently as it may experimentalize, in the rare and short-lived intervals of a nation's tranquillity; yet, let persecution or tribulation arise, and forthwith its imbecility is discovered. It is but a theory; it

cannot cope with difficulties ; it imparts no strength
or loftiness of mind ; it gains no influence over others.
It is at once shattered and crushed in the stern conflict of good and evil ; disowned, or rather overlooked,
by the combatants on either side, and vanishing, no
one knows how or whither.

The opinions alluded to in the foregoing remarks,
when assuming a definite doctrinal basis, will be found
to centre in Socinianism or Theophilanthropism, the
name varying according as it admits or rejects the
authority of Scripture.   And the spirit of this system
will be found to infect great numbers of men, who
are unconscious of the origin and tendency of their
opinions.   The essential dogmas of Socinianism are
such as these ; that the rule of Divine government
is one of benevolence, and nothing but benevolence ;
that evil is but remedial and temporary ; that sin is
of a venial nature; that repentance is a sufficient
atonement for it ; that the moral sense is substan-
tially but an instinct of benevolence, and that doctrinal opinions do not influence the character or prospects, nor deserve our serious attention.   On the
other hand, sentiments of this character are evidently
the animating principle of the false cheerfulness, and
the ill-founded hope, and the blind charitableness,
which have already been assigned to the man of the
world.

In order to illustrate the untenableness of such
positions as have just been adduced, and hence to
show, by way of instance, the shallowness and

feebleness of the minds which maintain them, their
real feebleness in all practical matters, plausibly or
loudly as they may speak during the hour of tranquillity in which they display themselves, it may be useful to make some remarks on what appears to be the
real judgment of God upon human sin, as far as it
is discernible by the light of nature; not as if anything new could be said on the subject, but in order
to remind ourselves of truths which are peculiarly
important in these times.

The consideration chiefly adduced by the advocate
for the absolute, unmixed benevolence of the Divine
government, and for the venial nature of sin according
to the provisions of that government, is an *à priori*
argument, founded on an appeal to a supposed instinct
of our nature. It has before now been put familiarly
thus:—"Is there any man living who would not, if he
could, accomplish the final restitution and eternal
happiness of every individual? and are we more benevolent than God?" Or, again, the same general
argument is sometimes stated more cautiously as follows; that "no man can be in a perfectly right state
of mind, who, if he consider general happiness at all,
is not ready to acknowledge that a good man must
regard it as being in its own nature the most desirable
of *all* objects; and that any habitual disposition
clearly discerned to be, in its whole result, at variance
with general happiness, is unworthy of being cultivated, or fit to be rooted out; that accordingly, we are
compelled to attribute God's *whole* government to

benevolence; that it is as much impossible for us to love and revere a Being, to whom we ascribe a mixed or imperfect benevolence, as to believe the most positive contradictions in terms; that is, as religion *consists* in love and reverence, *it* cannot subsist without a belief in benevolence as the *sole* principle of Divine government."

Now first, it is surely not true that benevolence *is* the only, or the chief, principle, of our moral nature. To say nothing of the notion of duty to an Unseen Governor, implied in the very authoritativeness with which conscience dictates to us (a notion which suggests to the mind that there *is*, in truth, some object more " desirable in its own nature " than " the general happiness " of mankind,—viz. the approbation of our Maker), not to insist on this, it may be confidently asserted, that the instincts of justice and of purity are natural to us in the same sense in which benevolence is natural. If it be natural to pity and wish well to men in general, without reference to their character, or our personal knowledge of them, or any other attendant circumstance, it is also natural to feel indignation when vice triumphs, and to be dissatisfied and uneasy till the inequality is removed.

In order to meet this objection, it is maintained by the writers under consideration, that the good of mankind is the ultimate end to which even the principle of justice, planted in us, tends; that the rule of reward and punishment is a chief means of making men happy; and therefore that the feelings of indignation, resentment, and the like, must be considered as given us, not for their own sake (granting them given us), but in order to ensure the general good of mankind; in other words, that they are no evidence of the existence of justice as an original and absolute principle of the moral law, but only of that infinite unmixed benevolence of God, to which the feelings in question are in our case subservient. But this is nothing but an assertion, and will not stand examination; for true as it is, that the instinct of justice, implanted in us, tends to *general* good,—good on the whole,—it evidently does not tend to *universal* good, the good of each individual; and nothing short of this can be the scope of absolute and simple benevolence. Our indignation at vice tends to the actual misery of the vicious (whether such be many or few)—nay, to their *final* misery, except indeed there be provisions in the world's system, hitherto concealed, securing the ultimate destruction of vice; for *while* it remained, it and all connected with it would ever be the natural objects of our abhorrence, and this natural abhorrence evidently interferes with the hypothesis, that universal good is the one end to which the present system of Divine governance tends.

On the other hand, so far from its being " impossible (as the theory under consideration affirms) to love and revere a Being to whom we ascribe a mixed benevolence," while undoubtedly benevolence excites our love and reverence, so does a perfect justice too; we are under a natural attraction to admire and

adore the great sight, just as we are led on (to compare small things with great) to dwell rapturously
upon some exquisite work of man's designing, the
beautiful and harmonious result of the highest and
most accomplished genius.   If we do not habitually
thus search out and lovingly hang over the traces of
God's justice, which are around us, it is because we
are ourselves sinners; because, having a bad conscience, we have a personal interest in denying them,
and a terror in having them forced upon us.   In proportion as we grow in habits of obedience, far from
our vision of the eternal justice of God vanishing from
our minds, and being disowned by our feelings, as if
it were but the useful misconception of a less advanced virtue, doubtless it increases, as fear is cast
out.   The saints in heaven ascribe glory to God,
" for *true and righteous* are His judgments."   " Great
and marvellous are Thy works, Lord God Almighty;
just and true are Thy ways, Thou King of saints [1]."
If, then, the infinite benevolence of God wins our
love, certainly His justice commands it; and were
we able, as the saints made perfect are able, to combine the notion of both in their separate perfections,
as displayed in the same acts, doubtless our awe and
admiration of the glorious vision would be immeasur-
ably increased.

Moreover, that justice is a primary notion in our
minds, and does not admit of resolution into other

[1] Rev. xv. 3.

elements, may be argued from its connexion with
that general love of order, congruity, and symmetry,
to which I have been alluding,—that very desire of
arranging and simplifying, which is made use of for
the purpose of denying its elementary nature, and
which must, in its essence, be considered, if any
thing is considered, an original principle of human
nature.

Nay, it may be doubted whether the notion of justice be not more essential to the mental constitution
of free agents, than benevolence can be. For our
very consciousness of being free, and so responsible,
includes in it the idea of an unchangeable rule of
justice, on which the judgment is hereafter to be conducted; or rather excludes, as far as it goes, the notion
of a simply benevolent Governor; a simply benevolent end being relinquished (as we may speak) by
the Creator, so soon as He committed the destinies
of man to his own hands, and made him a first cause,
a principle of origination, in the moral world.

But even if the general happiness of mankind
could be assigned in hypothesis, as the one end to
which all our moral instincts tended, and though
nothing could be adduced in behalf of the intrinsic
authority of the notion of justice, it would not be
allowable thence to infer the unmixed benevolence
of the Divine Mind, seeing we have actual evidences of
His justice in the course of the world, such as cannot
be explained away by a mere argument from the
analogy of our own nature. Should any one attempt

here to repeat the process of simplification, and refer in turn Divine justice, as seen in the world, to Divine benevolence, as if reward and punishment were but means to the one end of general good, let such a venturous speculator bethink himself what he is essaying, when he undertakes to simplify such attributes of the Divine mind, as the course of things happens to manifest to him. Not to insist on the presumption (as I may well call it) of the attempt, let him ask himself, merely as a philosopher, whether there is no difference between referring phenomena to an hypothetical law or system for convenience-sake (as, for instance, he is accustomed to refer the movements of the physical world to gravitation), and on the other hand undertaking to assign and fix, as a matter of fact, the real, primary and universal principles which guide the acts of a Mind, unknown and infinite, and that, from a knowledge of merely one or two characteristics of His mode of acting. After all, what is meant by affirming that God has, strictly speaking, *any* end or design in what He does, external to Himself? We see the world, physical and moral, as a fact ; and we see the Attributes of God, as they are called, displayed in it ; but before we attempt to decide whether or not the happiness of His creatures is the solitary all·absorbing end of His government, let us try to determine by the way of Reason what was His particular view in creating us at all. What indeed Revelation has told us, that we are able to speak confidently about, and it is our blessedness to be able;

but Revelation does not come into this question. By
the use of unaided Reason, we are utterly incapable
of conceiving, why a Being supremely blessed in Himself from eternity should ever commence the work
of creation; what the design of creation is, as such;
whether, if there be any end in it, it is not one different in kind, utterly removed from any which ear
hath heard or mind conceived; and whether the creation of man in the first instance, and therefore his happiness inclusively, may not be altogether subservient
to further ends in the scope of His purposes. Doubtless it is our wisdom, both as to the world and as to
Scripture, to take things as we find them; not to be
wise above what is written, whether in nature or in
grace; not to attempt a theory where we must
reason without data; much less could we frame one,
to mistake it for a fact instead of what it is, an arbitrary arrangement of our own knowledge, whatever
that may be, and nothing more.

Considerations such as these are sufficient for the
purpose for which I have employed them; sufficient
to repel and retort upon those who would undermine
our faith, little as they may mean to do so, with their
own weapons; nay, rather who would lead us, not
merely to a rejection or perversion of Christianity,
but even to a denial of the visible course of things as
it actually exists; that is, to that unreal and unpractical view of human nature which was described in the
outset.   And now, before concluding, let us observe
what the world teaches us, in matter of fact, con-

cerning the light in which sin is regarded by our great Governor and Judge.

Here it is usual to insist on the visible consequences of single sins, as furnishing some foreboding of the full and final judgment of God upon all we do; and the survey of such instances is very striking. A solitary act of intemperance, sensuality, or anger, a single rash word, a single dishonest deed, is often the cause of incalculable misery in the sequel to the person who has been betrayed into it. Our fortunes are frequently shaped by the thoughtless and seemingly inconsiderable sins of our early life. The quarrel of an hour, the sudden yielding to temptation, will throw a man into an unadvantageous line of life, bring him into trouble, ruin his prospects; or again, into circumstances unfavourable to his religious interests, which unsettle his mind, and ultimately lead him to abandon his faith. All through life we may suffer the penalty of past disobedience; disobedience, too, which we now can hardly enter into and realize, which is most foreign to our present principles and feelings, which we can hardly recognize as belonging to us, just as if no identity existed between our present and our former selves.

Should it be said that this does not in all or in most cases happen, I answer, that were there but a few such cases they would be sufficient to destroy the hypothesis, already remarked upon, of the unmixed benevolence of the Divine government. For they are in many instances too definite and significant to

be explained as remedial measures, or as any thing
short of judgments on sin; and in fact, they have
been acknowledged as such by the common sense of
mankind in every age; and on the other hand, it con-
stantly happens that they neither effect, nor evince a
tendency towards effecting, the moral benefit of the
individuals thus punished.   But further, granting
they are but isolated instances of God's judgment
concerning the guilt of disobedience; yet, if we believe that His Providence proceeds on any fixed
plan, and that all deeds are impartially recompensed
according to their nature, it seems to follow, that
since some sins evidently do receive an after punishment, therefore all have the prospect of the like;
and consequently that those who escape here, will
suffer hereafter: that this is the rule; and if there
be any additional law counteracting it, this has to be
proved.   What measure of punishment is reserved
for us, we cannot tell; but the actual consequences
which we witness of apparently slight offences, make
the prospect before us alarming.   If any law is traceable in this awful subject, it would appear to be this,
that the greater the delay, the greater the punishment,
if it comes at length; as if a suspension of immediate vengeance were an indulgence only to be com-
pensated by an accumulated suffering afterwards.

Then, as to the efficacy of repentance, which is so
much insisted on,—when repentance is spoken of
as being a sufficient substitute in itself, by a self-
evident fitness, though not for the consequences of

sin in this life, yet for the future punishment, let the following remark be considered, which is a solemn one.   I ask, does death, which is supposed to terminate the punishment of the penitent, terminate the consequences of his sins upon others?   Are not these consequences continued long after his death, even to the end of time?   And do they not thus seem to be a sort of intimation or symbol to survivors, that, in spite of his penitence, God's wrath is hot against him?   A man publishes an irreligious or immoral book; afterwards he repents, and dies.   What does Reason, arguing from the visible course of things, suggest concerning the efficacy of that repentance?   The sin of the penitent lives; it continues to disseminate evil; it corrupts multitudes.   *They* die many of them *without* repenting; many more receive permanent, though not fatal injury to their souls, from the perusal.   Surely no evidence is here, in the course of Divine Governance, of the efficacy of repentance.   Shall *he* be now dwelling in Abraham's bosom, who hears on the other side of the gulf the voices of those who curse his memory as being the victims of his guilt?

Against these fearful traces or omens of God's visitation upon sin, we are, of course, at liberty to set all the gracious intimations given us in nature of His placability.   Certain as it is, that all our efforts and all our repentance are often unable to rid us of the consequences of previous disobedience, yet doubtless they often alleviate these, and often remove them.

And this goes to show that His Governance is not one of absolute unmixed justice, which, of course, (were it so,) would reduce every one of us to a state of despair.   Nothing, however, is told us in nature of the limits of the two rules, of love and of justice, or how they are to be reconciled; nothing to show that the rule of mercy, as acting on moral agents, is more than the supplement, not the substitute, of the fundamental law of justice and holiness.   And, let it be added, taking us even as we are, much as each of us has to be forgiven, yet a religious man would hardly wish the rule of justice obliterated.   It is a something which he can depend on and recur to; it gives a character and a certainty to the course of Divine Governance; and, tempered by the hope of mercy, it suggests animating and consolatory thoughts to him; so that, far from readily acquiescing in the theory of God's unmixed benevolence, he will rather protest against it as the invention of those who, in their eagerness to conciliate the enemies of the Truth, care little about distressing and sacrificing its friends.

Different, indeed, is his view of God and of man, of the claims of God, of man's resources, of the guilt of disobedience, and of the prospect of forgiveness, from those flimsy self-invented notions, which satisfy the reason of the mere man of letters, or the prosperous and self-indulgent philosopher!   It is easy to speak eloquently of the order and beauty of the physical world, of the wise contrivances of visible nature, and the benevolence of the objects proposed in them;

but none of those topics throw light upon the subject which it most concerns us to understand, the character of the moral governance under which we live; yet, is not this the way of the wise in this world, viz. instead of studying that governance as a primary subject of inquiry, to assume they know it, or to conceive of it after the truths of Natural Theology, or, at best, to take their notions of it from what appears on the mere surface of human society?—as if men did not put on their gayest and most showy apparel when they went abroad!   To see truly the cost and misery of sinning, we must quit the public haunts of business and pleasure, and be able, like the Angels, to see the tears shed in secret,—to witness the anguish of pride and impatience, where there is no sorrow,—the stings of remorse, where yet there is no repentance,—the wearing, never-ceasing struggle between conscience and sin,—the misery of indecision,—the harassing, haunting fears of death, and a judgment to come,—and the superstitions which these engender. Who can name the overwhelming total of the world's guilt and suffering,—suffering crying for vengeance on the authors of it, and guilt foreboding it!

Yet one need not shrink from appealing even to the outward face of the world, as proving to us the extreme awfulness of our condition, as sinners against the law of our being; for a strange fact it is, that, boldly as the world talks of its own greatness and its enjoyments, and easily as it deceives the mere theophilanthropist, yet, when it proceeds to the thought of

its Maker, it has ever professed a gloomy religion, in
spite of itself. This has been the case in all times
and places. Barbarous and civilized nations here
agree. The world cannot bear up against the Truth,
with all its boastings. It makes an open mock at
sin, yet secretly attempts to secure an interest against
its possible consequences in the world to come.
Where has not the custom prevailed of propitiating,
if possible, the unseen powers of heaven?—but why,
unless man were universally conscious of his danger,
and feared the punishment of sin, while he " hated
to be reformed?" Where have not sacrifices been in
use, as means of appeasing the Divine displeasure?—
and men have anxiously sought out what it was they
loved best, and would miss most painfully, as if to
strip themselves of it might move the compassion of
God. Some have gone so far as to offer their sons
and their daughters as a ransom for their own sin,—
an abominable crime doubtless, and a sacrifice to
devils, yet clearly witnessing man's instinctive judgment upon his own guilt, and his foreboding of punishment. How much more simple a course had it
been, merely to have been sorry for disobedience,
and to profess repentance, were it a natural doctrine
(as some pretend), that repentance is an atonement
for offences committed!

Nor is this all. Not only in their possessions and
their offspring, but in their own persons, have men
mortified themselves, with the hope of expiating
deeds of evil. Burnt-offerings, calves of a year old,

thousands of rams, and ten thousands of rivers of oil, their first-born for their transgression, the fruit of their body for the sin of their soul; even these are insufficient to lull the sharp throbbings of a heavy-laden conscience. Think of the bodily tortures to which multitudes have gloomily subjected themselves, and that for years, under almost every religious system, with a view of ridding themselves of their sins, and judge what man conceives of the guilt of disobedience. You will say that such fierceness in self-tormenting is a mental disease, and grows on a man. But this answer, granting there is truth in it, does not account for the reverence in which such persons have usually been held. Have we no instinct of self-preservation? Would these same persons gain the admiration of others, unless their cruelty to their own flesh arose from a religious motive? Would they not be derided as madmen, unless they sheltered themselves under the sanction of an awful, admitted truth, the corruption and the guilt of human nature?

But it will be said, that Christians, at least, must admit that these frightful exhibitions of self-torture are superstition. Here I may refer to the remarks with which I began. Doubtless these desperate and dark struggles are to be called superstition, when viewed by the side of true religion; and it is easy enough to speak of them as superstition, when we have been informed of the gracious and joyful result in which the scheme of Divine Governance issues.

But it is man's truest and best religion, *before* the Gospel shines on him. If our race *be* in a fallen and depraved state, what ought our religion to be but anxiety and remorse, till God comfort us? Surely, to be in gloom,—to view ourselves with horror,—to look about to the right hand and to the left for means of safety,—to catch at every thing, yet trust in nothing,—to do all we can, and try to do more than all,—and, after all, to wait in miserable suspense, naked and shivering, among the trees of the garden, for the hour of His coming, and meanwhile to fancy sounds of woe in every wind stirring the leaves about us,—in a word, to be superstitious,—is nature's best offering, her most acceptable service, her most mature and enlarged wisdom, in the presence of a holy and offended God. They who are not superstitious without the Gospel, will not be religious with it: and I would that even in us, who have the Gospel, there were more of superstition than there is; for much is it to be feared that our security about ourselves arises from defect in self-knowledge rather than in fulness of faith, and that we appropriate to ourselves promises which we cannot read.

To conclude. Thoughts concerning the Justice of God, such as those which have engaged our attention, though they do not, of course, explain to us the mystery of the great Christian Atonement for sin, show the use of the doctrine to us sinners. Why Christ's death was requisite for our salvation, and how it has obtained it, will ever be a mystery in this life.   But, on the other hand, the contemplation of our guilt is so growing and so overwhelming a misery, as our eyes open on our real state, that some strong act (so to call it) was necessary, on God's part, to counterbalance the tokens of His wrath which are around us, to calm and reassure us, and to be the ground and the medium of our faith.   It seems, indeed, as if, in a practical point of view, no mere promise was sufficient to undo the impression left on the imagination by the facts of Natural Religion; but in the death of His Son we have His *deed*—His irreversible deed—making His forgiveness of sin, and His reconciliation with our race, no contingency, but an event of past history.   He has vouchsafed to evidence His faithfulness and sincerity towards us (if we may dare so to speak) as we must show ours towards Him, not in word, but by action; which, therefore, becomes the pledge of His mercy, and the plea on which we draw near to His presence;—or, in the words of Scripture, whereas " all have sinned, and come short of the glory of God," Christ Jesus is " set forth as a propitiation for the remission of sins that are past," to declare and assure us, that, without departing from the just rule, by which all men must, in the main, be tried, still He will pardon and justify " him that believeth in Jesus."

SERMON VI.

CONTEST BETWEEN FAITH AND SIGHT.

Preached May 27, 1832.

1 John v. 4.

" This is the victory that overcometh the world, even our faith."

THE danger to which Christians are exposed from the
influence of the visible course of things, or the world,
(as it is called in Scripture,) is a principal subject of
St. John's general Epistle.   He seems to speak of
the world as some False Prophet, promising what it
cannot fulfil, and gaining credit by its confident tone.
Viewing it as resisting Christianity, he calls it the
" spirit of anti-Christ," the parent of a numerous
progeny of evil, false spirits like itself, the teachers
of all lying doctrines, by which the multitude of men
are led captive.   The antagonist of this great tempter
is the spirit of Truth, which is " greater than he
that is in the world;" its victorious antagonist, as
gifted with those piercing eyes of Faith, which are

able to scan the world's shallowness, and to see
through the mists of error into the glorious kingdom
of God beyond them. "This is the victory that
overcometh the world," says the text, " even our
Faith." And if we inquire what are the sights which
our faith sees, the Apostle answers by telling us of
" the spirit that beareth witness, because the Spirit
is Truth." The world witnesses to an untruth, which
which will one day be exposed; and Christ, our Lord
and Master, is " the Amen, the faithful and true
witness," who came into the world " by water and
blood," to " bear witness unto the Truth;" that, as
the many voices of error bear down and overpower
the inquirer by their tumult and importunity, so, on
the other hand, Truth might have its living and
visible representative, no longer cast, like the bread,
at random on the waters, or painfully gained from
the schools and traditions of men, but committed to
One " come in the flesh," to One who has an earthly
name and habitation, who, in one sense, is one of the
powers of this world, who has His train and retinue,
His court and kingdom, His ministering servants,
bound together by the tie of brotherly love among
themselves, and of zeal against the Prophets of error.
" Who is he that overcometh the world, but he that
believeth that Jesus is the Son of God?" St. John
then compares together the force of the world's testimony, and of that which the Gospel provides. " If
we receive the witness of men, the witness of God is
greater; for this is the witness of God which He has

testified of His Son;" as if " the spirit, the water, and the blood," spoke for God more loudly than the world speaks for the Evil one. In the very opening of the Epistle, he had set before us in another form the same gracious truth, viz., that the Gospel, by affording us, in the Person and history of Christ, a witness of the invisible world, addresses itself to our senses and imagination, after the very manner in which the false doctrines of the world assail us. " That which was from the beginning, ... which we have looked upon, ... that which we have seen and heard, declare we unto you."

Now, here we have incidentally suggested to us an important truth, which, obvious as it is, may give rise to some profitable reflections; viz., that the world overcomes us, not merely by appealing to our reason, or exciting our passions, but by imposing on our imagination. So much do the systems of men swerve from the Truth as set forth in Scripture, that their very presence becomes a standing fact against Scripture, even when our reason condemns them, by their persevering assertions, and they gradually overcome those who set out by contradicting them. In all cases, what is often and unhesitatingly asserted, at length finds credit with the mass of mankind ; and so it happens, in this instance, that admitting, as we do, from the first, that the world is one of our three chief enemies, maintaining rather than merely granting that the outward face of things speaks a different language from the word of God; yet, when

we come to act in the world, we find this very thing
a trial, not merely of our obedience, but even of our
faith, that is, the mere fact, that the world turns out
to be what we began by confessing concerning it.

Let us now direct our attention to this subject, in
order to see what it means, and how it is exemplified
in the ordinary course of the world.

And let us commence with the age when men are
first exposed, in any great degree, to the temptation
of trusting the world's assertions,—when they enter
into life, as it is called. Hitherto they have learned
revealed truths only as a creed or system; they are
instructed and acquiesce in the great Christian doctrines; and having virtuous feelings, and desiring to
do their duty, they think themselves really and practically religious. They read in Scripture of the course
of the world, but they have little notion what it
really is; they believe it to be sinful, but how it acts
in seducing from the Truth, and making evil seem
good and good evil, is beyond them. Scripture, indeed, says much about the world; but they cannot
learn practically what it is from Scripture; for, not
to mention other reasons, Scripture being written by
inspiration, represents things such as they really are
in God's sight, such as they will seem to us in proportion as we learn to judge of them rightly, not as
they appear to those " whose senses are" not yet
" exercised to discern both good and evil."

Under these circumstances, men are brought to
their trial. The simple and comparatively retired

2

life which they have hitherto enjoyed is changed for the varied and attractive scenes of mixed society. Its numberless circles and pursuits open upon them, the diversities and contrarieties of opinion and conduct, and of the subjects on which thought and exertion are expended. This is what is called seeing the world. Here, then, all at once they lose their reckoning, and let slip the lessons which they thought they had so accurately learned. They are unable to apply in practice what they have received by word of mouth; and, perplexed at witnessing the multiplicity of characters and fortunes which human nature assumes, and the range and intricacy of the social scheme, they are gradually impressed with the belief that the religious system which they have hitherto received is an inadequate solution of the world's mysteries, and a rule of conduct too simple for its complicated transactions. All men, perhaps, are, in their measure, subjected to this temptation. Even their ordinary and most innocent intercourse with others, their temporal callings, their allowable recreations, captivate their imaginations, and, on entering into this new scene, they look forward with interest towards the future, and form schemes of action, and indulge dreams of happiness, such as this life has never fulfilled. Now, is it not plain, that, after thus realizing to themselves the promises of the world, when they look back to the Bible and their former lessons, these will seem not only uninteresting and dull, but a theory too?—dull, colourless, indeed, as a sober landscape, after we have

been gazing on some bright vision in the clouds,—
but, withal, unpractical, unnatural, unsuitable to the
exigencies of life and the constitution of man?

For consider how little is said in Scripture about
subjects which necessarily occupy a great part of the
attention of all men, and which, being there unnoticed,
become thereby the subject-matter of their trial.
Their private conduct day by day; their civil, social,
and domestic duties; their relation towards those
events which mark out human life into its periods,
and, in the case of most men, are the source of its
best pleasures, and the material of its deepest affections, are, as if purposely, passed over, that they themselves may complete the picture of true faith and
sanctity which Revelation has begun.

And thus (as has already been said) what is primarily a trial of our obedience, becomes a trial of
our faith also. The Bible seems to contain a world
in itself, and not the same world as that which we
inhabit; and those who profess to conform to its rules
gain from us respect indeed, and praise, and yet strike
us withal in some sort as narrow-minded and fanciful; tenderly to be treated, indeed, as you would
touch cautiously any costly work of art, yet, on the
whole, as little adapted to do good service in the
world as it is, as a weapon of gold or soft clothing on
a field of battle.

And much more, of course, does this delusion
hang about the mind, and more closely does it wrap
it round, if, by yielding to the temptations of the

flesh, a man predisposes himself to the influence of it. The palmary device of Satan is to address himself to the pride of our nature, and, by the promise of independence, to seduce us into sin. Those who have been brought up in ignorance of the polluting fashions of the world, too often feel a rising in their minds against the discipline and constraint kindly imposed upon them; and, not understanding that their ignorance is their glory, and that they cannot really enjoy both good and evil, they murmur that they are not allowed to essay what they do not wish to practise, or to choose for themselves in matters where the very knowledge seems to them to give a superiority to the children of corruption. Thus the temptation of becoming as gods works as in the beginning, pride opening a door to lust; and then, intoxicated by their experience of evil, they think they possess real wisdom, and take a larger and more impartial view of the nature and destinies of man than religion teaches; and, while the customs of society restrain their avowals within the bounds of propriety, yet in their hearts they learn to believe that sin is a matter of course, not a serious evil, a failing, in which all have share, indulgently to be spoken of, or rather, in the case of each individual, to be taken for granted, and passed over in silence; and believing this, they are not unwilling to discover or to fancy weaknesses in those who have the credit of being superior to the ordinary run of men, to insinuate the possibility of human passions influencing them, this or that of a more refined

VI.]   FAITH AND SIGHT.   115

nature, when the grosser cannot be imputed, and, ex-
tenuating at the same time the guilt of the vicious,
to reduce in this manner all men pretty much to a
level.   A more apposite instance of this state of soul
cannot be required than is given us in the celebrated
work of an historian of the last century, who, for his
great abilities, and, on the other hand, his cold heart,
impure mind, and scoffing spirit, may justly be accounted as, in this country at least, one of the masters of a new school of error, which seems not yet to
have accomplished its destinies, and is framed more
exactly after the received type of the author of evil,
than the chief anti-Christs which have, in these last
times, occupied the scene of the world.

The temptation I have been speaking of, of trusting the world, because it speaks boldly, and thinking
that evil must be acquiesced in, because it exists, will
be still stronger and more successful in the case of
one who is in any situation of active exertion, and
has no very definite principles to secure him in the
narrow way.   He was taught to believe that there
was but one true faith, and, on entering into life, he
meets with numberless doctrines among men, each
professing to be the true one.   He had learned that
there was but one Church, and he falls in with countless religious sects, nay, with a prevalent opinion that
all these are equally good, and that there is no divine-
ly-appointed Church at all.   He has been accustomed
to class men into good and bad, but he finds their
actual characters no how reducible to system ; good

and bad mixed in every variety of proportion, virtues and vices in endless combinations; and, what is stranger still, a deficient creed seemingly joined to a virtuous life, and inconsistent conduct disgracing a sound profession. Further still, he finds that men in general will not act on high motives, in spite of all that divines and moralists profess; and his experience of this urges him, till he begins to think it unwise and extravagant to insist upon the mass of mankind doing so, or to preach high morals and high doctrines; and at length he looks on the religious system of his youth as beautiful indeed in itself, and practical perhaps in private life, and useful for the lower classes, but as utterly unfit for those who live in the world; and, while unwilling to confess this, lest he should set a bad example, he tacitly concedes it, never is the champion of his professed principles when assailed, nor acts upon them in an honest way in the affairs of life.

Or, should he be led by a speculative turn of mind, or a natural philanthropy, to investigate the nature of man, or exert himself in plans for the amelioration of society, then his opinions become ultimately impressed with the character of a more definite unbelief. Sometimes he is conscious to himself that he is opposing Christianity; not indeed opposing it wantonly, but, as he conceives, unavoidably, as finding it in his way. This is a state of mind into which benevolent men are in danger of falling, in the present age. While they pursue objects tending, as they conceive, towards the good of mankind, it is by degrees forced upon their minds that Revealed Religion thwarts their proceedings, and, averse alike to relinquish their plans, and to offend the feelings of others, they determine letting matters take their course, and, believing fully that Christianity must fall before the increasing illumination of the age, yet they wish to secure it against direct attacks, and to provide that it no otherwise falls than as it unavoidably must, at one time or other; as every inflexible instrument, and every antiquated institution, crumbles under the hands of the Great Innovator, who creates new influences for new emergencies, and recognizes no right divine in a tumultuous and shifting world.

Sometimes, on the other hand, while he takes the spirit of the world as his teacher, such a one is drifted away unawares from the Truth as it is in Jesus, and, merely from ignorance of Scripture, maintains theories which Scripture anathematizes. Thus he dreams on for a time, as loath to desert his first faith; then, by accident, meeting with some of the Revealed doctrines which he learned when a child—the Incarnation, or the eternal punishment of the wicked—he stumbles. Then he will attempt to remove these, as if accidentally attached to the Scripture creed,— little thinking that they are its very peculiarities and essentials, nor reflecting that the very fact of his stumbling at them should be taken as a test that his views coincide but in appearance with the revealed system altogether; and so he will remain at the door

of the Church, witnessing against himself by his lingering there, yet missing the reward bestowed even
on the proselyte of the gate in heathen times, in
that he might have " known the way of righteousness," yet has " turned from the holy commandment
delivered unto him."

And some there are who, keeping their faith in
the main, give up the notion of its importance.
Finding that men will not agree together on points
of doctrine and discipline, and imagining that union
must be effected on any terms, they consent to abandon articles of faith as the basis of Christian fellowship, and try to effect what they call a union of
hearts, as a bond of fellowship among those who differ
in their notions of the One God, One Lord, One
Spirit, One baptism, and One body ; forgetful of the
express condemnation pronounced by our Saviour
upon those who " believe not" the preaching of His
servants [1]; and that he who denieth the Son, the
same hath not the Father [2].

And others, not being able to acquiesce in the un-
importance of doctrinal truth, yet perplexed at the
difficulties in the course of human affairs, which follow on the opposite view, accustom themselves gra-
tuitously to distinguish between their public and private duties, and to judge of them by separate rules.
These are often such as begin by assuming some
extravagant or irrelevant test for ascertaining the

---

[1] Mark xvi. 16.   [2] 1 John ii. 22.

existence of religious principle in others, and so are
led to think it is nowhere to be found, not in the
true Church more than in the sects which surround it;
and thus, regarding all men (to speak generally) as
equally far from the Truth, and strangers to that
Divine regeneration which Christ bestows on His
elect few, and, on the other hand, seeing that men,
as cast together in society, must co-operate on some
or other principles, they drop the strict principles of
Scripture in their civil relations, give no preference
to those who honour the Church over those who profess opinions disrespectful towards it; perhaps take
up the notion that the State, as such, has nothing to
do with the subject of religion; praise and blame
according to a different standard from that which
Christianity reveals; and all this while cherish, perhaps, in their secret thoughts a definite creed, rigid
in its decisions, stimulating in its influence, in spite
of the mildness, and submissiveness, and liberality of
sentiment, which their public mode of speaking and
acting seems to evidence.

Nor are even the better sort of men altogether
secure from the impression of the world's teaching,
which is so influential with the multitude. He truly
is a rare and marvellous work of heavenly grace,
who, when he comes into the din and tumult of the
world, can view things just as he calmly contemplated
them in the distance, before the time of action came.
So many are the secondary reasons which can be
assigned for and against every measure and every

principle, so urgent are the solicitations of interest
or passion when the mind is once relaxed or excited,
so difficult then to compare and ascertain the relative
importance of conflicting considerations, that the
most sincere and zealous of ordinary Christians will,
to their surprise, confess to themselves that they have
lost their way in the wilderness, which they could
accurately measure out before descending into it, and
have missed the track which lay like a clear thread
across the hills, when seen in the horizon. And
it is from their experience of this their own un-
skilfulness and weakness, that serious men have been
in the practice of making vows concerning purposes
on which they were fully set, that no sudden gust of
passion, or lure of worldly interest, should gain the
mastery over a heart which they desire to present
without spot or blemish, as a chaste virgin, to Christ.

Let the above be taken as a few illustrations out
of many, of the influence exerted, and the doctrine
enforced, in the school of the world; that school which
we all set out by acknowledging to be at enmity with
the school of Christ, but from which we are content
to take our lessons of practical wisdom as life goes
on. Such is the triumph of Sight over Faith. The
world really brings no new argument to its aid,—nothing beyond its own assertion. In the very outset
Christians allow that its teaching is contrary to Revelation, and not to be taken as authority; nevertheless, afterwards this mere unargumentative teaching,
which, when viewed in theory, formed no objection

to the truth of the Inspired Word, yet, when actually heard in the intercourse of life, converts them, more or less, to the service of the " prince of the power of the air, the spirit which now worketh in the children of disobedience." It assails their *imagination.* The world sweeps by in long procession; its principalities and powers, its Babel of languages, the astrologers of Chaldæa, the horse and its rider and the chariots of Egypt, Baal, and Ashtoreth, and their false worship; and those who witness, feel its fascination; they flock after it; with a strange fancy, they ape its gestures, and dote over its mummeries; and then, should they perchance fall in with the simple solemn services of Christ's Church, and hear its witnesses going the round of Gospel truths as when they left them: " I am the Way, the Truth, and the Life;" " Be sober, be vigilant;" " Strait is the gate, narrow the way;" " If any man will come after Me, let him deny himself;" " He is despised and rejected of men, a Man of sorrows and acquainted with grief:"—how utterly unreal do these appear, and the preachers of them, how irrational, how puerile!—how extravagant in their opinions, how weak in their reasoning! —and if they profess to pity and bear with them, how nearly does their compassion border on contempt!

The contempt of men!—why should we be unwilling to endure it? We are not better than our fathers. In every age it has been the lot of Christians far more highly endowed than we are with the

riches of Divine wisdom.   It was the lot of Apostles
and Prophets, and of the Saviour of mankind Himself.   When He was brought before Pilate, the
Roman Governor felt the same surprise and disdain
at His avowal of His unearthly office, which the
world now expresses.   " To this end was I born,
. . . . that I should bear witness unto the *Truth*.
Pilate saith, What is Truth ?"   Again, when Festus
would explain to King Agrippa the cause of the dispute between St. Paul and the Jews, he says, " The
accusers . . . . brought no accusations of such things
as I supposed, but certain questions against him of
their own superstition, and of one Jesus, which was
dead, whom Paul affirmed to be alive."

Such, however, are the words of men, who, not
knowing the strength of Christianity, had not the
guilt of deliberate apostasy.   But what serious
thoughts does it present to the mind, to behold
parallels to heathen blindness and arrogance in a
Christian country, where men might know better, if
they would inquire !—and what a warning to us all
is the sight of those who, though nominally within
the Church, are avowedly indifferent to it !   For all
of us surely are on our trial, and, as we go forth into
the world, so we are winnowed, and the chaff gradually separated from the true seed.   This is St.
John's account of it.   " They went out from us, but
they were not of us; for, if they had been of us,
they would no doubt have continued with us; but
they went out, that they might be made manifest

that they were not of us." And our Lord stands by
watching the process, telling us of " the hour of
temptation which shall come upon all the earth," ex-
horting us to " try them which say they are apostles,
and are not," and to " hold fast that which we have,
that no man take our crown."

Meanwhile, it is an encouragement to us to think
how much may be done in way of protest and teaching, by the mere example of those who endeavour to
serve God faithfully. In this way we may use against
the world its own weapons; and as its success lies in
the mere boldness of assertion with which it maintains that evil is good, so by the counter assertions of
a strict life and a resolute profession of the truth, we
may retort upon the imaginations of men, that religious obedience is not impracticable, and that Scripture has its persuasives. A martyr or a confessor is
a fact, and has its witness in itself; and while it dis-
arranges the theories of human wisdom, it also
breaks in upon that security and solitude into which
men of the world would fain retire from the thought
of religion. One prophet against four hundred dis-
turbed the serenity of Ahab, King of Israel. When
the witnesses in St. John's vision were slain, though
they were but two, then " they that dwelt on the
earth rejoiced over them, and made merry, and sent
gifts one to another, because these two prophets
tormented them that dwelt on the earth." Nay, such
confessors have a witness even in the breasts of those
who oppose them, an instinct originally from God,

which may indeed be perverted into a hatred, but scarcely into an utter disregard of the Truth, when exhibited before them. The instance cannot be found in the history of mankind, in which an anti-Christian power could long abstain from persecuting. The disdainful Festus at length impatiently interrupted his prisoner's speech; and in our better regulated times, whatever be the scorn or malevolence which is directed against the faithful Christian, these very feelings show that he is really a restraint on vice and unbelief, and a warning and guide to the feeble-minded, and to those who still linger in the world with hearts more religious than their professed opinions; and thus even literally, as the text expresses it, he overcomes the world, conquering while he suffers, and willingly accepting overbearing usage and insult from others, so that he may in some degree benefit them, though the more abundantly he loves them, the less he be loved.

SERMON VII.

HUMAN RESPONSIBILITY, AS INDEPENDENT OF
CIRCUMSTANCES.

Preached November 4, 1832.

GEN. iii. 13.

" The serpent beguiled me, and I did eat."

THE original temptation set before our first parents,
was that of proving their freedom, by using it without
regard to the will of Him who gave it. The original
excuse offered by them after sinning was, that they
were not really free, that they had acted under a constraining influence, the subtilty of the tempter. They
committed sin that they might be independent of
their Maker; they defended it on the ground that
they were dependent upon Him. And this has been
the course of lawless pride and lust ever since; to
lead us, first, to exult in our uncontrollable liberty of
will and conduct; then, when we have ruined ourselves, to plead that we are the slaves of necessity.

Accordingly, it has been always the office of Religion to protest against the sophistry of Satan, and to preserve the memory of those truths which the unbelieving heart corrupts, both the freedom and the responsibility of man;—the sovereignty of the Creator, the supremacy of the law of conscience as His representative within us, and the irrelevancy of external circumstances in the judgment which is ultimately to be made upon our conduct and character.

That we are accountable for what we do and what we are,—that, in spite of all aids or hindrances from without, each soul is the cause of its own happiness or misery,—is a truth certified to us both by Nature and Revelation. Nature conveys it to us in the feeling of guilt and remorse which implies *self*-condemnation. In the Scriptures, on the other hand, it is the great prevailing principle throughout, in every age of the world, and through every Dispensation. The change of times, the varieties of religious knowledge, the gifts of grace, interfere not with the integrity of this momentous truth. Praise to the obedient, punishment on the transgressor, is the revealed rule of God's government from the beginning to the consummation of all things. The fall of Adam did not abolish, nor do the provisions of Gospel-mercy supersede it.

At the creation it was declared, " In the day that thou eatest . . . thou shalt surely die." On the calling of the Israelites, the Lord God was proclaimed in sight of their lawgiver as "merciful and gracious, long-suffering, and abundant in goodness and truth ; keeping mercy for thousands, forgiving iniquity and transgression and sin, and that will by no means clear the guilty." And when Moses interceded for the people, with an earnestness which tended to the infringement of the Divine Rule, he was reminded that he could not himself be really responsible for others. " Whosoever hath sinned against Me, him will I blot out of My book." The Prophetical Dispensation enforced the same truth still more clearly. " With the pure Thou wilt show Thyself pure, and with the froward Thou wilt show Thyself froward." " The soul that sinneth, it shall die ; make you a new heart and a new spirit, for why will ye die ? " And after Christ had come, the most explicit of the inspired expounders of the New Covenant is as explicit in his recognition of the original rule. " Every man shall bear his own burden . . . Be not deceived: God is not mocked ; for whatsoever a man soweth, that shall he also reap." Even in his Epistle to the Romans, where he is directly engaged in declaring another, and at first sight opposite doctrine, he finds opportunity for confessing the principle of accountableness. Though exalting the sovereign power and inscrutable purposes of God, and apparently referring man's agency altogether to Him as the vessel of His good pleasure, still he forgets not in the very opening of his exposition to declare the real independence and responsibility of the human will. " He will render to every man according to his deeds ; . . . tri-

2

bulation and anguish upon every soul of man that doeth evil . . . but glory, honour, and peace, to every man that worketh good ; . . . for there is no respect of persons with God ; " declarations, which I will not say are utterly irreconcileable in their very structure with (what is called) the Calvinistic creed, but which it is certain would never have been written by an assertor of it in a formal exposition of his views to his fellow-believers.   Lastly, we have the testimony of the book which completes and seals up for ever the divine communications.   " My reward is with Me; to give every man according as his work shall be. Blessed are they that do His commandments, that they may have right to the tree of life [1]."

Moreover, we have the limits of external aids and hindrances distinctly stated to us, so as to guarantee to us, in spite of existing influences of whatever kind, even of our original corrupt nature, the essential freedom and accountableness of our will.   As regards external circumstances: " God is faithful, who will not suffer you to be tempted above that ye are able ; but will with the temptation also make a way to escape, that ye may be able to bear it." As regards the corrupt nature in which we are born : " Let no man say when he is tempted, I am tempted of God ; but every man is tempted, when he is drawn away of his own lust, and enticed ; then, when lust hath con-

[1] Gen. ii. 17.   Exod. xxxiv. 7 ; xxxii. 33.   Ps. xviii. 26. Ez. xviii. 4. 31.   Gal. vi. 5—7.   Rom. ii. 6—11.   Rev. xxii. 12, 13.

ceived, it bringeth forth sin; and sin, when it is finished, bringeth forth death." And as regards divine assistances : " It is impossible for those who were once enlightened . . . . if they fall away, to renew them again unto repentance[2]."

Far be it from any one to rehearse triumphantly, and in the way of controversy, these declarations of our privilege as moral agents ; rather, so fearful and burdensome is this almost divine attribute of our nature, that when we consider it attentively, it requires a strong faith in the wisdom and love of our Maker not to start sinfully from His gift ; and at the mere prospect, not the memory of our weakness, to attempt to transfer it from ourselves to the agents, animate and inanimate, by which we are surrounded, and to lose our immortality under the shadows of the visible world. And, much more, when the sense of guilt comes upon us, do we feel the temptation of ridding ourselves of our conviction of our own responsibility ; and, instead of betaking ourselves to Him who can reverse what we cannot disclaim, to shelter ourselves under the original unbelief of our first parents, as if the serpent gave it to us and we did eat.

It is my wish now to give some illustrations of the operation of this sophistry in the affairs of life ; not that it is a subject which admits of novelty in the discussion, but with the hope of directing attention to a mode of deceiving our consciences, common in

[2] 1 Cor. x. 13.   James i. 13—15.   Hebr. vi. 4—6.

all ages since the original transgression, and not least successful in our own.

To find fault with the circumstances in which we find ourselves, is our ready and familiar excuse when our conduct is arraigned in any particular. Yet even the heathen moralist saw, that all those actions are voluntary, in which we ourselves are in any way ultimately the principle of action; and that praise and blame are awarded, not according to the mode in which we should have behaved, had circumstances been different, but according as we actually conduct ourselves, things being as they are. Commenting on goods thrown overboard in a storm, he remarks "that such acts must be considered voluntary, as being the objects of our choice *at the time* when they are done, for our conduct is determined according to the emergency[3]." In truth, nothing is more easy to the imagination than duty in the abstract, that is, duty in name and not in reality. It is when it assumes a definite and actual shape, when it comes upon us under circumstances, (and it is obvious it can come in no other way,) then it is difficult and troublesome. Circumstances are the very trial of obedience. Yet, plain as this is, it is very common to fancy our particular condition peculiarly hard, and that we should be better and happier men in any other.

Thus, for instance, opportunity, which is the means of temptation in the case of various sins, is converted

---

[3] Arist. Eth. Nicom. iii. 17.

into an excuse for them. Perhaps it is very plain that, except for some unusual combination of circumstances, we could never have been tempted at all; yet, when we fall on such an occasion, we are ready to excuse our weakness, as if our trial were extraordinary.

Again, the want of education is an excuse common with the lower classes for a careless and irreligious life.

Again, it is scarcely possible to resist the imagination, that we should have been altogether other men than we are, had we lived in an age of miracles, or in the visible presence of our Lord; that is, we cannot persuade ourselves that whatever be the force of things external to us in modifying our condition, it is we, and not our circumstances, that are, after all, the main causes of what we do and what we are.

Or, again, to take a particular instance, which will perhaps come home to some who hear me, when a young person is in prospect of ordination, he has a conceit that his mind will be more fully his own, when he is actually engaged in the sacred duties of his new calling, than at present; and, in the event he is perhaps amazed and frightened, to find how little influence the change of circumstances has had in sobering and regulating his thoughts, whatever greater decency his outward conduct may exhibit.

Further, it is the common excuse of wilful sinners, that there are peculiarities in their present engagements, connexions, plans, or professions, incompatible

with immediate repentance; according to the memo-
rable words of Felix, "When I have a convenient
season I will send for thee."

The operation of the same deceit discovers itself
in our mode of judging the conduct of others;
whether, in the boldness with which we blame in
them what, under other circumstances, we allow in
ourselves; or again, in the false charity which we
exercise towards them. For instance, the vices of
the young are often regarded by beholders with an
irrational indulgence, on the ground (as it is said) that
youth ever will be wanton and impetuous; which is
only saying, if put into plain language, that there are
temptations which are not intended as trials of our
obedience. Or when, as lately, the lower orders rise
up against the powers that be, in direct opposition to
the word of Scripture, they are excused on the
ground of their rulers being bigoted and themselves
enlightened ; or because they feel themselves capable
of exercising more power; or because they have the
example of other nations to incite them to do so; or
simply (the more common excuse) because they have
the means of doing so; as if loyalty could be called
a virtue when men cannot be disloyal, or obedience
had any praise when it became a constraint. In like
manner, there is a false charity, which on principle
takes the cause of heresy under its protection ; and,
instead of condemning it, as such, busies itself in
fancying the possible circumstances which may, in
this or that particular instance, excuse it; as if out-

ward fortunes could change the nature of truth or of moral excellence, or as if, admitting the existence of unavoidable misbelief to be conceivable, yet it were not the duty of the Christian to take things as they are given us in Scripture, as they are in themselves, and as they are on the whole, instead of fastening upon exceptions to the rule, or attempting to ascertain that combination and balance of circumstances, in the case of individuals, which is only known to the Omniscient Judge.

The following apology for the early profligacy of the notorious French infidel of the last century is found among even the respectable literature of the present day, and is an illustration of the kind of fatalism now under consideration. "It is certain," the apologist says, "that a brilliant, highly-gifted, and more than commonly vivacious young man, like Voltaire, who moved in the high tide of Parisian society, must necessarily be imbued with the levity and laxity that on every side surrounded him, and which has rendered the period in question proverbial for profligacy and debauchery. . . . . This is not observed in defence of his moral defects, or of any one else, but in answer to those who expect the virtues of a sage from the education of an Alcibiades. His youthful career seems to have been precisely that of other young men of his age and station, neither better nor worse. It is scarcely necessary to prove the tinge which such a state of society must bestow upon every character, however intellectually gifted, which is formed in the midst of it." No one can say that the doctrine contained in this extract is extravagant, as opinions go, and unfair as a specimen of what is commonly received in the world, however boldly it is expressed. Yet it will be observed, that vice is here pronounced to be the necessary effect of a certain state of society, and, as being such, not extenuated merely, as regards the individual (as it may well be), but exculpated; so that, while the actions resulting from it are allowed to be intrinsically bad, yet the agent himself is acquitted of the responsibility of committing them.

The sophistry in question sometimes has assumed a bolder form, and has displayed itself in the shape of system. Let us, then, now direct our attention to it in some of those fortified positions which at various times it has taken up against the plain declarations of Scripture and Conscience.

1. Fatalism is the refuge of a conscience-stricken mind, maddened at the sight of evils which it has brought upon itself, and cannot remove. To believe and tremble is the most miserable of dooms for an immortal spirit; and bad men, whose reason has been awakened by education, resolved not to be "tormented before their time," seek in its intoxication a present oblivion of their woe. It is wretched enough to suffer, but self-reproach is the worm which destroys the inward power of resistance. Submission alone makes pain tolerable in any case; and they who refuse the Divine yoke are driven to

seek a sedative in the notion of an eternal necessity. They deny that they ever could have been other than they are. "What heaven has made me, I must be," is the sentiment which hardens them into hopeless pride and rebellion.

And it must be confessed, so great is the force of passion and of habit, when once allowed to take possession of the heart, that these men seem to have in their actual state, nay in their past experience, long before the time of their present obduracy, an infallible witness in behalf of their doctrine. In subduing our evil nature, the first steps alone are in our own power; a few combats seem to decide the solemn question, to decide whether the sovereignty is with the spirit or the flesh; *nisi paret, imperat,* is become a proverb. When once the enemy of our souls "comes in like a flood," what hope is there that he ever will be expelled? And what servitude can be compared to the bondage which follows, when we wish to do right, yet are utterly powerless to do it? whether we be slaves to some imperious passion, hushed indeed in its victim's ordinary mood, and allowing the recurrence of better thoughts and purposes, but rising suddenly and sternly, in his evil hour, to its easy and insulting triumph; or, on the other hand, to some cold sin which overhangs and deadens the mind, sloth, for instance, or cowardice, binding it down with ten thousand subtle fastenings to the earth, nor suffering it such motion as might suffice it for a renewal of the contest. Such, in its worst forms, is the condition of the obdurate sinner; who, feeling his weakness, but forgetting that he ever had strength, from the promise of aid from above, at length learns to acquiesce in his misery as the lot of his nature, and resolves neither to regret nor to hope.   Next he amuses his reason with the melancholy employment of reducing his impressions into system ; and proves, as he thinks, from the confessed influence of external events, and the analogy of the physical world, that all moral phenomena proceed according to a fixed law, and that we are not more to blame when we sin than when we die.

2. The Calvinistic doctrine, if not the result, is at least the forerunner of a similar neglect of the doctrine of human responsibility.   Whatever be the fallacies of its argumentative basis, viewed as a character of mind, it miscalculates the power of the affections, as fatalism does that of the passions.   Its practical error is that of supposing that certain motives and views, presented to the heart and conscience, produce certain effects as their necessary consequence, no room being left for the resistance of the will, or for self-discipline, as the medium by which faith and holiness are connected together.   It is the opinion of a large class of religious people, that faith being granted, works follow as a matter of course, without our own trouble ; and they are confirmed in their opinion by a misconception of our Church's 12th Article, as if to assert that works " spring out necessarily of a true and lively faith" could only mean that

they follow by a kind of physical law. When this
notion is once entertained, it follows that nothing remains to be done but to bring these sovereign principles before the mind, as a medicine which must work
a cure, or as sights which suddenly enlighten and win
the imagination.   To care for little duties, to set
men right in the details of life, to instruct and refine
their conscience, to tutor them in self-denial, the
Scripture methods of working onwards towards higher
knowledge and obedience become superfluous, nay,
and despicable, while these master visions are with-
held.   A system such as this will of course bring with
it full evidence of its truth to such debilitated minds
as have already so given way to the imagination,
that they find themselves unable to resist its impressions as they recur.   Nor is there among the theories
of the world any more congenial to the sated and
remorseful sensualist, who, having lost the command
of his will, feels that if he is to be converted, it must
be by some sudden and violent excitement.   On the
other hand, it will always have its advocates among
the young and earnest-minded, who, not having that
insight into their hearts which experience gives, think
that to know is to obey, and that their habitual love
of the Truth may be measured by their momentary
admiration of it.   And it is welcomed by the indo-
lent, who care not for the Scripture warnings of the
narrowness of the way of life, so that they can but
assure themselves that it is easy to those who are in
it ; and who readily ascribe the scantiness of those

who find it, not to the difficulty of connecting faith
and works, but to a Divine frugality in the dispensation of the gifts of grace.

Such are some of the elements of that state of
mind which, when scientifically developed, assumes
the shape of Calvinism; the characteristic error, both
of the system and of the state of mind, consisting in
the assumption that there are things external to the
mind, whether doctrines or influences, such, that
when once presented to it, they suspend its independence and involve certain results, as if by way of
physical consequence; whereas, on studying the New
Testament, we shall find, that amid all that is said
concerning the inscrutable decrees of God, and His
mysterious interposition in the workings of the human
mind, still everywhere the practical truths with which
Revelation started are assumed and recognized; that
we shall be judged by our good or evil doings, and that
a principle within us is ultimately the cause of the one
and the other. So that it is preposterous in us to
attempt to direct our course by the distant landmarks
of the Divine counsels, which are but dimly revealed
to us, overlooking the clear track close before our
eyes provided for our need. This perverse substitution in matters of conduct of a subtle argumentative rule for one that is plain and practical, is set before us, by way of warning, in the parable of the
talents. "Lord, I knew Thee that Thou art a hard
man ... and I was afraid, and went and hid Thy talent
in the earth."

3. One more illustration shall be given of the systematic disparagement of human responsibility, and the consequent substitution of outward events for the inward rule of conscience in matters of conduct.

The influence of the world, viewed as the enemy of our souls, consists in its hold upon our imagination. It seems to us incredible that anything is said everywhere and always can be false. And our faith is shown in preferring the testimony of our hearts and Scripture to its declarations, and our obedience in acting against it. It is the very function of the Christian to be moving against the world, and to be protesting against the majority of voices. And though a doctrine such as this may be perverted into a contempt of authority, a neglect of the Church, and an arrogant reliance on self, yet there is a sense in which it is true, as every part of Scripture teaches. " Thou shalt not follow a multitude to do evil," is its uniform injunction. Yet so irksome is this duty, that it is not wonderful that the wayward mind seeks a release from it ; and, looking off from what is within to what is without, it gradually becomes perplexed and unsettled. And, should it so happen that the face of society assumes a consistent appearance, and urges the claims of the world upon the Conscience as if on the ground of principle and system, then still greater is the difficulty in which it has entangled itself. Then it is that acts which exhibited in individual instances would have been condemned as crimes, acquire a dignity from the number of the delinquents,

or their assumption of authority, and venture to claim
our acquiescence as a matter of right. What would
be insubordination, or robbery, or murder, when done
by one man, is hallowed by the combination of the
great or the many.

Thus, for instance, what is more common at the
present day than for philosophers to represent society
as moving by a certain law through different stages,
and its various elements as coming into operation at
different periods; and then, not content with stating
the fact (which is undeniable), to go on to speak as if
what has been, and is, ought to be; and as if because
at certain eras this or that class of society gains the
ascendancy, therefore it lawfully gained it; whereas
in truth the usurpation of an invader, and the development (as it is called) of the popular power, are
alike facts, and alike sins, in the sight of Him who
forbids us to oppose constituted power. And yet the
credulous mind hangs upon the words of the world,
and falls a victim to its sophistry; as if, forsooth,
Satan could not work his work upon a law, and oppose God's will upon system. But the Christian,
rejecting this external guide of conduct, acts on
Faith, and far from being perplexed to find the world
consistent in its disobedience, recollects the declarations of Scripture which foretel it.

Yet so contrary to common sense is it thus to
assert that our conduct ought to be determined
merely by what is done by a mixed multitude, that it
was to be expected that the ingenious and eager minds

who practically acknowledge the principle, should wish to place it on some more argumentative basis. Accordingly, attempts have been made by foreign writers to show that society moves by a law which is independent of the conduct of its individual members, who cannot materially retard its progress, nor are answerable for it,—a law which in consequence is referrible only to the will of the Creator.   " Historical causes and their effects being viewed, at one glance, through a long course of years, seem," it has been said, "from their steady progression, to be above any human control ; an impulse is given, which beats down resistance, and sweeps away all means of opposition ; century succeeds to century, and the philosopher sees the same influence still potent, still undeviating and regular ; to him, considering these ages at once, following with rapid thought the slow pace of time, a century appears to dwindle to a point ; and the individual obstructions and accelerations, which within that period have occurred to impede or advance the march of events, are eliminated and forgotten."   This is the theory; and hence it is argued that it is our wisdom to submit to a power which is greater than ourselves, and which can neither be circumvented nor persuaded ; as if the Christian dare take any guide of conscience except the rule of duty, or might prefer expediency (if it be such) to principle.   Nothing, for instance, is more common than to hear men speak of the growing intelligence of the present age, and to insist upon the Church's supply-

ing its wants; the previous question being entirely
left out of view, whether those wants are healthy
and legitimate, or unreasonable,—whether real or
imaginary,—whether they ought to be gratified or
repressed: and it is urged upon us, that unless we
take the lead in the advance of mind ourselves, we
must be content to fall behind.   But, surely our first
duty is, not to resolve on satisfying a demand at any
price, but to determine whether it be innocent.   If
so, well; but if not, let what will happen.   Even
though the march of society be conducted on a superhuman law, yet, while it moves against Scripture
Truth, it is not God's ordinance,—it is but the creature of Satan; and, though it shiver all earthly obstacles to its progress, the gods of Sepharvaim and
Arphad, fall it must, and perish it must, before the
glorious fifth kingdom of the Most High, when He
visits the earth, who is called Faithful and True,
whose eyes are as a flame of fire, and on His head
many crowns, who smites the nations with a rod of
iron, and treadeth the winepress of the fierceness and
wrath of Almighty God.

My object in the foregoing remarks has been to
illustrate, in various ways, the operation of an all-
important truth; that circumstances are but the subject-matter, and not the rule of our conduct, nor in
any true sense the cause of it.   Let me conclude
with one more exemplification of it, which I address
to the junior part of my audience.

In this place, where the stated devotional services

of the Church are required of all of us, it is very
common with our younger members to slight them,
while they attend on them, on the ground of their
being forced upon them. A like excuse is sometimes urged in behalf of an unworthy participation
of the Lord's Supper, as if that Communion could
not be considered real, or dangerous to the impeni-
tent, which was performed under constraint.

Now, let such an apologist be taken on his own
ground. Let it be granted to him, for argument's sake,
though in no other way, that this general exaction
of religious duties is unwise; let him be allowed the
full force of his objections to a system which he has
not yet experience to understand.   Yet do these outward circumstances change the nature of the case in
any practical respect, or relieve him of his responsibility? Rather, is it not his plain duty to take things
as he finds them, since he has not the power of
changing them ; and, leaving to his superiors what
pertains to them, the task of deciding on the system
to be pursued, to inquire how he ought to act under
it, and to reflect what his guilt will be in the day of
account, if week after week he has come into the
presence of God with a deliberate profanation in his
right hand, or at least with irreverence of manner,
and an idle mind?

And, again, as regards the Holy Communion, how
do the outward circumstances which bring us thither
affect the real purpose of God respecting it?   Can
we in earthly matters remove what we dislike, by

wishing it away?—and shall we hope, by mere unbelief, to remove the Presence of God from His ordinance? As well may we think of removing thereby the visible emblems of bread and wine, or of withdrawing ourselves altogether from the Omnipresent Eye of God itself. Though Christ is savingly revealed in the Sacrament only to those who receive Him in faith, yet we have the express word of Scripture for saying, that the thoughtless communicant, far from remaining as if he did not receive it, is guilty of the actual Body and Blood of Christ,—guilty of the crime of crucifying Him anew, as not discerning that which lies hid in the rite. This does not apply, of course, to any one who communicates with a doubt merely about his own state—far from it!—nor to those who resolve heartily, yet in the event fail to perform, as is the case with the young; nor to those even who may happen to sin both before and after the reception of the Sacrament. Where there is earnestness, there is no condemnation; but it applies fearfully to such as view the Blessed Ordinance as a thing of course, from a notion that they are passive subjects of a regulation which others enforce; and, perhaps, the number of these is not small. Let such persons seriously consider that, were their argument correct, they need not be considered in a state of trial at all, and might escape the future judgment altogether. They would have only to protest (as we may speak) against their creation, and they would no longer have any duties to bind them. But what says

the word of God?   " That which cometh into your
mind, shall not be at all, that ye say, We will be as
the heathen, as the families of the countries, to serve
wood and stone."   And then follows the threat, addressed to those who rebel :—" As I live, saith the
Lord God, surely with a mighty hand, and with a
stretched out arm, and with fury poured out, will I
rule over you . . . . . And I will cause you to pass
under the rod, and I will bring you into the bond of
the covenant."

And these words apply to the whole subject which
has engaged us.   We may amuse ourselves, for a
time, with such excuses for sin as a perverted ingenuity furnishes ; but there is One who is justified in
His sayings, and clear when He judgeth.   Our worldly
philosophy and our well-devised pleadings will profit
nothing at a day when the heaven shall depart as a
scroll is rolled together, and all who are not clad in
the wedding garment of faith and love will be speech-
less.   Surely it is high time for us to wake out of
sleep, to chase from us the shadows of the night, and
to realize our individuality, and the coming of our
Judge.   "The night is far spent, the day is at hand,"
—" let us be sober, and watch unto prayer."

SERMON VIII.

WILFULNESS, THE SIN OF SAUL.

Preached December 2, 1832.

1 Sam. xv. 11.

" It repenteth Me that I have set up Saul to be king; for he is turned back from following Me, and hath not performed My commandments."

THE three chief religious patterns and divine instruments under the first Covenant, have each his counterpart in the Sacred History, that we may have warning as well as instruction. The distinguishing virtue, moral and political, of Abraham, Moses, and David, was their faith; by which I mean an implicit reliance in God's command and promise, and a zeal for His honour; a surrender and devotion of themselves, and all they had, to Him. At His word they each relinquished the dearest wish of their hearts, Isaac, Canaan, and the Temple; the Temple was not to be built, the land of promise not to be entered, the child of promise not to be retained. All three were tried by the anxieties and discomforts of exile and wandering; all three, and especially Moses and David, were very zealous for the Lord God of Hosts.

The faith of Abraham is illustrated in the lukewarmness of Lot, who, though a true servant of God, and a righteous man, chose for his dwelling-place the fertile country of a guilty people. To Moses, who was faithful in all God's house, is confronted the untrue prophet Balaam, who, gifted from the same Divine Master, and abounding in all knowledge and spiritual discernment, mistook words for works, and fell through love of lucre. The noble self-consuming zeal of David, who was at once ruler of the chosen people, and type of the Messiah, is contrasted with a still more conspicuous and hateful specimen of unbelief, as disclosed to us in the history of Saul. To this history it is proposed now to draw your attention, not indeed with the purpose of surveying it as a whole, but with hope of gaining thence some such indirect illustration, in the way of contrast, of the nature of religious Faith, as it is calculated to supply.

It cannot be denied that the designs of Providence towards Saul and David are, at first sight, of a perplexing nature, as implying distinctions in the moral character of the two individuals, which their history does not clearly warrant. Accordingly, it is usual, with a view of meeting the difficulty, to treat them as mere instruments in the Divine Governance of the Israelites, and to determine their respective virtues and defects, not by a moral, but by a political stand-

L 2

ard. For instance, the honourable title by which
David is distinguished, as " a man after God's own
heart," is interpreted with reference merely to his
activity and success in enforcing the principles of the
Mosaic system, no account being taken of the motives
which influenced him, or of his general character, or
of his conduct in other respects. Now, it is by no
means intended here to dispute the truth of such
representations, or to deny that the Church, in its
political relations, must even treat men with a certain
reference to their professions and outward acts, such
as it withdraws in its private dealings with them;
yet, to consider the difference between Saul and
David to be of a moral nature, is more consistent
with the practical objects with which we believe
Scripture to have been written, and more reverent,
moreover, to the memory of one whose lineage the
Saviour almost gloried in claiming, and whose devotional writings have edified the Church even to this
day. Let us then drop, for the present, the political
view of the history which it is proposed to consider,
and attempt to discover the moral lesson intended to
be conveyed to us in the character of Saul, the contrast of the zealous David.

The unbelief of Balaam discovers itself in a love
of secular distinction, and was attended by self-decep-
tion. Saul seems to have had no base ends in view;
he was not self-deceived; his temptation and his fall
consisted in a certain perverseness of mind, founded
on some obscure feelings of self-importance, very com-

monly observable in human nature, and sometimes called pride,—a perverseness which shows itself in a reluctance absolutely to relinquish its own independence of action, in cases where dependence is a duty, and interferes a little, and alters a little, as if with a view of satisfying its own fancied dignity, though it is afraid altogether to oppose itself to the voice of God. Should this seem, at first sight, to be a trifling fault, it is the more worth while to trace its operation in the history of Saul. If a tree is known by its fruit, it is a great sin.

Saul's character is marked by much that is considered to be the highest moral excellence,—generosity, magnanimity, calmness, energy, and decision. He is introduced to us as " a choice young man, and a goodly," and as possessed of a striking personal presence, and as a member of a wealthy and powerful family [1].

The first announcement of his elevation came upon him suddenly, but apparently without unsettling him. He kept it secret, leaving it to Samuel, who had made it to him, to publish it. " Saul said unto his uncle, He (that is, Samuel) told us plainly that the asses were found. But of the matter of the kingdom, whereof Samuel spake, he told him not." Nay, it would even seem as if he were averse to the dignity intended for him ; for when the Divine lot fell upon

[1] Some sentences which follow have already been inserted in the Author's Parochial Sermons, Vol. iii. Serm. 3.

him he had hid himself, and was not discovered by the people without Divine assistance.

The appointment was at first unpopular. "The children of Belial said, How shall this man save us?" Here again his highmindedness is discovered, and his remarkable force and energy of character. He showed no signs of resentment at the insult. "They despised him, and brought him no presents. But he held his peace." Soon the Ammonites invaded the country beyond Jordan, with the avowed intention of reducing its inhabitants to slavery. They, almost in despair, sent to Saul for relief; and the panic spread in the interior, as well as among those whose country was immediately threatened. The conduct of their new king brings to mind the celebrated Roman story. "Behold, Saul came after the herd out of the field; and Saul said, What aileth the people that they weep? And they told him the tidings of the men of Jabesh. And the Spirit of God came upon Saul, and his anger was kindled greatly." His order for an immediate gathering throughout Israel was obeyed with the alacrity with which, in times of alarm, the many yield themselves up to the will of the strongminded. A decisive victory over the enemy followed. Then the popular cry became, "Who is he that said, Shall Saul reign over us? Bring the men, that we may put them to death. And Saul said, There shall not a man be put to death this day: for to-day the Lord hath wrought salvation in Israel."

We seem here to find noble traits of character; at the same time it must not be forgotten that sometimes such exhibitions are also the concomitants of a certain strangeness and eccentricity of mind, which are very perplexing to those who study it, and very unamiable.   Reserve, sullenness, headstrong self-confidence, pride, caprice, sourness of temper, scorn of others, a scoffing at natural feeling and religious principle; all those characters of mind which, though distinct from mental aberration, are temptations to it, frequently take the form, and have in some degree the nature, of magnanimity.   It is probable, from the sequel of Saul's history, that the apparent nobleness of his first actions was connected with some such miserable principles and feelings, which then existed only in their seeds, but which afterwards sprang up and ripened to his destruction; and this in consequence of that one fatal defect of mind which has been already noticed, as corrupting the integrity of his faith.

Sight prevailed over the faith of Balaam; a more subtle, though not a rare temptation, overcame the faith of Saul; wilfulness, the unaccountable desire of acting short of simple obedience to God's will, a repugnance of unreserved self-surrender and submission to Him.   This, it will at once be seen, was one characteristic of the Jewish nation; so that the king was but a type of the people; nor, indeed, was it likely to be otherwise, born as he was in the original sin of that very perverseness which led them to

2

choose a king, instead of God. It is scarcely necessary to refer to the details of their history for instances of a like wilfulness,—such as their leaving the
manna till the morning, their going out to gather it
on the seventh day, Nadab and Abihu's offering
strange fire, their obstinate transgression of the Second Commandment, their presumptuous determination to fight with the Canaanites, though Moses fore-
told their defeat, and, when possessed of the promised land, their putting under tribute the idolaters
whom they were bid exterminate. The same was the
sin of Jeroboam, who is almost by title the Apostate; when God had promised him the kingdom of
Israel, he refused to wait God's time, but impatiently
forced a crisis, which ought to have been left to Him
who promised it. On the other hand, Abraham and
David, with arms in their hands, waited upon Him
for the fulfilment of the temporal promise in His
good time. It is on this that the distinction turns,
so much insisted on in the Books of Kings, of serving
God with a " perfect," or not with a perfect, heart.
" Ahaz went to Damascus to meet Tiglath-pileser,
King of Assyria, and saw an altar that was at Damascus; and King Ahaz sent to Urijah the priest the
fashion of the altar, . . . and Urijah . . . built an altar
according to all that king Ahaz had sent from Damascus." Here was a wanton innovation on received
usages, which had been appointed by Almighty God.
The same evil temper is protested against in Heze-
kiah's proclamation to the remnant of the Israelites:

" Be ye not like your fathers, and like your brethren, which trespassed against the Lord God of their fathers, who therefore gave them up to desolation, as ye see. Now be ye not stiff-necked, as your fathers were, but yield yourselves unto the Lord, and enter into His sanctuary." It is indirectly condemned, also, in the precept given to the Israelites, before their final deliverance from Pharaoh. When they were on the Red Sea shore, Moses said, " Fear ye not, stand still, and see the salvation of the Lord . . . . . . The Lord shall fight for you, and ye shall hold your peace." Again, in the Book of Psalms, " Be still, and know that I am God.   I will be exalted among the heathen, I will be exalted in the earth ;" the very trial of the people consisting in their doing nothing out of their place, but implicitly following when the Almighty took the lead.

The trial and sin of the Israelites were continued to the end of their history. They fell from their election on Christ's coming, in consequence of this very wilfulness ; refusing to receive the terms of the New Covenant, *as* they were vouchsafed to them, and attempting to incorporate them into their own ceremonial system. " They being ignorant of God's righteousness, and going about to establish their own righteousness, have not submitted themselves unto the righteousness of God."

Such was one distinguishing sin of the Israelites as a nation ; and, as it proved the cause of their rejection, so had it also, ages before, corrupted the faith, and forfeited the privileges, of their first king. The signs of wilfulness run through his history from first to last; but his formal trial took place at two distinct times, and in both cases terminated in his deliberate fall. Of these, the latter is more directly to our purpose. When sent to inflict a Divine judgment upon the Amalekites, he spared those whom he was bid slay; their king Agag, the best of the sheep and cattle, and all that was good. We are not concerned with the general state of mind and opinion which led him to this particular display of wilfulness. Much might be said of that profaneness, which, as in the case of Esau, was a distinguishing trait in his character. Indeed, we might even conjecture that from the first he was an unbeliever in heart; that is, that he did not recognize the exclusive divinity of the Mosaic theology, compared with those of the surrounding nations, and that he had by this time learned to regard the pomp and splendour of the neighbouring monarchies with an interest which made him ashamed of the seeming illiberality and the singularity of the institutions of Israel. A perverse will easily collects together a system of notions to justify itself in its obliquity. The real state of the case was this, that he preferred his own ways to that which God had determined. When directed by the Divine Hand towards the mark for which he was chosen, he started aside like a broken bow. He obeyed, but with a reserve, yet distinctly professing to Samuel that he had performed the commandment of the Lord, because the sheep and cattle were reserved for a pious purpose, a sacrifice to the Lord. The Prophet, in his reply, explained the real moral character of this limited and discretionary obedience, in words which are a warning to all who are within the hearing of Revealed Religion to the end of time : " Hath the Lord as great delight in burnt offerings and sacrifices, as in obeying the voice of the Lord ?   Behold, to obey is better than sacrifice; and to hearken, than the fat of rams. For rebellion is as the sin of witchcraft, and stubbornness is as iniquity and idolatry."

The moral of Saul's history is forced upon us by the events which followed this deliberate offence. By wilful resistance to God's will, he opened the door to those evil passions which till then, at the utmost, only served to make his character unamiable, without stamping it with guilt.   The reserve and mysteriousness, which, when subordinate to such magnanimity as he possessed, were even calculated to increase his influence as a ruler, ended in an overthrow of his mind, when they were allowed full scope by the removal of true religious principle, and the withdrawal of the Spirit of God.   Derangement was the consequence of disobedience.   The wilfulness which first resisted God next preyed upon himself, as a natural principle of disorder ; his moods and changes, his compunctions and relapses, what were they but the convulsions of the spirit, when the governing power was lost ?   At length the proud heart, which thought it much to obey its Maker, was humbled to seek comfort in a witch's cavern; essaying, by means which he had formerly denounced, to obtain advice from that Prophet when dead, whom in his lifetime he had dishonoured.

In contemplating this miserable termination of a history which promised well in the beginning, it should be observed, how clearly the failure of the divine purpose which takes place in it is attributable to man. Almighty God chose an instrument adapted, as far as external qualifications were concerned, to fulfil His purpose; adapted in all those respects which He reserved in His own hands, when he created a free agent; in character and gifts, in all respects except in that in which all men are, on the whole, on a level,—in will. No one could be selected in talents or conduct more suitable for maintaining political power at home than the reserved mysterious monarch whom God gave to His people; none more suitable for striking terror into the surrounding nations than a commander gifted with his coolness and promptitude in action. But he fell from his election, because of unbelief,—because he would take another part, and not the very part which was actually assigned him in the decrees of the Most High.

And again, considering his character according to the standard of moral excellence, here also it was one not without great promise. It is from such stern materials that the highest and noblest specimens of our kind are formed. The pliant and amiable by nature,

generally speaking, are not the subjects of great purposes. They are hardly capable of extraordinary discipline; they yield or they sink beneath the pressure
of those sanctifying processes which do but mature
the champions of holy Church. "Unstable as water,
thou shalt not excel," is a representation true in its
degree in the case of many, who nevertheless serve
God acceptably in their generation, and whose real
place in the ranks of the unseen world we have no
means of ascertaining. But those minds, which naturally most resemble the aboriginal chaos, contain
within them the elements of a marvellous creation
of light and beauty, if they but open their hearts to
the effectual power of the Holy Spirit. Pride and
sullenness, obstinacy and impetuosity, then become
transformed into the zeal, firmness, and high-minded-
ness of religious Faith. It depended on Saul himself
whether or not he became the rival of that exalted
saint, who, being once a fierce avenger of his brethren,
at length became "the meekest of men," yet not losing
thereby, but gaining moral strength and resoluteness.
Or again, a comparison of him in this respect
with the Apostle who originally bore his name, is not
perhaps so fanciful as it may appear at first sight. St.
Paul was distinguished by a furiousness and vindic-
tiveness equally incongruous as Saul's pride, with the
obedience of Faith. In the first persecution against
the Christians, he is described by the sacred writer
as ravening like a beast of prey. And he was exposed to the temptation of a wilfulness similar to

that of Saul—the wilfulness of running counter to God's purposes, and interfering in the course of Dispensations which he should have humbly received. He indeed was called miraculously, but scarcely more so than Saul, who, when he least expected it, was called by Samuel, and was, at his express prediction, suddenly filled by the Spirit of God, and made to prophesy. But, while Saul profited not by the privilege thus vouchsafed to him, St. Paul was "not disobedient to the heavenly vision," and matured in his after life in those exalted qualities of mind which Saul forfeited. Every attentive reader of his Epistles must be struck with the frequency and force of the Apostle's declarations concerning unreserved submission to the Divine Will, or rather of his exulting confidence in it. But the wretched king of Israel, what is his ultimate state, but the most forlorn of which human nature is capable? "How are the mighty fallen!" was the lament over him of the loyal though injured friend who succeeded to his power. He, who might have been canonized in the catalogue of the eleventh of Hebrews, is but the prototype of that vision of obduracy and self-inflicted destitution, which none but unbelieving poets of these latter ages have ever thought worthy of aught but the condemnation and abhorrence of mankind.

Two questions must be answered before we can apply the lesson of Saul's history to our own circumstances. It is common to contrast Christianity with Judaism, as if the latter were chiefly a system of positive commands, and the former addressed itself to the Reason and natural Conscience; and accordingly, it will perhaps be questioned whether Christians can be exposed to the temptation of wilfulness, that is, disobedience to the external word of God, in any way practically parallel to Saul's trial. And secondly, granting it possible, the warning against wilfulness, contained in his history and that of his nation, may be met by the objection that the Jews were a peculiarly carnal and gross-minded people, so that nothing can be argued concerning our danger at this day, from their being exposed and yielding to the temptation of perversity and presumption.

1. But such an assumption evidences a great want of fairness towards the ancient people of God, in those who make it, and is evidently perilous in proportion as it is proved to be unfounded. All men, not the Jews only, have a strange propensity, such as Eve evidenced in the beginning, to do what they are told not to do. It is plainly visible in children, and in the common people; and in them we are able to judge what we all are, before education and habit lay restraints upon us. Need we even do more than appeal to the events of the past year, to the conduct of the lower classes when under that fearful visitation, from which we are now, as we trust, recovering, in order to detect the workings of that innate spirit of scepticism and obduracy which was the enemy of Jewish faith? Of course, all places did not afford the same evidence of it; but on the whole there was

enough for my present allusion to it. A suspicion
of the most benevolent exertions in their favour, a
jealousy of the interference of those who knew more
than themselves, a perverse rejection of their services, and a counteraction of their plans and advice,
an unthankful credulity in receiving all the idle tales
told in disparagement of their knowledge and prudence; these were admonitions before our eyes, not
to trust those specious theories which are built on the
supposition, that the actual condition of the human
mind is better now than it was among the Jews. This
is not said without regard to the difference of guilt in
disobeying a Divine and a human command; nor,
again, in complaint of the poorer classes, of whom
we are especially bound to be tender, and who are
not the worse merely because they are less disguised
in the expression of their feelings; but as pointing
out for our own instruction the present existence of
a perversity in our common nature, like that which
appears in the history of Israel. Nor, perhaps, can
any one doubt, who examines himself, that he has
within him an unaccountable and instinctive feeling
to resist authority as such, which conscience or the
sense of interest is alone able to overcome.

Or, again, to take the case of young persons who
have not yet taken their place in the serious business
of life; consider the false shame they feel at being
supposed to be obedient to God or man; their endeavours to be more irreligious than they really can
be; their affected indifference to domestic feelings,

and the sanctity and the authority of relationship; their adoption of ridicule as an instrument of retaliation on the constraints of duty or necessity. What does all this show us, but that our nature likes its own way, not as thinking it better or safer, but simply because it is its own? In other words, that the principle of Faith is resisted, not only by our attachment to objects of sense and sight, but by an innate rebellious principle, which disobeys as if for the sake of disobedience.

2. Now if wilfulness be a characteristic of human nature, it is idle to make any such distinction of Dispensations, as will deprive us of the profitableness of the history of Saul, which was the second question just now raised concerning it. Under any circumstances it must be a duty to subdue that which is in itself vicious; and it is no excuse for wilfulness to say that we are not under a positive system of commands, such as the Mosaic, and that there is no room for the sin in Christianity. Rather, it will be our duty to regard ourselves in all our existing religious relations, and not merely according to some abstract views of the Gospel Covenant, and to apply the principles of right and wrong, exemplified in the Jewish history, to our changed circumstances on the whole.

But, to speak plainly, it may be doubted whether there be any such great difference between the Jewish system and our own, in respect of positive institutions and commandments. Revealed Religion, as such, is of the nature of a positive rule, implying, as it does, an addition, greater or less, to the religion of nature, and the disclosure of facts, which are thus disclosed, because otherwise not discoverable. Accordingly, the difference between the state of Jews and Christians is one simply of degree. We have to practise submission as they had, and we can run counter to the will of God in the very same way as they did, and under the same temptations which overcame them. For instance, the reception of the Catholic faith is a submission to a positive command, as really as was that of the Israelites to the Second Commandment. And the belief in the necessity of such reception, in order to salvation, is an additional instance of submission. Adherence to the Canon of Scripture is a further instance of this obedience of Faith; and St. John marks it as such in the words with which the Canon itself closes, which contain an anathema parallel to that which we use in the Creed. Moreover, the duty of Ecclesiastical Unity is clearly one of positive institution; it is a sort of ceremonial observance, and as such, is the tenure on which the evangelical privileges are chartered to us. The Sacraments, too, are of the same positive character.

If these remarks be well founded, it is plain that instead of our being very differently situated from the Jews, all persons who are subjects of Revealed Religion, coincide in differing from all who are left under the Dispensation of Nature. Revelation puts us on a trial which exists but obscurely in Natural Religion; the trial of obeying for obedience-sake, or on Faith.   Deference to the law of Conscience, indeed, is of the nature of Faith; but it is easily perverted into a kind of self-confidence, namely, a deference to our own judgment.   Here, then, Revelation provides us with an important instrument for chastening and moulding our moral character, over and above the matter of its disclosures.   Christians as well as Jews must submit as little children.   This being considered, how strange are the notions of the present day concerning the liberty and irresponsibility of the Christian!   If the Gospel be a message, as it is, it ever must be more or less what the multitude of self-wise reasoners declare it shall not be,—a law; it must be of the nature of what they call a form, and a bondage; it must, in its degree, bring darkness, instead of flattering them with the promise of immediate illumination; and must enlighten them only in proportion as they first submit to be darkened.   This, then, if they knew their meaning, is the wish of the so-called philosophical Christians, and men of no party, of the present day; namely, that they should be rid altogether of the shackles of a revelation: and to this assuredly their efforts are tending and will tend,—to identify the Christian doctrine with their own individual convictions, to sink its supernatural character, and to constitute themselves the prophets, not the recipients, of Divine Truth; creeds and discipline being already in their minds severed from its substance, and being gradually shaken off by them in fact, as the circumstances of the times will allow.

M 2

Let us, then, reflect that, whatever be the trial of those who have not a revelation, the trial of those who have is one of Faith in opposition to self-will. Those very self-appointed ordinances which are praiseworthy in a heathen, and the appropriate evidence of his earnestness and piety, are inexcusable in those to whom God has spoken. Things indifferent become sins when they are forbidden, and duties when commanded. The emblems of the Deity might be invented by Egyptian faith, but were adopted by Jewish unbelief. The trial of Abraham, when called on to kill his son, as of Saul when bid slay the Amalekites, was the duty of quitting the ordinary rules which He prescribes to our obedience, upon a positive commandment distinctly conveyed to them by revelation.

And so strong is this tendency of Revealed Religion to erect positive institutions and laws, that it absorbs into its province even those temporal ordinances which are, strictly speaking, exterior to it. It gives to the laws of man the nature of a divine authority, and where they exist makes obedience to them a duty. This is evident in the case of civil government, the forms and officers of which, when once established, are to be received for conscience-sake by those who find themselves under them. The same principle is applied in a more remarkable manner to sanction customs originally indifferent, in the case of the Rechabites; who were rewarded with a promise of continuance as a family, on the ground of their observance of certain discomforts and austerities, imposed on them by the simple authority of an ancestor.

With these principles fresh in the memory, a number of reflections crowd upon the mind in surveying the face of society, as at present constituted. The present open resistance to constituted power, and (what is more to the purpose) the indulgent toleration of it, the irreverence towards Antiquity, the unscrupulous and wanton violation of the commands and usages of our forefathers, the undoing of their benefactions, the profanation of the Church, the bold transgression of the duty of Ecclesiastical Unity, the avowed disdain of what is called party religion, (though Christ undeniably made a party the vehicle of His doctrine, and did not cast it at random on the world, as men would now have it,) the growing indifference to the Catholic Creed, the sceptical objections to portions of its doctrine, the arguings and discussings, and comparings and correctings and rejectings, and all the train of presumptuous exercises, to which its sacred articles are subjected, the numberless discordant criticisms on the Liturgy, which have shot up on all sides of us; the general irritable state of mind, which is every where witnessed, and craving for change in all things ; what do all these symptoms show, but that the spirit of Saul still lives? — that wilfulness, which is the antagonist principle to the zeal of David, — the principle of cleaving and breaking down all divine ordinances, instead of building up. And with Saul's sin, Saul's portion awaits his fol-

lowers,—distraction, aberration; the hiding of God's
countenance; imbecility, rashness, and changeable-
ness in their counsels; judicial blindness; fear of the
multitude; the persecution of good men and faithful
friends; subserviency to their worst foes, the kings
of Amalek and the wizards of Endor. So was it
with the Jews, who rejected their Messiah only to
follow impostors; so is it with infidels, who become
the slaves of superstition; and such is ever the
righteous doom of those who trust their own wills
more than God's word, in one way or other to be
led eventually into a servile submission to usurped
authority. As the Apostle says of the Roman
Christians, they were but slaves of sin, while they
were emancipated from righteousness. " What fruit,"
he asks, " had ye then in those things whereof ye
are now ashamed ?"

These remarks may at first sight seem irrelevant
in the case of those who, like ourselves, are bound
by affection and express promises to the cause of
Christ's Church; yet it should be recollected that
very rarely have its members escaped the infection
of the age in which they lived: and there certainly is
the danger of our considering ourselves safe, merely
because we do not go the lengths of others, but protest against the extreme principles or measures to
which they commit themselves.

SERMON IX.

FAITH AND REASON, CONTRASTED AS HABITS OF
MIND.

Preached on the Epiphany, 1839.

HEB. xi. 1.

" Now Faith is the substance of things hoped for, the evidence of
things not seen."

THE subject of Faith is one especially suggested to
our minds by the event which we this day commemorate, and the great act of grace of which it was the
first fruits. It was as on this day that the wise men
of the East were allowed to approach and adore the
infant Saviour, in anticipation of those Gentile multitudes who, when the kingdom of God was preached,
were to take possession of it as if by violence, and to
extend it to the ends of the earth. To them Christ
was manifested as He is to us, and in the same way;
not to the eyes of the flesh, but to the illuminated
mind, to their Faith. As the manifestation of God
accorded to the Jews was circumscribed, and addressed
to their senses, so that which is vouchsafed to Chris-

tians is universal and spiritual. Whereas the gifts of
the Gospel are invisible, Faith is their proper recipient; and whereas its Church is Catholic, Faith is
its bond of intercommunion; things external, local,
and sensible being no longer objects to dwell upon
on their own account, but merely means of conveying
onwards the divine gifts from the Giver to their
proper home, the heart itself.

As, then, Catholicity is the note, so an inward
manifestation is the privilege, and Faith the duty, of
the Christian Church; or, in the words of the Apostle,
"the *Gentiles*" receive "the promise of the *Spirit*
through *Faith*."

I shall not, then, be stepping beyond the range of
subjects to which this great Festival draws our attention, if I enter upon some inquiries into the nature of that special Gospel grace, by which Jews and
Gentiles apprehend and enjoy the blessings which
Christ has purchased for them, and which accordingly
is spoken of in the Collect for the Festival, as the peculiarity of our condition in this life, as Sight will be in
the world to come. And in so doing, I shall be pursuing a subject, which is likely to be of main importance in the controversies which lie before us at this
day, and upon which I am not speaking now for the
first time from this place[1].

It is scarcely necessary to prove from Scripture, the
especial dignity and influence of Faith, under the
Gospel Dispensation, as regards both our spiritual and

[1] Vide Sermon III.

moral condition. Whatever be the particular faculty or frame of mind denoted by the word, certainly Faith is regarded in Scripture as the chosen instrument connecting heaven and earth, as a novel principle of action, most powerful in the influence which it exerts both on the heart and on the Divine view of us, and yet in itself of a nature to excite the contempt or ridicule of the world. These characteristics, its apparent weakness, its novelty, its special adoption, and its efficacy, are noted in such passages as the following:—" Have faith in God; for verily I say unto you, that whosoever shall say unto this mountain, Be thou removed and be thou cast into the sea, and shall not doubt in his heart, but shall believe that those things which he saith shall come to pass, he shall have whatsoever he saith. Therefore I say unto you, what things soever ye desire, when ye pray, believe that ye receive them, and ye shall have them." And again : " If thou canst believe, all things are possible to him that believeth." Again : " The preaching of the Cross is to them that perish foolishness, but unto us which are saved it is the power of God. Where is the wise ? where is the scribe ? where is the disputer of this world ? For after that in the wisdom of God the world by wisdom knew not God, it pleased God by the foolishness of preaching to save them that believe." Again: " The word is nigh thee, even in thy mouth and in thy heart, that is, the word of faith which we preach. . . . Faith cometh by hearing,

and hearing by the word of God." And again : "Yet
a little while, and He that shall come will come, and
will not tarry; now the just shall live by faith." . . .
And then, soon after, the words of the text : " Now
faith is the substance of things hoped for, the evidence of things not seen[2]."

Such is the great weapon which Christianity employs, whether viewed as a religious scheme, as a
social system, or as a moral rule ; and what it is described in the foregoing texts, it is also said to be
expressly or by implication in other passages too
numerous to cite. And I suppose that it will not
be denied, that the first impression made upon the
reader from all these is, that Faith is an instrument
of knowledge and action, unknown to the world before, a principle *sui generis*, distinct from those which
nature supplies, and in particular (which is the point
into which I mean to inquire) independent of what
is commonly understood by Reason. Certainly if,
after all that is said about Faith in the New Testament, as if it were what may be called a discovery
of the Gospel, and a special divine method of salvation ; if, after all, it turns out merely to be a believing upon evidence, or a sort of conclusion upon
a process of reasoning, a resolve formed upon a calculation, the inspired text is not level to the understanding, or adapted to the instruction, of the un-

[2] Mark xi. 22—24 ; ix. 23.   1 Cor. i. 18—21.   Rom. x. 8. 17.
Heb. x. 37, 38.

learned reader.   If Faith be such a principle, how is it novel and strange?

Other considerations may be urged in support of the same view of the case.   For instance: Faith is spoken of as having its life in a certain moral temper, but argumentative exercises are not moral; Faith, then, is not the same method of proof as Reason.

Again: Faith is said to be one of the supernatural gifts imparted in the Gospel.   "By grace have ye been saved, through faith, and that not of yourselves, it is the gift of God;" but investigation and proof belong to man as man, prior to the Gospel; therefore Faith is something higher than Reason.

Again:—That Faith is independent of processes of Reason, seems plain from their respective subject-matters.   "Faith cometh by hearing, and hearing by the word of God."   It simply accepts testimony. As then testimony is distinct from experience, so is Faith from Reason.

And again:—When the Apostles disparage "the wisdom of this world," "disputings," "excellency of speech," and the like, they seem to mean very much what would now be called trains of argument, discussion, investigation,—that is, exercises of Reason.

Once more:—Various instances are given us in Scripture of an acknowledgment of Christ and His Apostles upon Faith, which would not be considered by the world as a rational conviction upon evidence. For instance: The lame man who sat at the Beautiful gate was healed on his faith, after St. Peter had

2

but said, " Look on us." And that other lame man
at Lystra saw no miracle done by St. Paul, but only
heard him preach, when the Apostle, " stedfastly
beholding him, and perceiving that he had faith to
be healed, said with a loud voice, Stand upright on
thy feet." Again, St. Paul at Athens did no miracle, but preached, and yet "certain men clave unto
him and believed." To the same purpose are our
Lord's words, when St. John Baptist sent to Him
to ask if He were the Christ. He wrought miracles,
indeed, to re-assure him, but added, " Blessed is he
whosoever shall not be offended in Me." And when
St. Thomas doubted of His resurrection, He gave him
the sensible proof which he asked, but He added,
" Blessed are they that have not seen, and yet have
believed." On another occasion He said, " Except
ye see signs and wonders, ye will not believe [3]."

On the other hand, however, it may be urged, that
it is plainly impossible that Faith should be independent of Reason, and a new mode of arriving at truth;
that the Gospel does not alter the constitution of our
nature, and does but elevate it and add to it; that
Sight is our initial, and Reason is our ultimate informant concerning all knowledge. We are conscious
that we see; we have an instinctive reliance on our
Reason : how can the claims of a professed Revelation be brought home to us as Divine, except through
these? Faith, then, must necessarily be resolvable

[3] Acts iii. 4. ; xiv. 9, 10.; xvii. 34. Matt. xi. 6. John xx. 29.
Ib. iv. 48.

at last into Sight and Reason; unless, indeed, we agree with enthusiasts in thinking that faculties altogether new are implanted in our minds, and that perceptibly, by the grace of the Gospel; faculties which, of course, are known to those who have them without proof; and, to those who have them not, cannot be made known by any. Scripture confirms this representation, as often as the Apostles appeal to their miracles, or to the Old Testament. This is an appeal to Reason; and what is recorded, in some instances, was, probably or certainly (as it is presumed from the necessity of the case) made in the rest, even where not recorded.

Such is the question which presents itself to readers of Scripture, as to the relation of Faith to Reason: and it is usual at this day to settle it in disparagement of Faith,—to say that Faith is but a moral quality, dependent upon Reason,—that Reason judges both of the evidence on which Scripture is to be received, and of the meaning of Scripture; and then that Faith follows or not, according to the state of the heart; that we make up our minds by Reason without Faith, and then we proceed to adore and to obey by Faith apart from Reason; that, though Faith rests on testimony, not on reasonings, yet that testimony, in its turn, depends on Reason for the proof of its pretensions, so that Reason is an indispensable preliminary.

1. Now, in attempting to investigate what are the distinct offices of Faith and Reason in religious

matters, and the relation of the one to the other,
I observe, first, that undeniable though it be, that
Reason has a power of analysis and criticism in all
opinion and conduct, and that nothing is true or
right but what may be justified, and, in a certain
sense, proved by it, and undeniable, in consequence,
that, unless the doctrines received by Faith are
approvable by Reason, they have no claim to be
regarded as true, it does not therefore follow that
Faith is actually grounded on Reason in the believing mind itself; unless, indeed, to take a parallel
case, a judge can be called the origin, as well as the
justifier, of the innocence or truth of those who are
brought before him. A judge does not make men
honest, but acquits and vindicates them : in like
manner Reason need not be the origin of Faith, as
Faith exists in the very persons believing, though it
does test and verify it. This, then, is one confusion,
which must be cleared up in the question,—the
assumption that Reason must be the inward principle
of action in religious inquiries or conduct in the case
of this or that individual, because, like a spectator, it
acknowledges and concurs in what goes on ;—the mistake of a critical for a creative power.

This distinction we cannot fail to recognize as true
in itself, and applicable to the matter in hand. It is
what we all admit at once as regards the principle of
Conscience. No one will say that Conscience is
against Reason, or that its dictates cannot be thrown
into an argumentative form ; yet who will, therefore,

maintain, that it is not an original principle, but must depend, before it acts, upon some previous processes of Reason? Reason analyzes the grounds and motives of action : a reason is an analysis, but is not the motive itself. As, then, Conscience is a simple element in our nature, yet its operations admit of being surveyed and scrutinized by Reason; so may Faith be cognizable, and its acts be justified, by Reason, without therefore being, in matter of fact, dependent upon it ; and as we reprobate, under the name of Utilitarianism, the substitution of Reason for Conscience, so perchance it is a parallel error to teach that a process of Reason is the *sine quá non* for true religious Faith. When the Gospel is said to require a rational Faith, this need not mean more than that Faith is accordant to right Reason in the abstract, not that it results from it in the particular case.

A parallel and familiar instance is presented by the generally-acknowledged contrast between poetical or similar powers, and the art of criticism. That art is the sovereign awarder of praise and blame, and constitutes a court of appeal in matters of taste ; as then the critic ascertains what he cannot himself create, so Reason may put its sanction upon the acts of Faith, without in consequence being the source from which Faith springs.

On the other hand, Faith certainly does seem, in matter of fact, to exist and operate quite independently of Reason. Will any one say that a child or uneducated person may not savingly act on Faith, without being able to produce reasons why he so acts? What sufficient view has he of the Evidences of Christianity? What logical proof of its divinity? If he has none, Faith, viewed as a habit of the mind, does not depend upon inquiry and examination, but has its own special basis, whatever that is, as truly as Conscience has. We see, then, that Reason may be the judge, without being the origin, of Faith; and that Faith may be justified by Reason, without making use of it. This is what it occurs to mention at first sight.

2. Next, I observe, that, whatever be the real distinction and relation existing between Faith and Reason, which it is not to our purpose. at once to determine, the contrast that would be made between them, on a popular view, is this,—that Reason requires strong evidence before it assents, and Faith is content with weaker evidence.

For instance: when a well-known infidel of the last century argues, that the divinity of Christianity is founded on the testimony of the Apostles, in opposition to the experience of nature, and that the laws of nature are uniform, those of testimony variable, and scoffingly adds that Christianity is founded on Faith not on Reason, what is this but saying that Reason is severer in its demands of evidence than Faith?

Again, the founder of the recent Utilitarian School insists that all evidence for miracles, before it can be received, should be brought into a court of law, and subjected to its searching forms:—this too is to imply that Reason demands exact proofs, but that Faith accepts inaccurate ones.

The same thing is implied in the notion, which men of the world entertain, that Faith is but credulity, superstition, or fanaticism; these principles being notoriously such as are contented with insufficient evidence concerning their objects. On the other hand, scepticism, which shows itself in a dissatisfaction with evidence of whatever kind, is often called by the name of Reason. What Faith, then, and Reason are, when compared together, may be determined from their counterfeits, —from the mutual relation of credulity and scepticism, which no one can doubt about.

In like manner, when mathematics are said to incline the mind towards doubt and latitudinarianism, this arises, according to the statement of one[4] who felt this influence of the study, from its indisposing us for arguments drawn from mere probabilities.

Or, to take particular instances:—When the proof of Infant Baptism is rested by its defenders on such texts as, "Suffer little children to come unto Me[5]," a man of a reasoning turn will object to such an argument as not sufficient to prove the point in hand; he will say that it does not follow that infants ought to be baptized, because they ought to be

---

[4] Bishop Watson.   [5] Matt. xix. 14.

UNIV. S.   N

brought and dedicated to Christ; and that he waits
for more decisive evidence.

Again, when the religious observance of a Christian
Sabbath is defended from the Apostles' observance
of it, it may be captiously argued that, considering St.
Paul's express declaration, that the Sabbath, as such,
is abolished, a mere practice, which happens to be
recorded in the Acts, and which, for what we know,
was temporary and accidental, cannot restore what
was once done away, and introduce a Jewish rite
into the Gospel. Religious persons, who cannot answer this objection, are often tempted to impute it
to " man's wisdom," " the logic of the schools,"
" the pride of reason," and the like, and to insist on
the necessity of the teachable study of Scripture as
the means of overcoming it. We are not concerned
to defend the language they use; but it is plain
that they corroborate what has been laid down, as
implying that Reason requires more evidence for
conviction than Faith.

When, then, Reason and Faith are contrasted together, Faith means easiness, Reason, difficulty of conviction. Reason is called either strong sense or scepticism, according to the bias of the speaker; and
Faith, either teachableness or credulity.

3. The next question, beyond which I shall not
proceed to-day, is this:—If this be so, how is it con-
formable to Reason to accept evidence less than Reason requires? If Faith be what has been described,
it opposes itself to Reason, as being satisfied with the

less where Reason demands the more. If, then, Reason be the healthy action of the mind, then Faith must be its weakness. The answer to this question will advance us one step further in our investigation into the relation existing between Faith and Reason.

Faith, then, I have said, does not demand evidence so strong as is necessary for what is commonly considered a rational conviction, or belief on the ground of Reason; and why? For this reason, because it is mainly swayed by antecedent considerations. In this way it is, that the two principles are opposed to one another: Faith is influenced by previous notices, prepossessions, and (in a good sense of the word) prejudices; but Reason, by direct and definite proof. The mind that believes is acted upon by its own hopes, fears, and existing opinions; whereas it is supposed to reason severely, when it rejects antecedent proof of a fact,—rejects everything but the actual evidence producible in its favour. This will appear from a very few words.

Faith is a principle of action, and action does not allow time for minute and finished investigations. We may (if we will) think that such investigations are of high value; though, in truth, they have a tendency to blunt the practical energy of the mind, while they improve its scientific exactness; but, whatever be their character and consequences, they are impracticable in action. Diligent collection of evidence, sifting of arguments, and balancing of rival testimonies, may be suited to persons who have leisure and opportunity to act when and how they will; they are not suited to the multitude. Faith, then, as being a principle for the multitude and for conduct, is influenced more by what (in language familiar to us of this place) are called εἰκότα than by σημεῖα,—less by evidence, more by previously-entertained principles, views, and wishes.

This is the case with all Faith, and not merely religious. We hear a report in the streets, or read it in the public journals. We know nothing of the evidence; we do not know the witnesses, or anything about them: yet sometimes we believe implicitly, sometimes not; sometimes we believe without asking for evidence, sometimes we disbelieve till we receive it. Did a rumour circulate of a destructive earthquake in Syria or the south of Europe, we should readily credit it; both because it might easily be true, and because it was nothing to us though it were. Did the report relate to countries nearer home, we should try to trace and authenticate it. We do not call for evidence till antecedent probabilities fail.

Again, it is scarcely necessary to point out how much our inclinations have to do with our belief. It is almost a proverb, that persons believe what they wish to be true. They will with difficulty admit the failure of any cherished project, or listen to a messenger of ill tidings. It may be objected, indeed, that great desire of an object sometimes makes us incredulous that we have attained it. Certainly;

but this is only when we consider its attainment improbable, as well as desirable. Thus St. Thomas
doubted of the Resurrection; and thus Jacob, especially as having already been deceived by his children,
believed not the news of Joseph's being governor
of Egypt. " Jacob's heart fainted, for he believed
them not . . . but when he saw the waggons which
Joseph had sent to carry him, the spirit of Jacob
their father revived."

The case is the same as regards preconceived
opinions. Men readily believe reports unfavourable
to persons they dislike, or confirmations of theories
of their own. " Trifles light as air" are all that the
predisposed mind requires for belief and action.

Such are the inducements to belief which prevail
with all of us, by a law of our nature, and whether
they are in the particular case reasonable or not.
When the probabilities we assume do not really exist,
or our wishes are inordinate, or our opinions are
wrong, our Faith degenerates into weakness, extravagance, superstition, enthusiasm, bigotry, prejudice, as
the case may be; but when our prepossessions are
unexceptionable, then we are right in believing or
not believing, not indeed without, but upon slender
evidence.

Whereas Reason then (as the word is commonly
used) rests on the evidence, Faith is influenced by
presumptions; and hence, while Reason requires rigid
proofs, Faith is satisfied with vague or defective
ones.

4. It will serve to bring out this doctrine into a more tangible form, to set down some inferences and reflections to which it leads, themselves not unimportant.

(1.) First, then, I would draw attention to the coincidence, for such it would seem to be, of what has been said, with St. Paul's definition of Faith in the text. He might have defined it "reliance on the word of another," or "acceptance of a divine message," or "submission of the intellect to mysteries," or in other ways equally true and more theological; but instead of such accounts of it, he adopts a definition bearing upon its nature, and singularly justifying the view which has been here taken of it. "Faith," he says, "is the substance" or realizing "of things hoped for." It is the reckoning that to be, which it hopes or wishes to be; not "the realizing of things proved by evidence." Its desire is its main evidence; or, as the Apostle expressly goes on to say, it makes its own evidence, "being the *evidence* of things not seen." And this is the cause, as is natural, why Faith seems to the world so irrational, as St. Paul says in other Epistles. Not that it has no grounds in Reason, that is, in evidence; but because it is satisfied with so much less than would be necessary, were it not for the bias of the mind, that to the world its evidence seems like nothing.

(2.) Next it is plain in what sense Faith is a moral principle. It is created in the mind, not so much by facts, as by probabilities; and since probabilities

have no definite ascertained value, and are reducible
to no scientific standard, what are such to each individual, depends on his moral temperament. A good
and a bad man will think very different things probable. In the judgment of a rightly disposed mind,
objects are desirable and attainable, which irreligious
men will consider to be but fancies. Such a correct
moral judgment and view of things, is the very medium in which the argument for Christianity has its
constraining influence; a faint proof under circumstances being more availing than a strong one, apart
from those circumstances. This holds good as regards
the matter as well as the evidence of the Gospel. It
is difficult to say where the evidence, whether for
Scripture or the Creed, would be found, if it were
deprived of those adventitious illustrations which
it extracts and absorbs from the mind of the inquirer, and which a merciful Providence places there
for that very purpose. Texts have their illuminating
power, from the atmosphere of habit, opinion, usage,
tradition, through which we see them. On the
other hand, irreligious men are adequate judges of the
value of mere evidence, when the decision turns upon
it; for evidence is addressed to the Reason, compels
the Reason to assent so far as it is strong, and allows
the Reason to doubt or disbelieve so far as it is weak.
The blood on Joseph's coat of many colours was as
perceptible to enemy as to friend; miracles appeal
to the senses of all men, good and bad; and, while

their supernatural character is learned from that
experience of nature which is common to the just
and to the unjust, the fact of their occurrence depends on considerations about testimony, enthusiasm,
imposture, and the like, in which there is nothing inward, nothing personal.   It is a sort of proof which
a man does not make for himself, but which is made
for him.   It exists independently of him, and is apprehended from its own clear and objective character.
It is its very boast that it does but require a candid
hearing; nay, it especially addresses itself to the unbeliever, and engages to convert him as if against his
will.   There is no room for choice; there is no merit,
no praise or blame, in believing or disbelieving; no
test of character in the one or the other.   But a man
is responsible for his faith, because he is responsible
for his likings and dislikings, his hopes and his opinions,
on all of which his faith depends.   And whereas unbelievers do not see this distinction, they persist in
saying that a man is as little responsible for his faith
as for his bodily functions; that both are from
nature; that the will cannot make a weak proof a
strong one; that if a person thinks a certain reason
goes only a certain way, he is dishonest in attempting
to make it go farther; that if he is after all wrong
in his judgment, it is only his misfortune, not his
fault; that he is acted on by certain principles from
without, and must obey the laws of evidence, which
are necessary and constant.   But in truth, though

a given evidence does not vary in force, the antecedent probability attending it does vary indefinitely,
according to the temper of the mind surveying it.

(3.) Again : it is plain from what has been said, why
our great divines, Bull and Taylor, not to mention
others, have maintained that justifying faith is *fides
formata charitate*, or in St. Paul's words, πίστις δι'
ἀγάπης ἐνεργουμένη. For as Faith, which is not moral,
but depends upon evidence, is *fides formata ratione*,—
dead Faith, which an infidel may have ; so that which
justifies or is acceptable in God's sight, lives in and
from a desire after those things which it accepts and
confesses.

(4.) And here, again, we see what is meant by saying
that Faith is a supernatural principle.   The laws of
evidence are the same in regard to the Gospel as to
profane matters.   If they were the sole arbiters of
Faith, of course Faith could have nothing supernatural
in it.   But love of the great Object of Faith, watchful attention to Him, readiness to believe Him near,
easiness to believe Him interposing in human affairs,
fear of the risk of slighting or missing what may
really come from Him ; these are feelings not natural
to fallen man, and they come only of supernatural
grace ; and these are the feelings which make us think
evidence sufficient, which falls short of a proof in itself.
The natural man has no heart for the promises of the
Gospel, and dissects its evidence without reverence,
without hope, without suspense, without misgivings ;
and, while he analyzes it perhaps more philosophi-

cally than another, and treats it more luminously, and
sums up its result with the precision and propriety
of a legal tribunal, he rests in it as an end, and
neither attains the further truths at which it points,
nor inhales the spirit which it breathes.

(5.) And this remark bears upon a fact which has
sometimes perplexed Christians,—that those philosophers[6], ancient and modern, who have been eminent
in physical science, have not unfrequently shown a
tendency to infidelity. The system of physical causes
is so much more tangible and satisfying than that of
final, that unless there be a pre-existent and independent interest in the inquirer's mind, leading him
to dwell on the phenomena which betoken an Intelligent Creator, he will certainly follow out those which
terminate in the hypothesis of a settled order of
nature and self-sustained laws. It is indeed a great
question whether atheism is not as philosophically
consistent with the phenomena of the physical world,
taken by themselves, as the doctrine of a creative
and governing Power. But, however this be, the
practical safeguard against atheism in the case of
scientific inquirers is the inward need and desire, the
inward experience, of that Power, existing in the
mind antecedent and independent of their examination of His material world.

(6.) And in this lies the main fallacy of the celebrated argument against miracles, already alluded to,
of a Scotch philosopher, whose depth and subtlety

[6] Vide Bacon, de Augm. Scient. § 5.

all must acknowledge.   Let us grant (at least for argument's sake) that judging from the experience of life, it is more likely that witnesses should deceive, than that the laws of nature should be suspended. Still there may be considerations distinct from this view of the question which turn the main probability the other way,—viz. the likelihood, *à priori*, that a revelation should be given.   Here, then, we see how Faith is and is not according to Reason; taken together with the antecedent probability that Providence will reveal Himself to mankind, such evidence of the fact, as is otherwise deficient, may be enough for conviction, even in the judgment of Reason.   But it need not be enough apart from that probability. That is, Reason, weighing evidence only, or arguing from external experience, is counter to Faith; but, admitting the full influence of the moral feelings, it concurs with it.

Hence it would seem as though Paley had hardly asked enough in the Introduction to his work on the Evidences, when he says of the doctrine of a future state and of a revelation relating to it, "that it is not necessary for our purpose that these propositions be capable of proof, or even that, by arguments drawn from the light of nature, they can be made out to be probable; it is enough that we are able to say concerning them, that they are not so violently improbable," that the propositions or the facts connected with them ought to be rejected at first sight.   This acute and ingenious writer here asks leave to do only

2

what the Utilitarian writer mentioned in a former
place demands should be done, namely, to bring his
case (as it were) into court; as if trusting to the
strength of his evidence, dispensing with moral and
religious considerations on one side or the other, and
arguing from the mere phenomena of the human
mind, the inducements, ·motives, and habits, according to which man acts. I will not say more of such
a procedure than that it seems to me dangerous. As
miracles, according to the common saying, are not
wrought to convince Atheists, and, when they claim
to be evidence of a revelation, presuppose the being
of an Intelligent Agent to whom they may be referred, so Evidences in general are grounded on the
admission that the doctrine they are brought to prove
is, not merely not inconsistent, but actually accordant with the laws of His moral governance. Miracles,
though they contravene the physical laws of the
universe, tend to the due fulfilment of its moral
laws. And in matter of fact, when they were wrought,
they addressed persons who were already believers, not
in the mere probability, but even in the truth of supernatural revelations. This appears from the preaching
of our Lord and His Apostles, who are accustomed to
appeal to the religious feelings of their hearers; and
who, though they might fail with the many, did thus
persuade those who were persuaded—not, indeed, the
sophists of Athens or the politicians of Rome, yet
men of very different states of mind one with another, the pious, the superstitious, and the dissolute,

different, indeed, but all agreeing in this, in the acknowledgment of truths beyond this world, whether
or not their knowledge was clear, or their lives consistent,—the devout Jew, the proselyte of the gate,
the untaught fisherman, the outcast Publican, and
the pagan idolater.

(7.) And last of all, we here see what divines mean,
who have been led to depreciate what are called the
Evidences of Religion.   The last century, a time
when love was cold, is noted as being especially the
Age of Evidences ; and now, when more devout and
zealous feelings have been excited, there is, I need
scarcely say, a disposition manifested in various quar-
ters to think lightly, as of the eighteenth century,
so of its boasted demonstrations.   I have not here to
make any formal comparison of the last century with
the present, or to say whether they are nearer the
truth, who in these matters advance with the present
age, or who loiter behind with the preceding.   I will
only state what seems to me meant when persons
disparage the Evidences,—viz. they consider that, as
a general rule, religious minds embrace the Gospel
mainly on the great antecedent probability of a revelation, and the suitableness of the Gospel to their
needs ; on the other hand, that on men of irreligious
minds Evidences are thrown away.   Further, they
perhaps would say, that to insist much on matters
which are for the most part so useless for any practical purpose, draws men away from the true view of
Christianity, and leads them to think that Faith is

mainly the result of argument, that religious Truth
is a legitimate matter of disputation, and that they
who reject it rather err in judgment than commit sin.
They think they see in the study in question a tendency to betray the sacredness and dignity of Religion, when those who profess themselves its champions allow themselves to stand on the same ground
as philosophers of the world, admit the same principles, and only aim at drawing different conclusions.
For is not this the error, the common and fatal error,
of the world, to think itself a judge of Religious Truth
without preparation of heart? "I am the good
Shepherd, and know My sheep, and am known of
Mine." "He goeth before them, and the sheep follow
Him, for they know His voice." "The pure in heart
see God:" "to the meek mysteries are revealed;"
"he that is spiritual judgeth all things." "The darkness comprehendeth it not." Gross eyes see not;
heavy ears hear not. But in the schools of the world
the ways towards Truth are considered high roads open
to all men, however disposed, at all times. Truth is
to be approached without homage. Every one is considered on a level with his neighbour; or rather the
powers of the intellect, acuteness, sagacity, subtlety,
and depth, are thought the guides into Truth. Men
consider that they have as full a right to discuss religious subjects, as if they were themselves religious.
They will enter upon the most sacred points of Faith
at the moment, at their pleasure,—if it so happen, in
a careless frame of mind, in their hours of recre-

ation, over the wine cup. Is it wonderful that they so frequently end in becoming Indifferentists, and conclude that Religious Truth is but a name, that all men are right and all wrong, from witnessing externally the multitude of sects and parties, and from the clear consciousness they possess that their own inquiries end in darkness ?

Yet, serious as these dangers may be, it does not therefore follow that the Evidences may not be of great service to persons in particular frames of mind. Careless persons may be startled by them as they might be startled by a miracle, which is no necessary condition of believing, notwithstanding. Again, they often serve as a test of honesty of mind; their rejection being the condemnation of unbelievers. Again, religious persons sometimes get perplexed and lose their way; are harassed by objections; see difficulties which they cannot surmount ; are a prey to subtlety of mind or over-anxiety. Under these circumstances the varied proofs of Christianity will be a stay, a refuge, an encouragement, a rallying point for Faith, a gracious economy ; and even in the case of the most established Christian are they a source of gratitude and reverent admiration, and a means of confirming faith and hope. Nothing need be detracted from the use of the Evidences on this score ; much less can any sober mind run into the wild notion that actually no proof at all is implied in the maintenance, or may be exacted for the profession of Christianity. I would only maintain that that proof

need not be the subject of analysis, or take a methodical form, or be complete and symmetrical, in
the believing mind; and that probability is its life.
I do but say that it is antecedent probability that
gives meaning to those arguments from facts which
are commonly called the Evidences of Revelation;
that, whereas mere probability proves nothing, mere
facts persuade no one; that probability is to fact, as
the soul to the body; that mere presumptions may
have no force, but that mere facts have no warmth.
A mutilated and defective evidence suffices for persuasion where the heart is alive; but dead evidences,
however perfect, can but create a dead faith.

To conclude: It will be observed, I have not yet said
what Reason really is, or what is its relation to Faith,
but have merely contrasted the two together, taking
Reason in the sense popularly ascribed to the word.
Nor do I aim at more than ascertaining the sense
in which the words Faith and Reason are used by
Christian and Catholic writers. If I shall succeed in
this, I shall be content, without attempting to defend
it. Half the controversies in the world are verbal
ones; and, could they be brought to a plain issue,
they would be brought to a prompt termination.
Parties engaged in them would then perceive, either
that in substance they agreed together, or that their
difference was one of first principles. This is the
great object to be aimed at in the present age, though
confessedly a very arduous one. We need not dis-

pute, we need not prove, — we need but define.   At all events, let us, if we can, do this first of all; and then see who are left for us to dispute with, what is left for us to prove.   Controversy, at least in this age, does not lie between the hosts of heaven, Michael and his Angels on the one side, and the powers of evil on the other; but it is a sort of night battle, where each fights for himself, and friend and foe stand together.   When men understand what each other mean, they see, for the most part, that controversy is either superfluous or hopeless.

SERMON X.

THE NATURE OF FAITH IN RELATION TO REASON.

Preached January 13, 1839.

1 Cor. i. 27.

" God hath chosen the foolish things of the world to confound the
wise, and God hath chosen the weak things of the world to
confound the things which are mighty."

It is usual at this day to speak as if Faith were
simply of a moral nature, and depended and followed
upon a distinct act of Reason beforehand,—Reason
warranting, on the ground of evidence, both ample
and carefully examined, that the Gospel comes from
God, and *then* Faith embracing it: on the other
hand, the more Scriptural representation seems to be
this, which is obviously more agreeable to facts also,
that, instead of there being really any such united
process of reasoning first, and then believing, the act
of Faith is sole and elementary, and complete in
itself, and depends on no process of mind previous to
it: and this doctrine is borne out by the common
opinion of men, who, though they contrast Faith and

Reason, yet rather consider Faith to be weak Reason, than a moral quality or act following upon Reason. The Word of Life is offered to a man; and, on its being offered, he has Faith in it. Why? On these two grounds,—the word of its human messenger, and the likelihood of the message. And why does he feel the message to be probable? Because he has a love for it, his love being strong, though the testimony is weak. He has a keen sense of the intrinsic excellence of the message, of its desirableness, of its likeness to what it seems to him Divine Goodness would vouch-safe did He vouchsafe any, of the need of a Reve-lation, and its probability. Thus Faith is the reason-ing of a religious mind, or of what Scripture calls a right or renewed heart, which acts upon presumptions rather than evidence, which speculates and ventures on the future when it cannot make sure of it.

Thus, to take the instance of St. Paul preaching at Athens: he told his hearers that he came as a mes-senger from that God whom they worshipped already, though ignorantly, and of whom their poets spoke. He appealed to the conviction that was lodged within them of the spiritual nature and the unity of God; and he exhorted them to turn to Him who had ap-pointed One to judge the whole world hereafter. This was an appeal to the antecedent probability of a Revelation, which would be estimated variously according to the desire of it existing in each breast. Now, what was the evidence he gave, in order to concentrate those various antecedent presumptions, to which he referred in behalf of the message which he brought? Very slight, yet something; not a miracle, but his own word that God had raised Christ from the dead; very like the evidence given to the mass of men now, or rather not so much. No one will say it was strong evidence; yet, aided by the novelty, and what may be called originality, of the claim, its strangeness and improbability considered as a mere invention, and the personal bearing of the Apostle, and supported by the full force of the antecedent probabilities which existed, and which he stirred within them, it was enough. It was enough, for some did believe,—enough, not indeed in itself, but enough for those who had love, and therefore were inclined to believe. To those who had no fears, wishes, longings, or expectations, of another world, he was but " a babbler;" those who had such, or, in the Evangelist's words in another place, were " ordained to eternal life," " clave unto him, and believed."

This instance, then, seems very fully to justify the view of Faith which I have been taking, that it is an act of Reason, but of what the world would call weak, bad, or insufficient Reason; and that, because it rests on presumption more, and on evidence less. On the other hand, I conceive that this passage of Scripture does not adjust at all with the modern theory now in esteem, that Faith is a mere moral act, dependent on a previous process of clear and cautious Reason. If so, one would think that St.

Paul had no claim upon the faith of his hearers, till he had first wrought a miracle, such as Reason might approve, in token that his message was to be handed over to the acceptance of Faith.

Now, that this difference of theories as regards the nature of religious Faith is not a trifling one, is evident, perhaps, from the conclusions which I drew from it last week, which, if legitimate, are certainly important: and as feeling it to be so, I now proceed to state distinctly what I conceive to be the relation of Faith to Reason. I observe, then, as follows:

We are surrounded by beings which exist quite independently of us,—exist whether we exist, or cease to exist, whether we have cognizance of them or no. These we commonly separate into two great divisions, material and immaterial. Of the material we have direct knowledge through the senses; we are sensible of the existence of persons and things, of their properties and modes, of their relations towards each other, and the courses of action which they carry on. Of all these we are directly cognizant through the senses; we see and hear what passes, and that immediately. As to immaterial beings, that we have faculties analogous to sense by which we have direct knowledge of their presence, does not appear, except indeed as regards our own soul and its acts. But so far is certain at least, that we are not conscious of possessing them; and we account it, and rightly, to be enthusiasm to profess such consciousness. At times, indeed, that consciousness has been imparted, as in some of the appearances of God to man contained in Scripture : but, in the ordinary course of things, whatever direct intercourse goes on between the soul and immaterial things ; whether we perceive them or not, and are influenced by them or not, certainly we have no consciousness of that perception or influence, such as our senses convey to us in the perception of things material. The senses, then, are the only instruments which we know to be granted to us for direct and immediate acquaintance with things external to us. Moreover, it is obvious that even our senses convey us but a little way out of ourselves, and introduce us to the external world only under circumstances, under conditions of time and place, and of certain media through which they act. We must be near things to touch them ; we must be interrupted by no simultaneous sounds to hear them ; we must have light to see them ; we can neither see, hear, nor touch things past or future.

Now, Reason is the faculty of the mind by which this deficiency is supplied ; by which knowledge of things external to us, of beings, facts, and events, is attained beyond the range of sense. It ascertains for us not natural things only, or immaterial only, or present only, or past, or future ; but, even if limited in its power, it is unlimited in its range, viewed as a faculty, though, of course, in individuals it varies in range also. It reaches to the ends of the universe, and to the throne of God beyond them ; it brings us

knowledge, whether clear or uncertain, still knowledge, in whatever degree of perfection, from every
side ; but, at the same time, with this characteristic,
that it obtains it indirectly, not directly.

Reason does not really perceive anything; but it
is a faculty of proceeding from things that are per-
ceived to things which are not ; the existence of which
it certifies to us on the hypothesis of something else
being known to exist, in other words, being assumed
to be true.

Such is Reason, simply considered ; and hence
the fitness of a number of words which are commonly
used to denote it and its acts.　For instance : it is
usually considered a process, which, of course, a progress of thought from one idea to another must be ; an
exercise of mind, which perception through the senses
can hardly be called ; or, again, an investigation, or
an analysis ; or it is said to compare, discriminate,
judge, and decide : all which words imply, not simply
assent to the reality of certain external facts, but a
search into grounds, and an assent upon grounds.
It is, then, the faculty of gaining knowledge upon
grounds given; and its exercise lies in asserting one
thing, because of some other thing ; and, when its
exercise is conducted rightly, it leads to knowledge;
when wrongly, to apparent knowledge, to opinion,
and error.

Now, if this be Reason, an act or process of Faith,
simply considered, is certainly an exercise of Reason;
whether a right exercise or not is a farther question ; and, whether so to call it, is a sufficient account

of it, is a farther question. It is an acceptance of things as real, which the senses do not convey, upon certain previous grounds; it is an instrument of indirect knowledge concerning things external to us,— the process being such as the following: " I assent to this doctrine as true, because I have been taught it;" or, " because superiors tell me so;" or, " because good men think so;" or, " because very different men think so," or " because all men," or " most men;" or, " because it is established;" or, " because persons whom I trust say that it was once guaranteed by miracles;" or, " because one who is said to have wrought miracles," or " who says he wrought them," " has taught it;" or, " because I have seen one who saw the miracles;" or, " because I saw what I took to be a miracle;" or, " for all," or " some of these reasons together." Some such exercise of Reason is the act of Faith, considered in its nature.

On the other hand, Faith plainly lies exposed to the popular charge of being a faulty exercise of Reason, as being conducted on insufficient grounds; and, I suppose, so much must be allowed on all hands, either that it is illogical, or that the mind has some grounds which are not fully brought out, when the process is thus exhibited. In other words, that when the mind savingly believes, the reasoning which that act involves, if it be logical, does not merely proceed from the actual evidence, but from other grounds besides.

I say, there is this alternative in viewing the par-

ticular process of Reason which is involved in Faith;
—to say either that the process is illogical, or the subject-matter more or less special and recondite; the
act of inference faulty, or the premises undeveloped;
that Faith is weak, or that it is unearthly. Scripture says that it is unearthly, and the world says that
it is weak.

This, then, being the imputation brought against
Faith, that it is the reasoning of a weak mind, whereas
it is in truth the reasoning of a divinely enlightened
one, let me now, in a few words, attempt to show
the analogy of this state of things, with what takes
place in regard to other exercises of Reason also;
that is, I shall attempt to show that Faith is not the
only exercise of Reason, which, when critically examined, would be called unreasonable, and yet is
not so.

1. In truth, nothing is more common among men
of a reasoning turn, than to consider that no one
reasons well but themselves. All men of course
think that they themselves are right and others wrong,
who differ from them; and so far all men must find
fault with the reasonings of others, since no one pro-
poses to act without reasons of some kind. Accordingly, so far as men are accustomed to analyze the
opinions of others and contemplate their processes of
thought, they are tempted to despise them as illogical.
If any one sets about examining why his neighbours
are on one side in political questions, not on another;
why for or against certain measures, of a social,

economical, or civil nature; why they belong to this
religious party, not to that; why they hold this or
that doctrine; why they have certain tastes in literature; or why they hold certain views in matters of
opinion; it is needless to say that if he measures their
grounds by the reasons which they produce, he will
have no difficulty in holding them up to ridicule, or
even to censure.   And so again as to the deductions
made from facts which come before us.   From the
sight of the same sky one may augur fine weather,
another bad; from the signs of the times one the
coming in of good, another of evil; from the same
actions of individuals one moral greatness, another
depravity or perversity, one simplicity, another craft;
upon the same evidence one justifies, another condemns.   The miracles of Christianity were in early
times imputed by some to magic, others they converted; the union of its professors was ascribed to
seditious and traitorous aims by some, while others
it moved to say, " See how these Christians love one
another."   The phenomena of the physical world have
given rise to a variety of theories, that is, of alleged
facts, at which they are supposed to point; theories
of astronomy, chemistry, and physiology; theories religious and atheistical.   The same events are considered to prove a particular providence, and not; to
attest the divinity of one religion or another.   The
downfall of the Roman Empire was to Pagans a refutation, to Christians an evidence of Christianity. Such
is the diversity with which men reason, showing us

that Faith is not the only exercise of Reason, which approves itself to some and not to others, or is, in the common sense of the word, irrational.

Nor can it fairly be said that such varieties do arise from deficiency of logical power in the multitude of men ; and that Faith, therefore, such as I have described it, is but proved thereby to be a specimen of such deficiency. This is what men of clear intellects are not slow to imagine. Clear, strong, steady intellects, if they are not deep, will look on these differences in deduction chiefly as failures in the reasoning faculty, and will despise them or excuse them accordingly. Such are the men who are commonly latitudinarians in religion on the one hand, or innovators on the other ; men of exact or acute but shallow minds, who consider all men wrong but themselves, yet think it no matter though they be ; who regard the pursuit of truth only as a syllogistic process, and failure in attaining it as arising merely from a want of mental conformity with the laws on which just reasoning is conducted. But surely there is no greater mistake than this. For the experience of life contains abundant evidence that in practical matters, when their minds are really roused, men commonly are not bad reasoners. Men do not mistake when their interest is concerned. They have an instinctive sense in which direction their path lies towards it, and how they must act consistently with self-preservation or self-aggrandisement. And so in the case of questions in which party spirit or political opinions, or ethical principle, or personal feeling, is concerned, men have a surprising sagacity, often unknown to themselves, in finding their own place. However remote the connexion between the point in question and their own creed, or habits, or feelings, the principles which they profess guide them unerringly to their legitimate issues; and thus it often happens that in apparently indifferent practices or usages or expressions, or in questions of science, or politics, or literature, we can almost prophesy beforehand, from their religious or moral views, where certain persons will stand, and often can defend them far better than they defend themselves. The same thing is proved from the internal consistency of such religious creeds as are allowed time and space to develope freely; such as Primitive Christianity, or the Medieval system, or Calvinism—a consistency which nevertheless is wrought out in and through the rude and inaccurate minds of the multitude. Again, it is proved from the uniformity observable in the course of the same doctrine in different ages and countries, whether it be political, religious, or philosophical; the laws of Reason forcing it on into the same developements, the same successive phases, the same rise, and the same decay, so that its recorded history in one century will almost suit its prospective course in the next.

All this shows, that in spite of the inaccuracy in expression, or (if we will) in thought, which prevails in the world, men on the whole do not reason incorrectly. If their reason itself were in fault, they would reason each in his own way: whereas they form into schools, and that not merely from imitation and sympathy, but certainly from internal compulsion, from the constraining influence of their several principles. They may argue badly, but they reason well; that is, their professed grounds are no sufficient measures of their real ones. And in like manner, though the evidence with which Faith is content is apparently inadequate to its purpose, yet this is no proof of real weakness or imperfection in its reasoning. It seems to be contrary to Reason, yet is not; it is but independent and distinct from what are called philosophical inquiries, intellectual systems, courses of argument, and the like.

So much on the general phenomena which attend the exercise of this great faculty, one of the characteristics of human over brute natures. Whether we consider processes of Faith or other exercise of Reason, men advance forward on grounds which they do not, or cannot produce, or if they could, yet could not prove to be true, on latent or antecedent grounds which they take for granted.

2. Next, let it be observed, that however full and however precise our producible grounds may be, however systematic our method, however clear and tangible our evidence, yet when our argument is traced down to its simple elements, there must ever something be assumed ultimately which is incapable of proof, and without which our conclusion will be as illogical as Faith is apt to seem to men of the world.

To take the case of actual evidence, and that of the strongest kind. Now, whatever it be, its cogency must be a thing taken for granted; so far it is its own evidence, and can only be received on instinct or prejudice. For instance, we trust our senses, and that in spite of their often deceiving us. They even contradict each other at times, yet we trust them. But even were they ever consistent, never unfaithful, yet their fidelity would not be thereby proved. We consider that there is so strong an antecedent probability that they are faithful, that we dispense with proof. We take the point for granted; or, if we have grounds for it, these either lie in our secret belief in the stability of nature, or in the preserving presence and uniformity of Divine Providence,—which, again, are points assumed. As, then, the senses may and do deceive us, and yet we trust them from a secret instinct, so it need not be weakness or rashness, if upon a certain presentiment of mind we trust to the fidelity of testimony offered for a revelation.

Again: we rely implicitly on our memory, and that, too, in spite of its being obviously unstable and treacherous. And we trust to memory for the truth of most of our opinions; the grounds on which we hold them not being at a given moment all present to our minds. We trust to memory to inform us what we do hold and what we do not. It may be said, that without such assumption the world could not go on: true; and in the same way the Church could not go on without Faith. Acquiescence in testimony, or in evidence not stronger than testimony, is the only method, as far as we see, by which the next world can be revealed to us.

The same remarks apply to our assumption of the fidelity of our reasoning powers; which in certain instances we implicitly believe, though we know they have deceived us in others.

Were it not for these instincts, it cannot be doubted but our experience of the deceivableness of Senses, Memory, and Reason, would perplex us much as to our practical reliance on them in matters of this world. And so, as regards the matters of another, they who have not that instinctive apprehension of the Omnipresence of God and His unwearied and minute Providence which holiness and love create within us, must not be surprised to find that the evidence of Christianity does not perform an office which was never intended for it,—viz. recommend itself as well as the revelation. Nothing, then, which Scripture says about Faith, however startling it may be at first sight, is inconsistent with the state in which we find ourselves by nature with reference to the acquisition of knowledge generally,—a state in which we must assume something to prove anything, and can gain nothing without a venture.

3. To proceed. Next let it be considered, that the following law seems to hold in our attainment of knowledge, that according to its desirableness, whether in point of excellence, or range, or intricacy, so is the vagueness of the evidence on which it is re-

ceived. We are so constituted, that if we insist upon
being as sure as is conceivable, in every step of our
course, we must be content to creep along the ground,
and can never soar. If we are intended for great
ends, we are called to great hazards; and, whereas
we are given absolute certainty in nothing, we must
in all things choose between doubt and inactivity,
and the conviction that we are under the eye of One
who, for whatever reason, exercises us with the less
evidence when He might give us the greater. He has
put it into our hands, who loves us; and He bids us
examine it, indeed, with our best judgment, reject this
and accept that, but still all the while as loving Him
in our turn; not coldly and critically, but with the
thought of His presence, and the reflection that perchance by the defects of the evidence He is trying
our love of its matter; and that perchance it is a
law of His Providence to speak less loudly the more
He promises. For instance, the touch is the most
certain and cautious, but it is the most circumscribed
of our senses, and reaches but an arm's length. The
eye, which takes in a far wider range, acts only in the
light. Reason, which extends beyond the province
of sense or the present time, is circuitous and indirect
in its conveyance of knowledge, which, even when
distinct, is traced out pale and faint, as distant objects
on the horizon. And Faith, again, by which we get
to know divine things, rests on the evidence of testimony, weak in proportion to the excellence of the
blessing attested. And as Reason, with its great

conclusions, is confessedly a higher instrument than Sense with its secure premisses, so Faith rises above Reason in its subject-matter, more than it falls below it in the obscurity of its process. And it is, I say, but agreeable to analogy, that divine Truth should be attained by so subtle and indirect a method, a method less tangible than others, less open to analysis, reducible but partially to the forms of Reason, and the ready sport of objection and cavil.

4. Further, much might be observed concerning the special delicacy and abstruseness of such reasoning processes as attend the acquisition of all higher knowledge. It is not too much to say that there is none of the greater achievements of the Reason, which would show to advantage, which would be apparently justified and protected from criticism, if thrown into the technical forms which the science of argument requires. The most remarkable victories of genius, remarkable both in their originality and the confidence with which they have been pursued, have been gained, as though by invisible weapons, by ways of thought so recondite and intricate that the mass of men are obliged to take them on trust, till the event or other evidence confirms them. Such are the methods which penetrating intellects have invented in mathematical science, which look like sophisms till they end in truth. Here, even in the severest of disciplines, and in absolutely demonstrative processes, the instrument of discovery is so subtle, that technical

expressions and formulæ are of necessity substituted
for it, to thread the labyrinth withal, by way of
tempering its difficulties to the grosser reason of
the many.   Or, let it be considered how rare
and immaterial (if I may use the words) is metaphysical proof; how difficult to embrace, even when
presented to us by philosophers in whose clearness
of mind and good sense we fully confide; and what
a vain system of words without ideas such men seem
to be piling up, while perhaps we are obliged to confess that it must be we who are dull, not they who
are fanciful; and that, whatever be the character of
their investigations, we want the vigour or flexibility
of mind to judge of them.   Or let us attempt to ascertain the passage of the mind, when slight indications in things present are made the informants of
what is to be.   Consider the preternatural sagacity
with which a great general knows what his friends
and enemies are about, and what will be the final
result, and where, of their combined movements,—
and then say whether, if he were required to argue
the matter in word or on paper, all his most brilliant
conjectures might not be refuted, and all his producible reasons exposed as illogical.

And, in an analogous way, Faith is a process of the
Reason, in which so much of the grounds of inference
cannot be exhibited, so much lies in the character of
the mind itself, in its general view of things, its estimate of the probable and the improbable, its im-

pressions concerning God's will, and its anticipations derived from its own inbred wishes, that it will ever seem to the world irrational and despicable ;—till, that is, the event confirms it.   The act of mind, for instance, by which an unlearned person savingly believes the Gospel, on the word of his teacher, may be analogous to the exercise of sagacity in a great statesman or general, supernatural grace doing for the uncultivated reason what genius does for them.

5. Now it is a singular confirmation of this view of the subject, that the reasonings of inspired men in Scripture, nay, of God Himself, are of this recondite nature ; so much so, that irreverent minds scarcely hesitate to treat them with the same contempt which they manifest towards the faith of ordinary Christians.   St. Paul's arguments have long ago been abandoned even by avowed defenders of Christianity.   Nor can it be said surely that the line of thought, (if I may dare so to speak,) on which some of our Ever-blessed Saviour's discourses proceed, is more intelligible to our feeble minds.   And here, moreover, let it be noted that, supposing the kind of reasoning which we call Faith to be of the subtle character which I am maintaining, and the instances of professed reasoning found in Scripture to be of a like subtlety, light is thrown upon another remarkable circumstance, which no one can deny, and which some have made an objection,—I mean, the indirectness of the Scripture proofs on which the Catholic

doctrines rest. Perchance, such a peculiarity in the inspired text is the proper correlative of Faith; such a text the proper matter for Faith to work upon; so that a Scripture such as we have, and not such as the Pentateuch was to the Jews, may be implied in our being under Faith and not under the Law.

6. Lastly, it should be observed, that the analogy which I have been pursuing extends to moral actions, and their properties and objects, as well as to intellectual exercises. According as objects are great, the mode of attaining them is extraordinary; and again, according as it is extraordinary, so is the merit of the action. Here, instead of going to Scripture, or to a religious standard, let me appeal to the world's judgment in the matter. Military fame, for instance, power, character for greatness of mind, distinction in experimental science, are all sought and attained by risks and adventures. Courage does not consist in calculation, but in fighting against chances. The statesman whose name endures, is he who ventures upon measures which seem perilous, and yet succeed, and can be only justified on looking back upon them. Firmness and greatness of soul are shown, when a ruler stands his ground on his instinctive perception of a truth which the many scoff at, and which seems failing. The religious enthusiast bends the hearts of men to a voluntary obedience, who has the keenness to see, and the boldness to appeal to, principles and feelings deep buried within them, which they know

not themselves, which he himself but by glimpses and at times realizes, and which he pursues from the intensity, not the steadiness of his view of them.   And so in all things, great objects exact a venture, and a sacrifice is the condition of honour.   And what is true in the world, why should it not be true also in the kingdom of God?   We must "launch out into the deep, and let down our nets for a draught;" we must in the morning sow our seed, and in the evening withhold not our hand, for we know not whether shall prosper, either this or that.   "He that observeth the wind shall not sow, and he that regardeth the clouds shall not reap."   He that fails nine times and succeeds the tenth, is a more honourable man than he who hides his talent in a napkin; and so, even though the feelings which prompt us to see God in all things, and to recognize supernatural works in matters of the world, mislead us at times, though they make us trust in evidence which we ought not to admit, and partially incur with justice the imputation of credulity, yet a Faith which generously apprehends Eternal Truth, though at times it degenerates into superstition, is far better than that cold sceptical critical tone of mind, which has no inward sense of an overruling ever-present Providence, no desire to approach its God, but sits at home waiting for the fearful clearness of His visible coming, whom it might seek and find in due measure amid the twilight of the present world.

To conclude : such is Faith as contrasted with

Reason;—how it is contrasted with Superstition, how separate from it, and by what principles and laws restrained from falling into it, is a most important question, without settling which any view of the subject of Faith is of course incomplete; but which it does not fall within my present scope to consider.

SERMON XI.

LOVE THE SAFEGUARD OF FAITH AGAINST SUPERSTITION.

Preached on Whit-Tuesday, May 21, 1839.

JOHN x. 4, 5.

" The sheep follow Him, for they know His voice. And a stranger will they not follow, but will flee from him, for they know not the voice of strangers."

FAITH, considered as an exercise of Reason, has this characteristic,—that it proceeds far more on antecedent grounds than on evidence; it trusts much to presumptions, and in doing this lies its special merit. Thus it is distinguished from Knowledge in the ordinary sense of that word. We are commonly said to know a thing, when we have ascertained it by the natural methods given us for ascertaining it. Thus we know mathematical truths, when we are possessed of demonstrative evidence concerning them; we know things present and material by our senses. We know the events of life by moral evidence; we know things past or things invisible, by reasoning from certain present consequences of the facts, such as testimony borne to them. When, for instance, we have ascertained the fact of a miracle by good testimony, the testimony of men who neither deceive nor are deceived, we may be said to know the fact; for we are possessed of those special grounds, of that distinct warrant in its behalf, which the nature of the case assigns and allows. These special grounds are often called the Evidence; and when we believe in consequence of them, we are said to believe upon Reason.

By Reason, indeed, is properly meant any process or act of the mind, by which from knowing one thing it advances on to know another; whether it be true or false Reason, whether it proceed from antecedent probabilities, by demonstration, or on evidence. And in this general sense it includes of course Faith, which is mainly an anticipation or presumption; but in its more popular sense (in which, as in former Discourses, I shall here for the most part use it) it is contrasted with Faith, as meaning in the main such inferences concerning facts, as are derived from the facts in question themselves, that is from Evidences, and which lead consequently to Knowledge.

Faith, then, and Reason, are popularly contrasted with one another; Faith consisting of certain exercises of Reason which proceed mainly on presumption, and Reason of certain exercises which proceed mainly upon proof. Reason makes the particular fact which is to be ascertained the point of primary im-

portance, contemplates it, inquires into its evidence,
not of course excluding antecedent considerations, but
not beginning with them.   Faith, on the other hand,
begins with its own previous knowledge and opinions,
advances and decides upon antecedent probabilities,
that is, on grounds which do not reach so far as to
touch precisely the desired conclusion, though they
tend towards it, and may come very near it.   It acts,
before actual certainty or knowledge, on grounds
which, for the most part, near as they may come, yet
in themselves stand clear of the definite thing which
is its object.   Hence it is said, and rightly, to be a
venture, to involve a risk, to be against Reason, to
triumph over Reason, to surpass or outstrip Reason,
to attain to what Reason falls short of, to effect what
Reason finds beyond its powers; or again, to be a
principle above or beyond argument, not to be subject to the rules of argument, not to be capable of
defending itself, to be illogical, and the like.

This is a view of Faith on which I insisted before
now; and though it is a subject which at first sight
is deficient in interest, yet I believe it will be found
to repay attention, as bearing immediately on practice.   It is, moreover, closely connected with the
doctrine laid down in the text, and with the great
revealed truth which we commemorate at this Season,
and with a view to which the Gospel for the day, of
which the text forms a part, has been selected.

To maintain that Faith is a judgment about facts
in matters of conduct, such, as to be formed, not so

much from the impression legitimately made upon
the mind by those facts, as from the reaching forward
of the mind itself towards them,—that it is a presumption, not a proving,—may sound paradoxical,
yet surely is borne out by the actual state of things
as they come before us every day.   Can it, indeed,
be doubted, that the great majority of those who
have sincerely and deliberately given themselves to
religion, who take it for their portion, and stake their
happiness upon it, have done so, not on an examination of evidence, but from a spontaneous movement
of their hearts towards it? They go out of themselves to meet Him who is unseen, and they discern
Him in such symbols of Him as they find ready
provided for them.   Whether they examine afterwards the evidence on which their faith may be justified or not, or how far soever they do so, still their
faith does not originate in the evidence, nor is it
strong in proportion to their knowledge of the evidence; but, though it may admit of being strengthened
by such knowledge, yet it may be quite as strong
without it as with it.   They believe on grounds
within themselves, not merely or mainly on the external testimony on which religion comes to them.
As to the multitude of professed Christians, they indeed believe on mere custom, or nearly so.   Not
having their hearts interested in religion, they may
fairly be called mere hereditary Christians.   I am
not speaking of these, but of the serious portion of
the community; and I say, that they also, though

2

not believing merely because their fathers believed, but with a faith of their own, yet, for that very reason, believe on something distinct from evidence, —believe with a faith more personal and living than evidence could create. Mere evidence would but lead to passive opinion and knowledge; but anticipations and presumptions are the creation of the mind itself; and the faith which exists in them is of an active nature, whether in rich or poor, learned or unlearned, young or old. They have heard or recollect nothing of " interruptions of the course of nature," " sensible miracles," " men neither deceivers nor deceived," and other similar topics; but they feel that the external religion offered them elicits into shape, and supplies the spontaneous desires and presentiments of their minds: certain, as they are, that some religion must be from God, though not absolutely certain or able to prove, at starting, nay, nor asking themselves, whether some other form is not more simply from Him than that which is presented to them.

The same view of Faith, as being a presumption, is also implied in our popular mode of regarding it. It is commonly and truly said, that Faith is a test of a man's heart. Now, what does this really mean, but that it shows what he thinks likely ?—and what he thinks likely, depends surely on nothing else than the general state of his mind, the state of his convictions, feelings, tastes, and wishes. A fact is asserted, and is thereby proposed to the acceptance or rejection of those who hear it. Each hearer will have his

own view concerning it, prior to the evidence; this
view will result from the character of his mind; nor
commonly will it be reversed by any ordinary varia-
tion in the evidence.   If he is indisposed to believe,
he will explain away very strong evidence; if he is
disposed, he will accept very weak evidence.   On
the one hand, he will talk of its being the safer side
to believe; on the other hand, that he does not feel
that he can go so far as to close with what is offered
him.   That the evidence is something, and not everything; that it tells a certain way, yet might be more;
he will hold, in either case: but then follows the
question, what is to come of the evidence, being what
it is, and this he decides according to (what is called)
the state of his heart.   I do not mean that there is no
extent or deficiency of evidence sufficient to convince
him against his will, or at least to silence him; but
that commonly the evidence for and against religion,
whether true religion or false religion, in matter of
fact, is not of this overpowering nature.   Neither do I
mean that the evidence does not bear one way more
than another, or have a determinate meaning, (for
Christianity and against Naturalism, for the Church
and against every other body,) but that, as things are,
amid the engagements, the confusion, and the hurry of
the world, and, considering the private circumstances
of most minds, few men are in a condition to weigh
things in an accurate balance, and to decide, after
calm and complete investigations of the evidence.
Most men must and do decide by the principles of

thought and conduct which are habitual to them ; that is, the antecedent judgment with which a man approaches the subject of religion, not only acts as a bearing this way or that,— causing him to go out to meet the evidence in a greater or less degree, and no more,—but it practically colours the evidence, even in a case in which he has recourse to evidence, and interprets it for him.

This is the way in which judgments are commonly formed concerning facts alleged or reported in political and social matters, and for the same reason, because it cannot be helped. Act we must, yet seldom indeed is it that we have means of examining into the evidence of the statements on which we are forced to act. Hence statements are often hazarded by persons interested, for the very purpose of bringing out the public mind on some certain point, ascertaining what it thinks, and feeling how their way lies, and what courses are feasible and safe. And, in like manner, startling or unexpected reports are believed or disbelieved, and acted on in this way or that, according as the hearer is or is not easy of belief, or desirous of the event, or furnished with precedents, or previously informed. And so in religious matters, on hearing or apparently witnessing a supernatural occurrence, men judge of it this way or that, according as they are credulous or not, or wish it to be true or not, or are influenced by such or such views of life, or have more or less knowledge on the subject of miracles. We decide one way or

another, according to the position of the alleged
fact, relatively to our existing state of religious knowledge and feeling. I am not saying that such religious judgments are parallel to those which we form
in daily and secular matters, as regards their respective chances of turning out correct in the event.
That is another matter.   Reports in matters of this
world are many, and our resources of mind for the
discrimination of them very insufficient.   Religions
are few, and the moral powers by which they are to
be accepted or rejected, strong and correspondent.
It does not follow, then, because even the most sa-
gacious minds are frequently wrong in their antecedent judgments in matters of this world, that therefore even common minds need be wrong in similar
judgments about the personal matters of another.   It
does not follow, because, in the insignificant matters
of this world, *à priori* judgments run counter to judgments on evidence, that therefore, in the weightier
matters of the next, a merciful Providence may not
have so ordered the relation between our minds and
His revealed will, that presumption, which is the
method of the many, may lead to the same conclusions as examination, which is the method of the
few.   But this is not the point. I am not speaking
of the trustworthiness of Faith, but of its nature :
it is generally allowed to be a test of moral character.
Now, I say that it is a test, as matters of this world
show, only so far as it goes upon presumptions, whatever follows from this as to the validity of its infer-

ences, which is another matter. As far, then, as its
being a test of moral character is of the essence of
religious Faith, so far its being an antecedent judgment or presumption is of its essence.   On the other
hand, when we come to what is called Evidence, or,
in popular language, exercises of Reason, prejudices
and mental peculiarities are excluded from the discussion, we descend to grounds common to all;
certain scientific rules and fixed standards for weighing testimony, and examining facts, are received.
Nothing can be urged, or made to tell, but what all
feel, all comprehend, all can put into words; current language becomes the measure of thought; only
such conclusions may be drawn as can produce their
reasons; only such reasons are in point as can be exhibited in simple propositions; the multiform and
intricate assemblage of considerations, which really
lead to judgment and action, must be attenuated or
mutilated into a major and a minor premiss.   Under
such circumstances, there is as little virtue or merit
in deciding a right as in working a mathematical pro-
blem correctly; as little guilt in deciding wrongly as
in mistakes in accounts, or in a faulty memory in
history.

And, again:—As Faith may be viewed as opposed
to Reason, in the popular sense of the latter word, it
must not be overlooked that Unbelief is opposed to
Reason also.   Unbelief, indeed, considers itself especially rational, or critical of evidence; but it criticises
the evidence of Religion, only because it does not like

it, and really goes upon presumptions and prejudices as much as Faith does, only presumptions of an opposite nature. This I have already implied. It considers a religious system so improbable, that it will not listen to the evidence of it; or, if it listens, it employs itself in doing what a believer could do, if he chose, quite as well, what he is quite as well aware can be done; viz., in showing that the evidence might be more complete and unexceptionable than it is. On this account it is that unbelievers call themselves rational; not because they decide by evidence, but because, after they had made their decision, they merely occupy themselves in sifting it. This surely is quite plain, even in the case of Hume, who first asks, " What have we to oppose to such a cloud of witnesses," in favour of certain alleged miracles he mentions, " but the absolute impossibility or miraculous nature of the events which they relate? And this surely," he adds, " in the eyes of all reasonable people, will alone be regarded as a sufficient refutation;" that is, the antecedent improbability is a sufficient refutation of the evidence. And next, he scoffingly observes, that " our most holy Religion is founded on Faith, not on Reason;" and that " mere Reason is insufficient to convince us of its veracity." As if his infidelity were " founded on Reason," in any more exact sense; or presumptions on the side of Faith could not have, and presumptions on the side of unbelief might have, the nature of proof.

Such, then, seems to be the state of the case, when

we carefully consider it. Faith is an exercise of
presumptive reasoning, or of Reason proceeding on
antecedent grounds: such seems to be the fact, whatever comes of it. Let us take things as we find
them: let us not attempt to distort them into what
they are not. True philosophy deals with facts. We
cannot make facts. All our wishing cannot change
them. We must use them. If Revelation has always
been offered to mankind in one way, it is in vain to
say that it ought to have come to us in another. If
children, if the poor, if the busy, can have true
Faith, yet cannot weigh evidence, evidence is not
the simple foundation on which Faith is built. If
the great bulk of serious men believe, not because
they have examined evidence, but because they are
disposed in a certain way,—because they are τεταγμένοι
εἰς ζωὴν αἰώνιον,—ordained to eternal life, this must be
God's order of things. Let us attempt to understand
it. Let us not disguise it, or explain it away. It
may have difficulties; if so, let us own them. Let
us fairly meet them: if we can, let us overcome
them.

Now, there is one very serious difficulty in the
view which I have taken of Faith, which most persons will have anticipated before I allude to it; that
such a view may be made an excuse for all manner
of prejudice and bigotry, and leads directly to credulity and superstition; and, on the other hand, in the
case of unbelief, that it affords a sort of excuse
for impenetrable obduracy. Antecedent probabilities

may be equally available for what is true, and what pretends to be true, for a revelation and its counterfeit, for Paganism, or Mahometanism, or Christianity. They seem to supply no intelligible rule what is to be believed, and what not; or how a man is to pass from a false belief to a true. If a claim of miracles is to be acknowledged because it happens to be advanced, why not for the miracles of India, as well as for those of Palestine? If the abstract probability of a Revelation be the measure of genuineness in a given case, why not in the case of Mahomet, as well as of the Apostles? How are we to manage (as I may say) the Argument from Presumption for Christianity, so as not to carry it out into an argument against it?

This is the difficulty. It is plain that some safeguard of Faith is needed, some corrective principle which will secure it from running (as it were) to seed, and becoming superstition or fanaticism. All parties who have considered the subject, seem to agree in thinking some or other corrective necessary. And here reasoners of a school, which has been in fashion of late years, have their answer ready, and can promptly point out what they consider the desired remedy. What, according to them, forms the foundation of Faith, is also its corrective. Faith is built upon Reason, and Reason is its safeguard. Cultivate the Reason, and in the same degree you lead men both to the acknowledgment, and also to the sober use of the Gospel. Their religion will be rational, inasmuch as they know why they believe, and what. The young, the poor, the ignorant, those whose reason is undeveloped, are the victims of an excessive faith. Give them, then, education; open their minds; enlighten them; enable them to reflect, compare, investigate, and infer; draw their attention to the Evidences of Christianity. While, in this way, you bring them into the right path, you also obviate the chance of their wandering from it; you tend to prevent enthusiasm and superstition, while you are erecting a bulwark against infidelity.

This, or something like this, is often maintained, and, if correctly, it must be confessed, nothing can be more extravagant than to call Faith an exercise or act of Reason, as I have done, when, in fact, it needs Reason; such language does but tend to break down the partition-wall which separates Faith from Superstition, and to allow it to dissipate itself in every variety of excess, and to throw itself away upon the most unworthy and preposterous objects.

This is what, perhaps, will be objected; and yet I am not unwilling to make myself responsible for the difficulty in question, by denying that any intellectual act is necessary for right Faith besides itself; that it need be much more than a presumption, or that it need be fortified and regulated by investigation; by denying, that is, that Reason is the safeguard of Faith. What, then, is the safeguard, if Reason is not? I shall give an answer, which may seem at once common-place and paradoxical; yet I believe is the true one. The safeguard of Faith is a right state of heart. This it is that gives it birth; it also disciplines it. This is what protects it from bigotry, credulity, and fanaticism. It is holiness, or dutifulness, or the new creation, or the spiritual mind, however we word it, which is the quickening and illuminating principle of true Faith, giving it eyes, hands, and feet. It is Love which forms it out of the rude chaos into an image of Christ; or, in scholastic language, justifying Faith, whether in Pagan, Jew, or Christian, is *fides formata charitate*.

"Verily, verily, I say unto you," says the Divine Speaker, "I am the Door of the sheep . . . . I am the Good Shepherd, and know My sheep, and am known of Mine."

"Ye believe not, because ye are not of My sheep, as I said unto you. My sheep hear My voice, and I know them, and they follow Me; and I give unto them eternal life, and they shall never perish, neither shall any one pluck them out of My hand."

"He that entereth in by the door, is the Shepherd of the sheep. To Him the porter openeth, and the sheep hear His voice, and He calleth His own sheep by name, and leadeth them out. And when He putteth forth His own sheep, He goeth before them, and the sheep follow Him, for they know His voice. And a stranger will they not follow, but will flee from him, for they know not the voice of strangers."

What is here said about exercises of Reason, in order to believing? What is there not said of sympathetic feeling, of newness of spirit, of love? It was from lack of love towards Christ that the Jews discerned not in Him the Shepherd of their souls. "Ye believe not, because ye are not of My sheep. My sheep hear My voice, and follow Me." It was the regenerate nature sent down from the Father of Lights which drew up the disciples heaven-ward,—which made their affections go forth to meet the Bridegroom, and fixed those affections on Him, till they were as cords of love staying the heart upon the Eternal. " All that the Father giveth Me, shall come to Me. No man can come unto Me, except the Father which hath sent Me draw him. It is written in the Prophets, And they shall be all taught of God. Every man, therefore, that hath heard and hath learned of the Father, cometh unto Me." It is the new life, and not the natural Reason, which leads the soul to Christ. Does a child trust his parents, because he has proved to himself that they are such, and that they are able and desirous to do him good, or from the instinct of affection? We *believe*, because we *love*. How plain a truth! What gain is it to be wise above that which is written? Why, O men, deface with your minute and arbitrary philosophy the simplicity, the reality, the glorious liberty of the inspired teaching? Is this your godly jealousy for Scripture? this, your abhorrence of human additions?

It is the doctrine, then, of the text, that those who believe in Christ, believe because they know Him to be the Good Shepherd; and they know Him by His voice; and they know His voice, because they are His sheep; that they do not follow strangers and robbers, because they know not the voice of strangers: moreover, that they know and follow Christ, upon His loving them. " I am come, that they might have life. . . . . The hireling fleeth, because he is a hireling, and careth not for the sheep." The divine-ly-enlightened mind sees in Christ the very Object whom it desires to love and worship,—the Object correlative of its own affections; and it trusts Him, or believes, from loving Him.

The same doctrine is contained in many other places, as in the second chapter of St. Paul's First Epistle to the Corinthians. In this passage, doubtless, there are one or two expressions, which, taken by themselves, admit, and may well be taken to include a distinct interpretation: as a whole, however, it distinctly teaches the nothingness of natural Reason, and the all-sufficiency of supernatural grace in the conversion of the soul. " And I, brethren, when I came to you, came not with excellency of speech or of wisdom," (with discussion, argument, elaborate proof, cumulation of evidence,) " declaring unto you the testimony of God. For I determined not to know anything among you, save Jesus Christ, and Him crucified. . . . . And my speech and my preaching was not with enticing words of man's wisdom," not with the reasonings of the schools, " but in demonstration of the Spirit, and of power," with an inward and spiritual conviction, " that your Faith should not

stand in the wisdom of men," natural Reason, "but in
the power of God," His regenerating and renewing
influences. " But the natural man receiveth not the
things of the Spirit of God, for they are foolishness
unto him; neither can he know them, because they
are spiritually discerned: but he that is spiritual
judgeth all things, yet he himself is judged of no man.
For who hath known the mind of the Lord, that he
may instruct Him? But we have the mind of Christ."
Here a certain moral state, and not evidence, is made
the means of gaining the Truth, and the beginning of
spiritual perfection.

In like manner St. John: " They went out from
us, but they were not of us; for if they had been of
us, they would no doubt have continued with us;
but they went out, that they might be made manifest
that they were not all of us. But ye have an unction
from the Holy One, and ye know all things." If this
unction and this knowledge, which God the Holy
Ghost bestows, be a moral gift, (as who will deny?)
then also must our departing from Christ arise from
the want of a moral gift, and our adhering to Him
must be the consequence of a moral gift.

Again:—" The anointing which ye have received
of Him abideth in you, and ye need not that any man
teach you, but as the same anointing teacheth you of
all things, and is true, and is no lie, and even as it
hath taught you, ye shall abide in Him[1]." Surely

---

[1] 1 Cor. ii. 1, 2. 4. 14—16.   1 John ii. 19, 20—27.

the faculty by which we know the Truth is here represented to us, not as a power of investigation, but as a moral perception.

If this, then, is the real state of the case, (as I do think would be granted by all of us, if, discarding systems, we allowed Scripture to make its legitimate and full impression upon our minds,) if holiness, dutifulness, or love, however we word it, and not Reason, is the eye of Faith, the discriminating principle which keeps it from fastening on unworthy objects, and degenerating into enthusiasm or superstition, it now follows to attempt to analyze the process by which it does so. I mean, let us examine *how* it happens, *what* in the actual course of thinking and determining is the mode, by which Love does regulate as well as animate Faith, guiding it in a clear and high path, neither enervated by excitement, nor depressed by bondage, nor distorted by extravagance. For till we have done this in some good measure, it is plain that we have made little advance towards grasping the meaning of the Scripture statements on the subject. I will make an endeavour this way, as far as time permits, and so bring my present remarks to an end.

Right Faith is the faith of a right mind. Faith is an intellectual act; right Faith is an intellectual act, done in a certain moral disposition. Faith is an act of Reason, viz. a reasoning upon presumptions; right Faith is a reasoning upon holy, devout, and enlightened presumptions. Faith ventures and hazards; right

Faith ventures and hazards deliberately, seriously, so-
berly, piously, and humbly, counting the cost and de-
lighting in the sacrifice. As far as, and wherever Love
is wanting, so far, and there, Faith runs into excess or
is perverted.   The grounds of Faith, when animated
by the spirit of love and purity, are such as these :—
that a revelation is very needful for man ; that it is
earnestly to be hoped from a merciful God; that it is to
be expected; nay, that of the two it is more probable,
that what professes to be a revelation should be or
should contain a revelation, than that there should
be no revelation at all ; that, if Almighty God inter-
poses in human affairs, His interposition will not be
in opposition to His known attributes, or to His
dealings in the world, or to certain previous revelations
of His will ; that it will be in a way worthy of Him ;
that it is likely to bear plain indications of His hand ;
that it will be for great ends, specified or signified ;
and moreover, that such and such ends are in their
nature great, such and such a message important,
such and such means worthy, such and such circumstances congruous. I consider that under the guidance
of such anticipations and calculations as these which
Faith—not mere Faith, but Faith working by Love—
suggests, the honest mind may, under ordinary circumstances, be led, and practically is led, into an acceptable, enlightened, and saving apprehension of divine
Truth, without that formal intimacy and satisfaction
with the special evidence existing for the facts believed,
which is commonly called Reasoning, or the use of

Reason, and which results in knowledge. Some instances will serve to explain how:—

1. Superstition, in its grossest form, is the worship of evil spirits. What the Gentiles sacrifice is done (we are told) "to devils, not to God;" their table is "the table of devils." "They offered their sons and their daughters unto devils[2]." It is needless to say, that the view above taken of the nature of Religious Faith has no tendency towards such impieties. Faith, indeed, considered as a mere abstract principle, certainly does tend to humble the mind before any thing which comes with a profession of being supernatural; not so the Faith of a religious mind, a right religious Faith, which is instinct with love towards God and towards man. Love towards man will make it shrink from cruelty; love towards God from false worship. This is idolatry, to account creatures as the primary and independent sources of providence and the ultimate objects of our devotion. I say, the principle of Love, acting not by way of inquiry or argument, but spontaneously and as an instinct, will cause the mind to recoil from cruelty, impurity, and the assumption of divinity, though coming with ever so superhuman a claim, real or professed. And though there are cases in which such a recoil is erroneous, as arising from partial views or misconceptions, yet on the whole it will be found a correct index of the state of the case, and a safe direction for our conduct.

[2] 1 Cor. x. 20.   Ps. cvi. 37.

2. Again: another kind of Superstition, as the word is usually understood, is the payment of religious honour to things forbidden. Such were some of the idolatries to which the Israelites surrendered themselves, as the worship of the golden calf. Moreover, when a ritual has directly been given from heaven, what is not commanded may be accounted forbidden, except a power of making additions has been granted; it being the same undutifulness to supersede or alter the revealed manner of approaching God, as to adopt means actually unlawful. Such might be the continued worship of the Brazen Serpent, which, though at a certain juncture an ordained symbol and instrument of God, nevertheless, in a rigid system of rites, such as the Mosaic, could not be honoured in continuance at the people's will, especially with self-devised rites, without great undutifulness, or lack of love. On the other hand, Nebuchadnezzar's homage to Daniel, when the king " fell on his face and worshipped him, and commanded that they should offer an oblation and sweet odours unto him," was accepted by the Prophet, as coming from a heathen, to whom such works of reverence had not been forbidden by any imposed ritual, and who on the other hand could not mean to acknowledge Daniel as the source of prophetic knowledge, both because the Prophet had himself just declared that there was a " God in heaven that revealeth secrets, and maketh known to the king Nebuchadnezzar what shall be in the latter days," and also because he him-

2

self, while commanding the oblation, proceeds to say, "Of a truth it is that your God is a God of gods, and a Lord of kings, and a Revealer of secrets, seeing thou couldest reveal this secret." Nebuchadnezzar then (it would seem) did not stop short of God; but honoured Daniel as God's visible emblem, and that without any revealed prohibition of his doing so. And if so, his faith did not evince any deficiency of love, or any superstition.

3. Here we may lay it down as a principle, that what is superstition in Jew or Christian is not necessarily such in heathen; or what in Christian is not in Jew. Faith leads the mind to communion with the invisible God; its attempts at approaching and pleasing Him are acceptable or not, according as they are or are not self-willed; and they are self-willed when they are irrespective of God's revealed will. It was a superstition in the Israelites, and not faith, to take the Ark to battle uncommanded, and they were punished with the loss of it. It was no superstition in the Philistines, abundantly superstitious and wicked as they otherwise were, to yoke the kine to the Ark, and to leave them to themselves to see what they would do; thus making trial of the Ark's sacredness. It was a trial which could but be unsuccessful, but might give them assurance; and whatever of heathen irreverence there was in the circumstances of the action, yet still it was to a certain extent a tacit, or (if we will) an unwilling, acknowledgment of the God of Israel. Again, sacrifices of blood were not ne-

cessarily superstitious in heathen; they would be most
superstitious and profane in Christians, as being superseded by the great Atonement made once for all, and
the continual Memory of it in Holy Communion.
On the other hand, the Sign of the Cross in Baptism would be superstitious, unless the Church had
"power to decree rites and ceremonies in the worship
of God."

4. Again : when the barbarous people of Melita
saw the viper fasten upon St. Paul's hand, first they
considered him a murderer, then a god.   What is to
be said of their conduct?   Plainly it evinced Faith ;
but was it healthy Faith or perverted?   On the one
hand, they had a sense of the probability of supernatural interference such, as to lead them to accept
this occurrence as more than ordinary, while they
doubted and wavered in their interpretation of it according as circumstances varied.   Faith accepted it
as supernatural; and in matter of fact they were
not wrong in the main point.   They judged rightly
in thinking that God's presence was in some immediate way with St. Paul ; Reason, following upon
Faith, attempted to deduce from it.   Their reasoning
was wrong, their faith was right.   But did it not involve Superstition?   We must distinguish here.   It
is no refinement, surely, to say that they were not
superstitious, though their conduct, viewed in itself,
was such.   Their reasoning was superstitious in *our*
idea of Superstition ; I mean, with our superior knowledge of religious truth, *we* are able to say that they

were seeing in things visible what was not there, and drawing conclusions which were not valid; but it needs to be proved that they acted preposterously or weakly under their circumstances. I am speaking, be it observed, of their incidental reasoning; and concerning this I say that it does not become us, who are blessed with light, which gives us freedom from the creature by telling us definitely where are the paths and dwelling-places of God in the visible world, to despise those who were " seeking Him, if haply they might feel after Him and find Him." Superstition is a faith which falls below that standard of religion which God has given us, whatever it is. We are accustomed naturally and fairly to define, according to our own standard, what are abstractedly superstitions and what are not; but we have no right to apply this standard, in particular cases, to other men whose circumstances are different.

5. The woman with the issue of blood, who thought to be healed by secretly touching our Lord's garment, may perhaps be more correctly called superstitious than the barbarians of Melita. Yet it is remarkable that even she was encouraged by our Lord, and that on the very ground of her faith. In His judgment, then, a religious state of mind, which is not free from Superstition, may still be Faith,—nay, and high Faith. "Daughter," He said, "be of good comfort; thy faith hath made thee whole; go in peace, and be whole of thy plague." I have said that she showed a more superstitious temper than the people of Me-

lita, inasmuch as what she did was inconsistent with
what she knew. Her faith did not rise to the standard
of her own light. She knew enough of the Good
Shepherd to have directed her faith to Him as the
one source of all good, instead of which she lingered
in the circumstances and outskirts of His Divine
Perfections. She in effect regarded the hem of
His garment as an original principle of miraculous
power, and thereby placed herself almost in the position of those who idolize the creature. Yet even
this seems to have arisen from great humbleness of
mind : like the servants of the ruler of the syna-
gogue, who were then standing by, she feared probably to " trouble the Master " with her direct in-
tercession ; or like the Apostles on a subsequent
occasion, who rebuked those who brought children
for His touch, she was unwilling to interrupt Him ;
or she was full of her own unworthiness, like the
centurion who prayed that Christ would not condescend to enter his roof, but would speak the word
instead, or send a messenger. She thought that a
little one, such as herself, might come in for the
crumbs from His table by chance, and without His
distinct bidding, by the perpetual operation and
spontaneous exuberance of those majestic general
laws on which He wrought miracles. In all this,—
in her faith and her humility, her faith tinged with
superstition, her abject humility,—she would seem to
resemble such worshippers in various ages and countries in the Christian Church, as have impaired their

simple veneration of the Invisible, by an undue lingering of mind upon the outward emblems which they have considered He had blessed.

6. One more instance shall be added,—that of the Prophet from Judah, who had a message brought him by a lying Prophet in the name of the Lord, bidding him go home with him. Had he not been a Prophet himself, had he known the other to have been a Prophet; nay, or even considering that he called himself such, and that prophets then were in Israel, there would have been nothing very superstitious or wrong in his yielding to his solicitations. But of course the character of the act was quite changed, considering his own commission, and the express directions which had been given him how to conduct himself in the apostate land. If he went back with his seducer merely to refresh himself, as would appear, of course neither Faith nor Superstition had anything to do with his conduct, which was a mere yielding to temptation; but if he did suppose that he was thereby commending himself to God, he showed credulousness, not Faith. And here we see why it is not Faith, but credulousness and superstition, to listen to idle tales of apparitions, charms, omens, and the like, which may be current even in a Christian land; viz. because we have already received a revelation. The miracles, we believe, indispose us to believe the report of other miracles external to the revealed system. We have found the Christ, we are not seeking. And much more, if the doctrine put forth in the professed

revelation of to-day contradicts or invalidates the doctrine of those revelations which have been received
from the beginning. Hence we are expressly warned
in Scripture, that though an Angel from heaven
preach unto us any other Gospel than that we have
received, he must be pronounced anathema. And this
was the sin of the Judaizers, that having received
the Spirit, they went back for perfection to the rites
of the Law then abolished. In like manner the Israelites had been warned by Moses: "If there arise
among you a prophet, or a dreamer of dreams, and
giveth thee a sign or a wonder, and the sign or the
wonder come to pass whereof he spake unto thee, saying, Let us go after other gods, which thou hast not
known, and let us serve them ; thou shalt not hearken
unto the words of that prophet or that dreamer of
dreams, for the Lord your God proveth you, to know
whether ye love the Lord your God with all your
heart and with all your soul." And hence it was a
point of especial moment with St. Paul to prove
that the Gospel was not an annulling of the Law, but
its fulfilment, built upon it and intended by it; and
that in the rejection of the Jews and the calling of
the Gentiles, the old Church as well as the old Commandment was still preserved. And thus, even in the
case of the heathen, the Apostle was anxious to pay
due respect to the truths which they already admitted,
and to show that the Gospel was rather the purification, explanation, development, and completion of

R

those scattered verities of Paganism than their abro-
gation³. " Whom therefore ye ignorantly worship,"
he says, " Him declare I unto you." In other words,
it was not his method to represent the faith, to which
he exhorted his hearers, as a state of mind utterly
alien from their existing knowledge, their convictions,
and their moral character. He drew them on, not by
unsettling them, but through their own system, as
far as might be,—by persuasives of a positive nature,
and which, while fitted to attract by their innate truth
and beauty, excluded by their very presence whatever
in Paganism was inconsistent with them. What they
already were, was to lead them on, as by a venture,
to what they were not ; what they knew was to lead
them on, upon presumptions, to what they as yet
knew not. Neither of Jew nor of Gentile did he
demand Faith in his message, on the bare antecedent
ground that God was everywhere, and therefore, if so
be, might be with himself in particular who spoke to
them ; nor, again, did he appeal merely to his miraculous powers ; but he looked at men stedfastly, to

³ Some admirable articles have appeared in the late numbers of the " British Critic," on the divinely appointed mode
of seeking truth where persons are in doubt and difficulty, viz.
No. lx. art. 2 ; lxii. art. 1 ; lxiii. art. 2 ; lxiv. art. 3 ; lxv.
art. 7. As they appear to be but the first sketches of a deep
and important theory which has possession of the writer's mind,
it is to be hoped that they will one day appear in a more systematic form.

see whether they had "faith to be healed;" he appealed
to that whole body of opinion, affection, and desire,
which made up, in each man, his moral self; which,
distinct from all guesses and random efforts, set him
forward steadily in one direction, which, if it was what
it should be, would respond to the Apostle's doctrine,
as the strings of one instrument vibrate with another,
which, if it was not, would either not accept it, or
not abide in it.   He taught men, not only that Almighty God was, and was every where, but that He
had certain moral attributes; that He was just, true,
holy, and merciful; that His representative was in
their hearts; that He already dwelt in them as a
lawgiver and a judge, by a sense of right and a
conscience of sin; and that what he himself was
then bringing fulfilled what was thus begun in them
by nature, by tokens so like the truth, as to constrain
all who loved God under the Religion of Nature to
believe in Him as revealed in the Gospel.

Such, then, under all circumstances, is real Faith;
a presumption, yet not a mere chance conjecture,—
a reaching forward, yet not of excitement or of passion,—a moving forward in the twilight, yet not
without clue or direction;—a movement from something known to something unknown, kept in the narrow path of truth by the Law of dutifulness which
inhabits it, the Light of heaven which animates and
guides it,—and which, whether feeble and dim as in

the Heathen, or bright and vigorous as in the Christian; whether merely the awakening and struggling conscience, or the " minding of the Spirit;" whether as a timid hope, or in the fulness of love; is, under every Dispensation, the one acceptable principle commending us to God for the merits of Christ. And it becomes superstition, or credulity, or enthusiasm, or fanaticism, or bigotry, in proportion as it emancipates itself from this spirit of wisdom and understanding, of counsel and ghostly strength, of knowledge and true godliness, and holy fear. And thus I would answer the question how it may be secured from excess, without the necessity of employing what is popularly called Reason for its protection: I mean processes of investigation, discrimination, discussion, argument, and inference. It is itself an intellectual act, and it takes its character from the moral state of the agent. It is perfected, not by mental cultivation, but by obedience. It does not change its nature or its function, when thus perfected. It remains what it is in itself, an initial principle of action; but it becomes changed in its quality, as being made spiritual. It is as before a presumption, but the presumption of a serious, sober, thoughtful, pure, affectionate, and devout mind. It acts because it is Faith; but the direction, firmness, consistency, and precision of its acts, it gains from Love.

Let these remarks suffice, insufficient as they are in

themselves, on the relation and distinction between Faith and Superstition.   Other important questions, however, remain, which have a claim on the attention of all who would gain clear notions on an important and difficult subject.

SERMON XII.

EXPLICIT AND IMPLICIT REASON.

Preached on St. Peter's Day, 1840.

1 Pet. iii. 15.

" Sanctify the Lord God in your hearts ; and be ready always to give an answer to every man that asketh you a reason of the hope that is in you, with meekness and fear."

St. Peter's faith was one of his characteristic graces. It was ardent, keen, watchful, and prompt. It dispensed with argument, calculation, deliberation, and delay, whenever it heard the voice of its Lord and Saviour: and it heard that voice even when its accents were low, or when it was unaided by the testimony of the other senses. When Christ appeared walking on the sea, and said, " It is I," Peter answered Him, and said, " Lord, if it be Thou, bid me come unto Thee on the water." When Christ asked His disciples who He was, " Simon Peter answered and said," as we have read in the Gospel for this day, " Thou art the Christ, the Son of the Living

God," and obtained our Lord's blessing for such clear and ready Faith. At another time, when Christ asked the Twelve whether they would leave Him as others did, St. Peter said, " Lord, to whom shall we go? Thou hast the words of eternal life ; and we believe and are sure that Thou art the Christ, the Son of the Living God." And after the Resurrection, when he heard from St. John that it was Christ who stood on the shore, he sprang out of the boat in which he was fishing, and cast himself into the sea, in his impatience to come near Him. Other instances of his faith might be mentioned. If ever Faith forgot self, and was occupied with its Great Object, it was the faith of Peter. If in any one Faith appears in contrast with what we commonly understand by Reason, and with Evidence, it so appears in the instance of Peter. When he reasoned, it was at times when Faith was lacking. " When he saw the wind boisterous he was afraid ;" and Christ in consequence called him, " Thou of little faith." When He had asked, " Who touched Me ?" Peter and others reasoned, " Master," said they, " the multitude throng Thee, and press Thee, and sayest Thou, Who touched Me ?" And in like manner, when Christ said that he should one day follow Him in the way of suffering, " Peter said unto Him, Lord, *why* cannot I follow Thee now ?"— and we know how his faith gave way soon afterwards.

Faith and Reason, then, stand in strong contrast in the history of Peter : yet it is Peter, and he not the fisherman of Galilee, but the inspired Apostle, who in the text gives us a precept which implies, in order to its due fulfilment, a careful exercise of our Reason, an exercise both upon Faith, considered as an act or habit of mind, and upon the Object of it. We are not only to " sanctify the Lord God in our hearts," not only to prepare a shrine within us in which our Saviour Christ may dwell, and where we may worship Him ; but we are so to understand what we do, so to master our thoughts and feelings, so to recognize what we believe, and how we believe, so to trace out our ideas and impressions, and to contemplate the issue of them, that we may be " ready *always* to give an answer to *every* man that asketh us an account of the hope that is in us."   In these words, I conceive, we have a clear warrant, or rather an injunction, to cast our religion into the form of Creed and Evidences.

It would seem, then, that though Faith is the characteristic of the Gospel, and Faith is the simple lifting of the mind to the Unseen God, without conscious reasoning or formal argument, still the mind may be allowably, nay, religiously engaged, in reflecting upon its own Faith ; investigating the grounds and Object of it, bringing it out into words, whether to defend, or recommend, or teach it to others. And St. Peter himself, in spite of his ardour and earnestness, gives us in his own case some indications of such an exercise of mind.   When he said, " Thou art the Christ, the Son of the Living God," he cast his faith, in a measure, into a dogmatic form : and

when he said, " To whom shall we go ? Thou hast
the words of eternal life," he gave " an account of the
hope that was in him," or grounded his faith upon
Evidence.

Nothing would be more theoretical and unreal
than to suppose that true Faith cannot exist except
when moulded upon a Creed, and based upon Evidence; yet nothing would indicate a more shallow
philosophy than to say that it ought carefully to be
disjoined from dogmatic and argumentative statements. To assert the latter is to discard the science
of theology from the service of religion; to assert
the former, is to maintain that every child, every
peasant, must be a theologian. Faith cannot exist
without grounds or without an object; but it does
not follow that all who have faith should recognize,
and be able to state what they believe, and how.
Nor, on the other hand, because it is not identical
with its grounds and its object, does it therefore
cease to be true Faith, on its recognizing them.   In
proportion as the mind reflects upon itself, it will be
able " to give an account" of what it believes and
hopes; as far as it has not thus reflected, it will not
be able. Such knowledge cannot be wrong, yet cannot be necessary, while reflection is at once a natural
faculty of our souls, yet needs cultivation. Scripture
gives instances of Faith in each of these states, when
attended by a conscious exercise of Reason, and when
not. When Nicodemus said, " No man can do these
miracles that Thou doest, except God be with him," he

reasoned or argued.   When the Scribe said, " There
is One God, and there is none other but He ; and to
love Him with all the heart . . . . . is more than all
whole burnt offerings and sacrifices," his belief was
dogmatical.   On the other hand, when the cripple at
Lystra believed, on St. Paul's preaching, or the man
at the Beautiful gate believed in the Name of Christ,
their faith was independent, not of objects or grounds,
(for that is impossible,) but of perceptible, recognized,
producible objects and grounds : they believed, they
could not say what or why.   True Faith, then, admits,
but does not require, the exercise of what is commonly understood by Reason.

I hope it will not seem any want of reverence towards a great Apostle, who reigns with Christ in
heaven, if, instead of selecting one of the many lessons to which his history calls our attention, or the
points of doctrine which might so profitably be enlarged upon, I employ his Day to continue a subject
to which I have already devoted such opportunities
of speaking from this place as have from time to time
occurred, though it be but incidentally connected
with him.   Such a continuation of subject has some
sanction in the character of our first Lessons for Holy
days, which, for the most part, instead of being appropriate to the particular Festivals on which they are
appointed, are portions of a course, and connected with
those which are assigned to others.   And I will add
that, if there is a question, the intrusion of which may
be excused in the present age, and to which the mind

is naturally led on the Days commemorative of the first Founders of the Church, it is the relation of Faith to Reason under the Gospel; and the means whereby, and the grounds whereon, and the subjects wherein, the mind is bound to believe and acquiesce in matters of religion.

In the Epistle for this Day we have an account of St. Peter, when awakened by the Angel, obeying him implicitly, yet not understanding, while he obeyed. He girt himself, and bound on his sandals, and cast his garment about him, and " went out and followed him;" yet " wist not that it was true which was done by the Angel, but thought he saw a vision." Afterwards, when he " was come to himself, he said, Now I know of a surety, that the Lord hath sent His Angel, and hath delivered me."   First he acted spontaneously, then he contemplated his own acts.   This may be taken as an illustration of the difference between the more simple faculties and operations of the mind, and that process of analyzing and describing them, which takes place upon reflection.   We not only feel, and think, and reason, but we know that we feel, and think, and reason; not only know, but can inspect and ascertain our thoughts, feelings, and reasonings; not only ascertain, but describe.   Children, for a time, do not realize even their material frames, or (as I may say) count their limbs : but, as the mind opens, and is cultivated, they turn their attention to soul as well as body; they contemplate all they are, and all they do; they are no longer beings of impulse, instinct, conscience, imagination, habit, or reason, merely; but they are able to reflect upon their own mind as if it were some external object; they reason upon their reasonings. This is the point on which I shall now enlarge.

Reason, according to the simplest view of it, is the faculty of gaining knowledge without direct perception, or of ascertaining one thing by means of another. In this way it is able, from small beginnings, to create to itself a world of ideas, which do or do not correspond to the things themselves for which they stand, or are true or not, according as it is exercised soundly or otherwise.   One fact may suffice for a whole theory; one principle may create and sustain a system; one minute token is a clue to a discovery. The mind ranges to and fro, and spreads out, and advances forward with a quickness which has become a proverb, and a subtlety and versatility which baffle investigation.   It passes on from point to point, gaining one by some indication ; another on a probability ; then availing itself of an association ; then falling back on some received law; next seizing on testimony; then committing itself to some popular impression, or some inward instinct, or some obscure memory ; and thus it makes progress not unlike a clamberer on a steep cliff, who, by quick eye, prompt hand, and firm foot, ascends how he knows not himself, by personal endowments and by practice, rather than by rule, leaving no track behind him, and unable to teach another. It is not too much to say that the stepping by which great geniuses scale the mountains of truth is as unsafe and precarious to men in general, as the ascent of a skilful mountaineer up a literal crag. It is a way which they alone can take; and its justification lies in their success. And such mainly is the way in which all men, gifted or not gifted, reason,—not by rule, but by an inward faculty.

Reasoning, then, or the exercise of Reason, is a living spontaneous energy within us, not an art. But when the mind reflects upon itself, it begins to be dissatisfied with the absence of order and method in the exercise, and attempts to analyze the various processes which take place during it, to refer one to another, and to discover the main principles on which they are conducted, as it might contemplate and investigate its faculty of memory or imagination. The boldest, simplest, and most comprehensive theory which has been invented for the analysis of the reasoning process, is the well-known science for which we are indebted to Aristotle, and which is framed upon the principle that every act of reasoning is exercised upon neither more nor less than three terms. Short of this, we have many general words in familiar use to designate particular methods of thought, according to which the mind reasons, (that is, proceeds from truth to truth,) or to designate particular states of mind which influence its reasonings. Such methods are antecedent probability, analogy, parallel cases, testimony, and circumstantial evidences; and such states of mind are prejudice, deference to authority, party spirit, attachment to such and such principles, and the like.   In like manner we distribute the Evidences of Religion into External and Internal; into *à priori* and *à posteriori*; into Evidences of Natural Religion and of Revealed; and so on.   Again, we speak of proving doctrines either from the nature of the case, or from Scripture, or from history; and of teaching them in a dogmatic, or a polemical, or a hortatory way.   In these and other ways we instance the reflective power of the human mind, contemplating and scrutinizing its own acts.

Here, then, are two processes, distinct from each other,—the original process of reasoning, and next, the process of investigating our reasonings.   All men reason, for to reason is nothing more than to gain truth from former truth, without the intervention of sense, to which brutes are limited; but all men do not reflect upon their own reasonings, much less reflect truly and accurately, so as to do justice to their own meaning; but only in proportion to their abilities and attainments.   In other words, all men have a reason, but not all men can give a reason. We may denote, then, these two exercises of mind as reasoning and arguing, or as conscious and unconscious reasoning, or as Implicit Reason and Explicit Reason.   And to the latter belong the words, science, method, development, analysis, criticism, proof, system, principles, rules, laws, and others of a like nature.

That these two faculties are not to be confounded together would seem too plain for remark, except

2

that they have been confounded. Clearness in argument certainly is not indispensable to reasoning well. Accuracy in stating doctrines or principles is not essential to feeling and acting upon them. The exercise of analysis is not necessary to the integrity of the process analyzed. The process of reasoning is complete in itself, and independent. The analysis is but an account of it; it does not make the conclusion correct; it does not make the inference rational. It does not cause an individual to reason better. It does but give him a sustained consciousness, for good or for evil, that he is reasoning. How a man reasons is as much a mystery as how he remembers. He remembers better and worse on different subject-matters, and he reasons better and worse. Some men's reason becomes genius in particular subjects, and is less than ordinary in others. The faculty or talent of reasoning may be distinct in different subjects, though the process of reasoning is the same. Now a good arguer or clear speaker is but one who excels in analyzing or expressing a process of reason, taken as his subject-matter. He traces out the connexion of facts, detects principles, applies them, supplies deficiencies, till he has reduced the whole into order. But his talent of reasoning, or the gift of reason as possessed by him, may be confined to such an exercise, and he may be as little expert in other exercises, as a mathematician need be an experimentalist; as little creative of the reasoning itself which he analyzes, as a critic need possess the gift of writing poems.

But if reasoning and arguing be thus distinct, what is to be thought of assertions such as the following? Certainly, to say the least, they are very inaccurately worded, and may lead, as they have led, to great error.

Tillotson, for instance, says: " Nothing ought to be received as a divine doctrine and revelation, *without good evidence* that it is so : that is, without some *argument* sufficient to *satisfy* a prudent and considerate man[1]." Again : " Faith . . . is an assent of the mind to something as revealed by God : now all assent must be *grounded upon evidence ;* that is, no man can believe anything, unless he have, or think he hath, some *reason* to do so. For to be confident of a thing without reason is not faith, but a presumptuous persuasion and obstinacy of mind[2]." Such assertions either have an untrue meaning, or are unequal to the inferences which the writers proceed to draw from them.

In like manner Paley and others [3] argue that miracles are not improbable unless a revelation is improbable, on the ground that there is no other conceivable way of ascertaining a revelation ; that is, they would imply the necessity of a conscious investigation and verification of its claims, or the possession of

---

[1] Serm. vol. ii. p. 260.   [2] Serm. vol. iv. p. 42.

[3] Prepar. Consid. p. 3 ; vid. also Farmer on Miracles, p. 539.

grounds which are satisfactory in argument ; whereas
considerations which seem weak and insufficient in an
explicit form may lead, and justly lead, us by an
implicit process to a reception of Christianity ; just
as a peasant may from the look of the sky foretel
to-morrow's weather, on grounds which, as far as they
are producible, an exact logician would not scruple
to pronounce inaccurate and inconsequent.   " In
what way," he asks, " can a revelation be made,"
that is, as the context shows, be ascertained, " but
by miracles?   In none which we are able to conceive."

Again : another writer says, " There are but two
ways by which God could reveal His will to mankind ; either by an immediate influence on the mind
of every individual of every age, or by selecting some
particular persons to be His instruments . . . . and
for this purpose vested by Him with such powers as
might carry the strongest evidence that they were really
divine teachers[4]."   On the other hand, Bishop Butler
tells us, that it is impossible to decide what evidence
will be afforded of a revelation, supposing it made ;
and certainly it might have been given without any
supernatural display at all, being left (as it is in a
manner even now) to be received or rejected by each
man according as his heart sympathised in it, that is,
on the influence of reasons, which, though practically

[4] Douglas, Criterion, pp. 21, 22.

persuasive, are weak when set forth as the argumentative grounds of conviction.

Faith, then, though in all cases a reasonable process, is not necessarily founded on investigation, argument, or proof; these processes being but the explicit form which the reasoning takes in the case of
particular minds.   Nay, so far from it, that the opposite opinion has, with much more plausibility, been
advanced, viz. that Faith is not even compatible with
these processes.   Such an opinion, indeed, cannot be
maintained, particularly considering the light which
Scripture casts upon the subject, as in the text; but
it may easily take possession of serious minds.   When
they witness the strife and division to which argument and controversy minister, the proud self-confidence which strength of the reasoning powers fosters,
the laxity of opinion which often accompanies the
study of the Evidences, the coldness, the formality, the
secular and carnal spirit which may be united to an
exact adherence to dogmatic formularies; and on the
other hand, when they recollect that Scripture represents religion as a divine life, seated in the
affections and manifested in spiritual graces, no wonder that they are tempted to rescue Faith from all connexion with faculties and habits which may exist in
perfection without Faith, and which too often usurp
from Faith its own province, and profess to be a substitute for it.   I repeat, such a persuasion is extreme,
and will not maintain itself, and cannot be acted on,

for any long time; it being as paradoxical to prohibit religious inquiry and inference, as to make it imperative.   Yet we should not dismiss the notice of it, on many accounts, without doing justice to it; and therefore I propose now, before considering some of the uses of our critical and analytical powers, in the province of Religion, to state certain of the inconveniences and defects; an undertaking which will fully occupy what remains of our time this morning.

Inquiry and argument may be employed, first, in ascertaining the divine origin of Religion, Natural and Revealed; next, in interpreting Scripture; and thirdly, in determining points of Faith and Morals; that is, in the Evidences, Biblical Exposition, and Dogmatic Theology.   In all three departments there is, first of all, an exercise of implicit reason, which is in its degree common to all men; for all men gain a certain impression, right or wrong, from what comes before them, for or against Christianity, for or against certain interpretations of Scripture, for or against certain doctrines.   This impression, made upon their minds, whether by the claim itself of Revealed Religion, or by its documents, or by its teaching, it is the object of science to analyze, verify, methodize, and exhibit.   We believe certain things, on certain grounds, through certain informants; and the analysis of these three, the why, the how, and the what, seems pretty nearly to constitute the science of divinity.

1. By the Evidences of religion I mean the systematic analysis of all the grounds on which we believe

Christianity to be true. I say " all," because the word
Evidence is often restricted to denote only such
arguments as arise out of the thing itself which is to
be proved; or, to speak more definitely, facts and circumstances which presuppose the point under inquiry as a condition of their existence, and which
are weaker or stronger arguments, according as it
approaches to be a necessary condition of them.
Thus blood on the clothes is an evidence of a murderer, just so far as a deed of violence is necessary to
the fact of the stains, or alone accounts for them.
Such are the Evidences as drawn out by Paley and
other writers; and though but a secondary part, they
are popularly considered the whole of the Evidences,
because they can be exhibited and studied with far
greater ease than antecedent considerations, presumptions, and analogies, which, vague and abstruse
as they are, still are more truly the grounds on
which religious men receive the Gospel; but on
this subject something has been said on a former
occasion.

2. Under the science of Interpretation is of course
included all inquiry into its principles; the question
of mystical interpretation, the theory of the double
sense, the doctrine of types, the phraseology of prophecy, the drift and aim of the several books of Scripture; the dates when, the places where, and persons
by and to whom they were written; the comparison
and adjustment of book with book; the uses of the
Old Testament; the relevancy of the Law to Chris-

tians ; its relation to the Gospel, and the historical fulfilment of prophecy. And previous to such inquiries are others still more necessary, such as the study of the original languages in which the sacred Volume is written.

3. Under Dogmatic Theology must be included, not only doctrine, such as that of the Blessed Trinity, or the theory of Sacramental Influence, or the settlement of the Rule of Faith, but questions of morals and discipline also.

Now, in considering the imperfections and defects incident to such scientific exercises, we must carefully exempt from our remarks all instances of them which have been vouchsafed to us from above, and therefore have a divine sanction ; and that such instances do exist, is the most direct and satisfactory answer to any doubts which religious persons may entertain, of the lawfulness of employing science in the province of Faith at all. Of such analyses and determinations as are certainly from man, we are at liberty to dispute both the truth and the utility : but what God has done is perfect, that is, perfect according to its subject-matter. Whether in the department of evidence, Scripture interpretation, or dogmatic teaching, what He has spoken must be received, not criticised ;—and in saying this, I have not to assign the limit or the channels of God's communications. Whether He speaks only by Scripture, or by private and personal suggestion, or by the first ages, or by Tradition, or by the Church collective, or by the Church

in Council, or by the Chair of Saint Peter, are
questions about which Christians may differ without
interfering with the principle itself, that what God
has given is true, and what He has not given
may, if so be, be not true. What He has not
given by His appointed methods, whatever they
be, may be venerable for its antiquity, or authori-
tative as held by good men, or safer to hold as held
by many, or necessary to hold because it has been
subscribed, or persuasive from its probability, or expedient from its good effects; but after all, except
that all good things are from God, it is, as far as we
know, a human statement, and is open to criticism,
because the work of man. To such human inferences
and propositions I confine myself in the remarks
that follow.

Now the great practical evil of method and
form in matters of religion,—nay, in all moral
matters,—is obviously this:—their promising more
than they can effect. At best the science of divinity
is very imperfect and inaccurate, yet the very name
of science is a profession of accuracy. Other and
more familiar objections readily occur; such as its
leading to familiarity with sacred things, and consequent irreverence; its fostering formality; its substituting a sort of religious philosophy and literature
for worship and practice; its weakening the springs
of action by inquiring into them; its stimulating to
controversy and strife; its substituting, in matters of
duty, positive rules which need explanation for an in-

stinctive feeling which commands the mind; its
leading the mind to mistake system for truth, and to
suppose that an hypothesis is real because it is consistent: but all such objections, though important,
rather lead us to a cautious use of science than to a
distrust of it in religious matters. But its insuffi-
ciency in so high a province is an evil which attaches
to it from first to last, an inherent evil which there
are no means of remedying, and which, perhaps, lies
at the root of those other evils which I have just
been enumerating. To this evil I shall now direct
my attention, having already incidentally referred to
it in some of the foregoing remarks.

No analysis is subtle and delicate enough to represent adequately the state of mind under which we
believe, or the subjects of belief, as they are presented to our thoughts. The end proposed is that of
delineating, or, as it were, painting what the mind sees
and feels; now let us consider what it is to pourtray
duly in form and colour things material, and we shall
surely understand the difficulty, or rather the impossibility, of representing the outline and character, the
hues and shades in which any intellectual view really
exists in the mind, or of giving it that substance and
that exactness in detail in which consists its likeness
to the original, or of sufficiently marking those minute
differences which attach to the same general state of
mind or tone of thought as found in this or that individual respectively. It is probable that given
opinions, as held by individuals, even when of the

most congenial views, are as distinct from each other
as their faces.   Now how minute is the defect in imitation which hinders the likeness of a portrait from
being successful! how easy is it to recognize who is
intended by it, without allowing that really he is represented! Is it not hopeless, then, to expect that
the most diligent and anxious investigation can end in
more than in giving some very rude description of the
living mind, and its feelings, thoughts, and reasonings.
And if it be difficult to analyze fully any state, or
frame, or opinion of our own minds, is it a less difficulty to delineate, as Theology professes to do, the
works, dealings, providences, attributes, or nature of
Almighty God?

In this point of view we may, without irreverence,
speak even of the words of inspired Scripture as imperfect and defective; and though they are not subjects for our judgment (God forbid), yet they will for
that very reason serve to enforce and explain better
what I would say, and how far the objection goes.   Inspiration is defective, not in itself, but in consequence
of the medium it uses and the beings it addresses.
It uses human language, and it addresses man; and
neither can man compass, nor can his hundred tongues
utter, the mysteries of the spiritual world, and God's
dealings in this.   This vast and intricate scene of
things cannot be generalized or represented through
or to the mind of man; and inspiration, in undertaking to do so, necessarily lowers what is divine
to raise what is human.   What, for instance, is

the mention made in Scripture of the laws of God's government, of His providences, counsels, designs, anger, and repentance, but a gracious mode (the more gracious because necessarily imperfect) of making man contemplate what is far beyond him? Who shall give method to what is infinitely complex, and measure to the unfathomable? We are as worms in an abyss of divine works; myriads upon myriads of years would it take, were our hearts ever so religious, and our intellects ever so apprehensive, to receive from without the just impression of those works as they really are, and as experience would convey them to us: sooner, then, than we should know nothing, Almighty God has condescended to speak to us so far as human thought and language will admit, by approximations, in order to give us practical rules for our own conduct amid His infinite and eternal operations.

And herein consists one great blessing of the Gospel Covenant, that in Christ's death on the Cross, and in other parts of that all-gracious Economy, are concentrated, as it were, and so presented to us those attributes and works which fill eternity. And with a like graciousness we are also told, in human language, things concerning God Himself, concerning His Son and His Spirit, and concerning His Son's incarnation, and the union of two natures in His One Person— truths which even a peasant holds implicitly, but which Almighty God, whether by His Apostles, or by His Church after them, has vouchsafed to bring together and methodize, and to commit to the keeping of science.

Now all such statements are likely at first to strike coldly or harshly upon religious ears, when taken by themselves, for this reason if for no other,—that they express heavenly things under earthly images, which are infinitely below the reality. This applies especially to the doctrine of the Eternal Sonship of our Lord and Saviour, as all know who have turned their minds to the controversies on the subject.

Again, it may so happen, that statements are only possible in the case of certain aspects of a doctrine, and that these seem inconsistent with each other, or mysteries, when contrasted together, apart from what lies between them; just as if one were shown the picture of a little child and an old man, and were told that they represented the same person,—a statement which would be incomprehensible to those who were unacquainted with the natural changes which take place, in the course of years, in the human frame.

Or doctrinal statements may be introduced, not so much for their own sake, as because many consequences flow from them, and therefore a great variety of errors may, by means of them, be prevented. Such is the doctrine that our Saviour's personality is in His Godhead, not in His manhood; that He has taken the manhood into God. It is evident that such statements, being made for the sake of something beyond, when viewed apart from their end, or in themselves, are abrupt, and may offend hearers.

Again, so it is, however it be explained, that frequently we do not recognize our sensations and ideas, when put into words ever so carefully. The representation seems out of shape and strange, and startles us, even though we know not how to find fault with it. This applies, at least in the case of some persons, to portions of the received theological analysis of the impression made upon the mind by the Scripture notices concerning Christ and the Holy Spirit. In like manner, such phrases as " good works are a condition of eternal life," or " the salvation of the regenerate ultimately depends upon themselves,"— though unexceptionable, are of a nature to offend certain minds.

This difficulty of analyzing our more recondite feelings happily and convincingly, has a most important influence upon the science of the Evidences. Defenders of Christianity naturally select as reasons for belief, not the highest, the truest, the most sacred, the most intimately persuasive, but such as best admit of being exhibited in argument; and these are commonly not the real reasons.

Nay, they are led, for the same reason, to select such arguments as all will allow; that is, such as depend on principles which are a common measure to all minds. A science certainly is, in its very nature, public property; when, then, the grounds of Faith take the shape of a book of Evidences, nothing properly can be assumed but what men in general will grant as true; that is, nothing but what is on a level with all minds, good and bad, rude and refined.

Again, as to the difficulty of detecting and expressing the real reasons on which we believe, let this be considered,—how very differently an argument strikes the mind at one time and another, according to its particular state, or the accident of the moment. At one time it is weak and unmeaning,—at another, it is nothing short of demonstration. We take up a book at one time, and see nothing in it; at another, it is full of weighty remarks and precious thoughts. Sometimes a statement is axiomatic,—sometimes we are at a loss to see what can be said for it. Such, for instance, are the following, many like which are found in controversy;—that true saints cannot but persevere to the end; or that the influences of the Spirit cannot but be effectual; or that there must be an infallible Head of the Church on earth; or that the Roman Church, extending into all lands, is the Catholic Church; or that a Church, which is Catholic abroad, cannot be schismatical in England; or that, if our Lord is the Son of God, He must be God; or that a Revelation is probable; or that, if God is All-powerful, He must be also All-good. Who shall analyze the assemblage of opinions in this or that mind, which occasions it almost instinctively to reject or to accept each of these and similar positions? Far be it from me to seem to insinuate that they are *but* opinions, neither true nor false, and approving themselves or not, according to the humour or prejudice of the individual : so far from it, that I would maintain that the recondite reasons which lead each person to take or decline them, are just the most important portion of the considerations on which his conviction depends; and I say so, by way of showing that the science of controversy, or again the science of Evidences, has done very little, since it cannot analyze and exhibit these momentous reasons; nay, so far has done worse than little, in that it professes to have done much, and leads the student to mistake what are but secondary points in debate, as if they were the most essential.

It often happens, for the same reason, that controversialists or philosophers are spoken of by this or that person as unequal, sometimes profound, sometimes weak.   Such cases of inequality, of course, do occur ; but we should be sure, when tempted so to speak, that the fault is not with ourselves, who have not entered into an author's meaning, or analyzed the implicit reasonings along which his mind proceeds in those parts of his writings which we not merely dissent from (for that we have a right to do), but criticise as inconsecutive.

These remarks apply especially to the proofs commonly brought, whether for the truth of Christianity, or for certain doctrines from texts of Scripture.   Such alleged proofs are commonly strong or slight, not in themselves, but according to the circumstances under which the doctrine professes to come to us, which they are brought to prove; and they will have a great or small effect upon our minds, according as we admit those circumstances or not. Now, the admission of those circumstances involves a variety of antecedent views, presumptions, admitted analogies, and the like, many of which it is very difficult to detect and analyze. One person, for instance, is convinced by Paley's argument from the Miracles, another is not; and why? Because the former admits that there is a God, that He governs the world, that He wishes the salvation of man, that the light of nature is not sufficient for man, that there is no other way of introducing a Revelation but miracles, and that men, who were neither enthusiasts nor impostors, could not have acted as the Apostles did, unless they had seen the miracles which they attested; the other denies some one, or more, of these statements, or does not feel the force of some other principle more recondite and latent still than any of these, which is nevertheless necessary to the validity of the argument.

Further, let it be considered, that, even as regards what are commonly called Evidences, that is, arguments *à posteriori*, conviction for the most part follows, not upon any one great and decisive proof or token of the point in debate, but upon a number of very minute circumstances together, which the mind is quite unable to count up and methodize in an argumentative form. Let a person only call to mind the clear impression he has about matters of every day's occurrence, that this man is bent on a certain object, or that that man was displeased, or another suspicious; or that one is happy, and another unhappy; and how much depends in such impressions on manner, voice, accent, words uttered, silence instead of words, and all the many subtle symptoms which are felt by the mind, but cannot be contemplated; and let him consider how very poor an account he gives of his impression, if he avows it, and is called upon to justify it. This, indeed, is meant by what is called moral proof, in opposition to legal. We speak of an accused person being guilty without any doubt; but still the evidences of his guilt being none of them broad and definite enough in themselves to admit of being forced upon the notice of those who are not obliged to see them.

Now, should the proof of Christianity, or the Scripture proof of its doctrines, be of this subtle nature, of course it cannot be exhibited to advantage in argument: and even if it be not, but contain strong and almost legal evidences, still there will always be a temptation in the case of writers on Evidences, or the Scripture proof of doctrine, to over-state and exaggerate, or to systematize in excess; as if they were making a case in a court of law, rather than simply and severely analyzing, as far as is possible, certain existing reasons why the Gospel is true, or why it should be considered of a certain doctrinal character. It is hardly too much to say, that almost all reasons formally adduced in moral

2

inquiries, are rather specimens and symbols of the real grounds, than those grounds themselves. They do but approximate to a representation of the general character of the proof which the writer wishes to convey to another's mind. They cannot, like mathematical proof, be passively followed with an attention confined to what is stated, and with the admission of nothing but what is urged. Rather, they are hints towards, and samples of, the true reasoning, and demand an active, ready, candid, and docile mind, which can throw itself into what is said, neglect verbal difficulties, and pursue and carry out principles. This is the true office of a writer, to excite and direct trains of thought; and this, on the other hand, is the too common practice of readers, to expect everything to be done for them,—to refuse to think,—to criticise the letter, instead of reaching forwards towards the sense,—and to account every argument as unsound which is illogically worded. Here is the fertile source of controversy, which may undoubtedly be prolonged without limit by those who desire it, while words are incomplete exponents of ideas, and complex reasons demand study, and involve prolixity. They, then, who wish to shorten the dispute, and to silence a captious opponent, look out for some strong and manifest argument which may be stated tersely, handled conveniently, and urged rhetorically; some one reason, which bears with it a show of vigour and plausibility, or a profession of clearness, simplicity, or originality, and may be easily reduced to mood and figure. Hence the stress often laid upon particular texts, as if decisive of the matter in hand : hence one disputant dismisses all parts of the Bible which relate to the Law,—another finds the high doctrines of Christianity revealed in the Book of Genesis,—another rejects certain portions of the inspired volume, as the Epistle of St. James,—another gives up the Apocrypha,—another rests the defence of Revelation on Miracles only, or the Internal Evidence only,—another sweeps away all Christian teaching but Scripture,—one and all from impatience at being allotted, in the particular case, an evidence which does no more than create an impression on the mind ; from dislike of an evidence, varied, minute, complicated, and a desire of something producible, striking, and decisive.

Lastly, since a test is in its very nature of a negative character, and since argumentative forms are mainly a test of reasoning, so far they will be but critical, not creative. They will be useful in raising objections, and in ministering to scepticism ; they will pull down, and will not be able to build up.

I have been engaged in proving the following points : that the reasonings and opinions which are involved in the act of Faith are latent and implicit ; that the mind reflecting on itself is able to bring them out into some definite and methodical form ; that Faith, however, is complete without this reflective faculty, which, in matter of fact, often does interfere with it, and must be used cautiously.

I am quite aware that I have said nothing but what must have often passed through the minds of others; and it may be asked whether it is worth while so diligently to traverse old ground. Yet perhaps it is never without its use to bring together in one view, and steadily contemplate truths, which one by one may be familiar notwithstanding.

May we be in the number of those who, with the Blessed Apostle whom we this day commemorate, employ all the powers of their minds to the service of their Lord and Saviour, who are drawn heavenward by His wonder-working grace, whose hearts are filled with His love, who reason in His fear, who seek Him in the way of His commandments, and who thereby believe on Him to the saving of their souls!

SERMON XIII.

WISDOM, AS CONTRASTED WITH FAITH AND WITH BIGOTRY.

Preached on Whit-Tuesday, 1841.

---

1 Cor. ii. 15.

" He that is spiritual judgeth all things, yet he himself is judged
of no man."

THE gift to which this high characteristic is ascribed
by the Apostle, is Christian Wisdom, and the Giver
is God the Holy Ghost. "We speak wisdom," he
says, shortly before the text, " among them that are
perfect, yet not the wisdom of this world . . . but we
speak the wisdom of God in a mystery, even the hidden
wisdom." And after making mention of the heavenly
truths which Wisdom contemplates, he adds: " God
hath revealed them unto us by His Spirit . . . we have
received, not the spirit of the world, but the Spirit
which is of God."

In a former verse St. Paul contrasts this divine
Wisdom with Faith. " My speech and my preaching was not with enticing words of man's wisdom,

but in demonstration of the Spirit and of power, that your faith should not stand in the wisdom of men, but in the power of God. Howbeit, we speak wisdom among them that are perfect." Faith, then, and Wisdom, are distinct, or even opposite gifts. Wisdom belongs to the perfect, and more especially to preachers of the Gospel; and Faith is the elementary grace which is required of all, especially of hearers. The two are introduced again in a later chapter of the same Epistle: "To one is given by the Spirit the word of Wisdom, to another the word of Knowledge by the same Spirit, to another Faith by the same Spirit." Such are the two gifts which will be found to lie at the beginning and at the end of our new life, both intellectual in their nature, and both divinely imparted; Faith being an exercise of the Reason, so spontaneous, unconscious, and unargumentative, as to seem at first sight even to have a moral origin, and Wisdom being that orderly and mature development of thought, which in earthly language goes by the name of science and philosophy.

In like manner, in the Services of this sacred Season, both these spiritual gifts are intimated, and both referred to the same heavenly source. The Collect virtually speaks of Faith, when it makes mention of Almighty God's "teaching the hearts of His faithful people by the sending to them the light of His Holy Spirit;" and of the Wisdom of the perfect, when it prays God, that "by the same Spirit" we may "have a right judgment in all things."

Again, in the Gospel for Whitsunday, the gift of Wisdom is surely implied in Christ's promise, that the Comforter should teach the Apostles " all things," and " bring all things to their remembrance whatsoever He had said unto them ;" and in St. Paul's exhortation, which we read yesterday, " In malice be children, but in understanding be men." Again, a cultivation of the reasoning faculty, near akin to Philosophy or Wisdom, is surely implied in the precepts, of which we have heard, or shall hear, from the same Apostle and St. John to-day, about " proving all things," and " holding fast that which is good," and about " trying the spirits whether they are of God."

Again, other parts of our Whitsun Services speak of exercises of Reason more akin to Faith, as being independent of processes of investigation or discussion. In Sunday's Gospel our Lord tells us, " He that loveth Me shall be loved of My Father, and I will love him, and will manifest Myself to him. . . . If a man love Me, he will keep My words, and My Father will love him, and We will come unto him, and make Our abode with him." This manifestation is doubtless made to us through our natural faculties ; but who will maintain that even so far as it is addressed to our Reason, it comes to us in forms of argument? Again, in the Gospel for yesterday, " He that doeth truth cometh to the light," and on the contrary, " Light is come into the world, and men loved darkness rather than light, because their deeds were evil ; for every one that doeth evil hateth the light." Men do not

choose light or darkness without Reason, but by an
instinctive Reason, which is prior to argument and
proof. And in the Gospel for to-day, " The sheep
hear His voice, and He calleth His own sheep by
name, and leadeth them out. The sheep follow Him,
for they know His voice, and a stranger will they not
follow, for they know not the voice of strangers."
The sheep could not tell *how* they knew the Good
Shepherd; they had not analyzed their own impressions or cleared the grounds of their knowledge,
yet doubtless grounds there were: they, however,
acted spontaneously on a loving Faith.

In proceeding, then, as I shall now do, to inquire
into the nature of Christian Wisdom, as a habit or
faculty of mind distinct from Faith, the mature fruit
of Reason, and nearly answering to what is meant
by Philosophy, it must not be supposed that I am
denying its spiritual nature or its divine origin. Almighty God influences us and works in us, through
our minds, not without them or in spite of them; as
at the fall we did not become other beings than what
we had been, but forfeited gifts which had been
added to us on our creation, so under the Gospel we
do not lose any part of the nature in which we are
born, but regain what we have lost. We are what
we were, and something more. And what is true of
God's dealings with our minds generally, is true in
particular as regards our reasoning powers. His grace
does not supersede, but uses them, and renews them
by using. We gain Truth by reasoning, whether im-

plicit or explicit, in a state of nature; we gain it in the same way in a state of grace. Both Faith and Wisdom, the elementary and the perfecting gift of the Holy Spirit, are intellectual habits, and involve the exercise of Reason, and may be examined and defined as any other power of the mind, and are subject to perversion and error, and may be fortified by rules, just as if they were not instruments in the hands of the Most High. It is no derogation, then, from the divine origin of Christian Wisdom, to treat it in its human aspect, to show what it consists in, and what are its counterfeits and perversions; to determine, for instance, that it is much the same as Philosophy, and that its perversions are such as love of system, theorizing, fancifulness, dogmatism, and bigotry,—as we shall be led to do. And now to enter upon our subject.

The words philosophy, a philosophical spirit, enlargement or expansion of mind, enlightened ideas, a wise and comprehensive view of things, and the like, are, I need hardly say, of frequent occurrence in the literature of this day, and are taken to mean very much the same thing. That they are always used with a definite meaning, or with any meaning at all, will be maintained by no one; that so many persons, and many of them men of great ability, should use them absolutely with no meaning whatever, and yet should lay such stress and rest so much upon them, is, on the other hand, not to be supposed. Yet their meaning certainly requires drawing out and

illustrating.   Perhaps it will be best ascertained by
setting down some cases, which are commonly understood, or will be claimed, as instances of this process
of mental growth or enlargement, in the sense in
which the words are at present used.

I suppose that, when a person whose experience
has hitherto been confined to our own calm and un-
pretending scenery, goes for the first time into parts
where physical nature puts on her wilder and more
awful forms, whether at home or abroad, as especially
into mountainous districts,—or when one who has
ever lived in a quiet village comes for the first time
to a great metropolis,—he will have a sensation of
mental enlargement, as having gained a range of
thoughts to which he was before a stranger.

Again, the view of the heavens, which the tele-
scope opens upon us, fills and possesses the mind,
and is called an enlargement, whatever is meant by
the term.

Again, the sight of an assemblage of beasts of
prey and other foreign animals, their strangeness and
startling novelty, the originality (if I may use the
term,) and mysteriousness of their forms, and gestures, and habits, and their variety and independence
of one another, expand the mind, not without its
own consciousness; as if knowledge were a real
opening, and as if an addition to the external objects
presented before it were an addition to its inward
powers.

Hence physical science, generally, in all its depart-

ments, as bringing before us the exuberant riches, the
active principles, yet the orderly course of the universe, is often set forth even as the only true philosophy, and will be allowed by all persons to have
a certain power of elevating and exciting the mind,
and yet to exercise a tranquillizing influence upon it.

Again, the knowledge of history, and again, the
knowledge of books generally—in a word, what is
meant by education, is commonly said to enlighten
and enlarge the mind, whereas ignorance is felt to
involve a narrow range and a feeble exercise of its
powers.

Again, what is called seeing the world, entering into
active life, going into society, travelling, acquaintance
with the various classes of the community, coming
into contact with the principles and modes of thought
of separate parties, interests, or nations, their opinions, views, aims, habits, and manners, their religious
creeds and forms of worship,—all this exerts a perceptible effect upon the mind, which it is impossible
to mistake, be it good or be it bad, and which is popularly called its enlargement or enlightenment.

Again, when a person for the first time hears the
arguments and speculations of unbelievers, and feels
what a very novel light they cast upon what he has
hitherto accounted most sacred, it cannot be denied,
that, unless he is shocked and closes his ears and
heart to them, he will have a sense of expansion and
elevation.

Again, sin brings with it its own enlargement of

mind, which Eve was tempted to covet, and of which she made proof. This, perhaps, in the instance of some sins, to which the young are especially tempted, is their great attraction and their great recompense. They excite the curiosity of the innocent, and they intoxicate the imagination of their miserable victims, whose eyes seem opened upon a new world, from which they look back upon their state of innocence with a sort of pity and contempt, as if it were below the dignity of men.

On the other hand, religion has its own enlargement. It is often remarked of uneducated persons, who hitherto have lived without seriousness, that on their turning to God, looking into themselves, regulating their hearts, reforming their conduct, and studying the inspired Word, they seem to become, in point of intellect, different beings from what they were before. Before, they took things as they came, and thought no more of one thing than of another. But now every event has a meaning ; they form their own estimate of whatever occurs ; they recollect times and seasons ; and the world, instead of being like the stream which the countryman gazed on, ever in motion and never in progress, is a various and complicated drama, with parts and with an object.

Again, those who, being used to nothing better than the divinity of what is historically known as the nonconformist school,—or, again, of the latitudinarian, —are introduced to the theology of the early Church, will often have a vivid sense of enlargement, and will feel they have gained something, as becoming aware of the existence of doctrines, opinions, trains of thought, principles, aims, to which hitherto they have been strangers.

And again, such works as treat of the Ministry of the Prophets under the various divine Dispensations, of its nature and characteristics, why it was instituted and what it has effected; the matter, the order, the growth of its disclosures; the views of divine Providence, of the divine counsels and attributes which it was the means of suggesting; and its contrast with the pretences to prophetical knowledge which the world furnishes in mere political partisans or popular fortune-tellers; such treatises, as all will admit, may fitly be said to enlarge the mind.

Once more, such works as Bishop Butler's Analogy, which carry on the characteristic lineaments of the Gospel Dispensation into the visible course of things, and, as it were, root its doctrines into nature and society, not only present before the mind a large view of the matters handled, but will be commonly said, and surely, as all will feel, with a true meaning, to enlarge the mind itself which is put in possession of them.

These instances show beyond all question that what is called Philosophy, Wisdom, or Enlargement of mind, has some intimate dependence upon the acquisition of Knowledge; and Scripture seems to say the same thing. "God gave Solomon," says the inspired writer, " wisdom and understanding, exceeding much, and largeness of heart even as the sand that is on the sea shore. . . . And he spake three thousand proverbs, and his songs were a thousand and five. And he spake of trees, from the cedar-tree that is in Lebanon, even unto the hyssop that springeth out of the wall. He spake also of beasts and of fowl, and of creeping things and of fishes." And again, when the Queen of Sheba came, "Solomon told her all her questions; there was not any thing hid from the king, which he told her not." And in like manner St. Paul, after speaking of the Wisdom of the perfect, calls it a revelation, a knowledge, of the things of God, such as the natural man " discerneth " not. And in another Epistle, evidently speaking of the same Wisdom, he prays that his brethren may be given to " comprehend with all saints what is the breadth and length and depth and height, and to know the love of Christ which passeth knowledge, that they might be filled with all the fulness of God."

However, a very little consideration will make it plain also, that knowledge itself, though a condition of the mind's enlargement, yet, whatever be its range, is not that very thing which enlarges it. Rather the foregoing instances show that this enlargement consists in the *comparison* of the subjects of knowledge one with another. We feel ourselves to be ranging freely, when we not only learn something, but also refer it to what we knew before. It is not the mere addition to our knowledge which is the enlargement, but the change of place, the movement onwards, of that moral centre, to which what we know and what we have been acquiring, the whole mass of our knowledge, as it were, gravitates.   And therefore a philosophical cast of thought, or a comprehensive mind, or wisdom in conduct or policy, implies a connected view of the old with the new; an insight into the bearing and influence of each part upon every other; without which there is no whole, and could be no centre.   It is the knowledge, not only of things, but of their mutual relations.   It is organized, and therefore living knowledge.

A number of instances might readily be supplied in which knowledge is found apart from this analytical treatment of the matter of it, and in which it is never associated with Philosophy, or considered to open, enlarge, and enlighten the mind.

For instance, a great memory is never made synonymous with Wisdom, any more than a dictionary would be called a treatise.   There are men who contemplate things both in the mass and individually, but not correlatively, who accumulate facts without forming judgments, who are satisfied with deep learning or extensive information.   They may be linguists, antiquarians, annalists, biographers, or naturalists; but, whatever their merits, which are often very great, they have no claim to be considered philosophers.

To the same class belong persons, in other respects very different, who have seen much of the world, and of the men who, in their own day, have played a conspicuous part in it, who are full of information, curious and entertaining, about men and things, but who, having lived under the influence of no very clear or settled principles, speak of every one and everything as mere facts of history, not attempting to illustrate opinions, measures, aims, or policy,—not discussing or teaching, but conversing.

Or take, what is again a very different instance, the case of persons of little intellect, and no education, who perhaps have seen much of foreign countries, and who receive in a passive, otiose, unfruitful way, the various facts which are forced upon them. Seafaring men, for example, range from one end of the earth to the other; but the multiplicity of phenomena which they have encountered, forms no harmonious and consistent picture upon their imagination; they, as it were, see the tapestry of human life on the wrong side of it. They sleep, and they rise up, and they find themselves now in Europe, now in Asia; they see visions of great cities and wild regions; they are in the marts of commerce, or amid the islands of the ocean; they gaze on the Andes, or they are ice-bound; and nothing which meets them carries them on to any idea beyond itself. Nothing has a meaning, nothing has a history, nothing has relations. Everything stands by itself, and comes and goes in its turn, like the shifting sights of a show, leaving the beholder where he was. Or, again, under other circumstances, everything seems

2

to such persons strange, monstrous, miraculous, and awful; as in fable, to Ulysses and his companions in their wanderings.

Or, again, the censure often passed on what is called undigested reading, shows us that knowledge without system is not Philosophy. Students who store themselves so amply with literature or science, that no room is left for determining the respective relations which exist between their acquisitions, one by one, are rather said to load their minds than to enlarge them.

Scepticism, in religious matters, affords another instance in point. Those who deliberately refuse to form a judgment upon the most momentous of all subjects; who are content to pass through life in ignorance, why it is given, or by whom, or to what it leads; and who bear to be without tests of truth and error in conduct, without rule and measure for the principles, persons, and events, which they encounter daily,—these men, though they often claim, will not by any Christian be granted, the name of philosophers.

All this is more than enough to show that some analytical process, some sort of systematizing, some insight into the mutual relation of things, is essential to that enlargement of mind or philosophical temper, which is commonly attributed to the acquisition of knowledge. In other words, Philosophy is Reason exercised upon Knowledge; for, from the nature of the case, where the facts are given, as is here sup-

posed, Reason is synonymous with analysis, having
no office beyond that of ascertaining the relations
existing between them.   Reason is the power of proceeding to new ideas by means of given ones. Where
but one main idea is given, it can employ itself in
developing this into its consequences.   Thus, from
scanty data, it often draws out a whole system, each
part with its ascertained relations, collateral or lineal,
towards the rest, and all consistent together, because
all derived from one and the same origin.   And
should means be found of ascertaining directly some of
the facts which it has been deducing by this abstract
process, then their coincidence with its *à priori*
judgments will serve to prove the accuracy of its
deductions.   Where, however, the facts or doctrines
in question are all known from the first, there, instead of advancing from idea to idea, Reason does
but connect fact with fact; instead of discovering, it
does but analyze; and what was, in the former case,
the tracing out of inferences, becomes a laying down
of relations.

Philosophy, then, is Reason exercised upon Knowledge; or the Knowledge not merely of things in
general, but of things in their relations to one
another.   It is the power of referring everything to
its true place in the universal system,—of understanding the various aspects of each of its parts,—of
comprehending the exact value of each,—of tracing
each backwards to its beginning, and forward to its
end,—of anticipating the separate tendencies of each,

and their respective checks or counteractions; and thus of accounting for anomalies, answering objections, supplying deficiencies, making allowance for errors, and meeting emergencies.   It never views any part of the extended subject-matter of knowledge, without recollecting that it is but a part, or without the associations which spring from this recollection.   It makes everything lead to everything else; it communicates the image of the whole body to every separate member, till the whole becomes in imagination like a spirit, everywhere pervading and penetrating its component parts, and giving them their one definite meaning. Just as our bodily organs, when mentioned, recal to mind their function in the body, as the word creation suggests the idea of a Creator, as subjects that of a sovereign, so in the mind of a philosopher, the elements of the physical and moral world, sciences, arts, pursuits, ranks, offices, events, opinions, individualities, are all viewed, not in themselves, but as relative terms, suggesting a multitude of correlatives, and gradually, by successive combinations, converging one and all to their true centre.   Men, whose minds are possessed by some one object, take exaggerated views of its importance, are feverish in their pursuit of it, and are startled or downcast on finding obstacles in the way of it; they are ever in alarm or in transport; and they, on the contrary, who have no firm grasp of principles, are perplexed and lose their way every fresh step they take.   They do not know what to think or say of new phenomena which meet

them, of whatever kind; they have no view, as it may
be called, concerning persons, or occurrences, or facts,
which come upon them suddenly; they cannot form
a judgment, or determine on a course of action; and
they ask the opinion or advice of others as a relief to
their minds.   But Philosophy cannot be partial, cannot be exclusive, cannot be impetuous, cannot be
surprised, cannot fear, cannot lose its balance, cannot
be at a loss, cannot but be patient, collected, and
majestically calm, because it discerns the whole in
each part, the end in each beginning, the worth of
each interruption, the measure of each delay, because it always knows where it is, and how its path
lies from one point to another.   There are men who,
when in difficulties, by the force of genius, originate
at the moment vast ideas or dazzling projects; who,
under the impulse of excitement, are able to cast a
light, almost as if from inspiration, on a subject or
course of action which comes before them; who have
a sudden presence of mind equal to any emergency,
rising with the occasion, and an undaunted heroic
bearing, and an energy and keenness, which is but
sharpened by opposition.   Faith is a gift analogous
to this thus far, that it acts promptly and boldly on
the occasion, on slender evidence, as if guessing and
reaching forward to the truth, amid darkness or confusion; but such is not the Wisdom of the perfect.
It is the clear, calm, accurate vision, and comprehension of the whole course, the whole work of God;
and though there is none who has it in its fulness

but He who " searcheth all things, yea, the deep
things of " the Creator, yet " by that Spirit " they
are, in a measure, " revealed unto us." And thus,
according to that measure, is the text fulfilled, that
" he that is spiritual judgeth all things, yet he himself is judged by no man." Others understand him
not, master not his ideas, fail to combine, harmonize,
or make consistent, those distinct views and principles
which come to him from the Infinite Light, and are
inspirations of the breath of God. He, on the contrary, compasses others, and locates them, and anti-
cipates their acts, and fathoms their thoughts, for, in
the Apostle's language, he " hath the mind of Christ,"
and all things are his, " whether Paul, or Apollos, or
Cephas, or the world, or life, or death, or things present, or things to come." Such is the marvellous-
ness of the Pentecostal gift, wherein we " have an
unction from the Holy One, and know all things."

Now, this view of the nature of Philosophy leads
to the following remark : that, whereas no arguments in favour of religion are of much account but
such as rest on a philosophical basis, Evidences of
Religion, as they are called, which are truly such,
must consist mainly in such investigations into the
relation of idea to idea, and developments of system,
as have been described, if Philosophy lie in these
abstract exercises of Reason. Such, for instance, is
the argument from analogy, or from the structure of
prophecy, or from the needs of human nature and
the fulness of time ; or from the Catholic Church.

From which it follows, first, that what may be called the rhetorical or forensic Evidences,—I mean those which are content with the proof of certain facts, motives, and the like, such as, that a certain miracle must have taken place, or a certain prophecy must have been both written before, and fulfilled in, a certain event; these, whatever their merits, which I have no wish to disparage, are not philosophical. And next, it follows that Evidences in general are not the essential groundwork of Faith, but its reward; since Wisdom is the last gift of the Spirit, and Faith the first.

In the foregoing observations I have, in fact, been showing,—in prosecution of a line of thought to which I have before now drawn attention,—what is the true office, and what the legitimate bounds of those abstract exercises of Reason which may best be described by the name of systematizing. They are in their highest and most honourable place, when they are employed upon the vast field of Knowledge, not conjecturing unknown truths, but comparing, adjusting, connecting, explaining facts and doctrines ascertained. Such a use of Reason is Philosophy; such employment was it to which the reason of Newton dedicated itself; and the reason of Butler; and the reason of those ancient Catholic Divines, nay, in their measure, of those illustrious thinkers of the middle ages, who have treated of the Christian faith on system, Athanasius, Augustine, Aquinas. But where the exercise of Reason much outstrips our Know-

ledge; where Knowledge is limited, and Reason active; where ascertained truths are scanty, and courses
of thought abound; there indulgence of system is
unsafe, and may be dangerous. In such cases there
is much need of wariness, jealousy of self, and habitual dread of presumption, paradox, and unreality,
to preserve our deductions within the bounds of
sobriety, and our guesses from assuming the character
of discoveries. System, which is the very soul, or,
to speak more precisely, the formal cause of Philosophy, when exercised upon adequate knowledge,
does but make, or tend to make, theorists, dogmatists,
philosophists, and sectarians, when or so far as Knowledge is limited or incomplete.

This statement, which will not be questioned, perhaps, in the abstract, requires to be illustrated in
detail, and that at a length inconsistent with my
present limits.   At the risk, however, of exceeding
them, I will attempt so much as this,—to show that
Faith, distinct as it is from argument, discussion, investigation, philosophy, nay, from Reason altogether,
in the popular sense of the word, is at the same time
perfectly distinct also from narrowness of mind in all
its shapes, though sometimes accidentally connected
with it in particular instances. I am led to give attention to this point from its connection with subjects, of
which I have already treated on former occasions.

It is as if a law of the human mind, ever to do
things in one and the same way. It is not various
in its modes of action, except by an effort; but, if

left to itself, it becomes almost mechanical, as a matter of course. Its doing a thing in a certain way to-day, is the cause of its doing it in the same way to-morrow. The order of the day perpetuates itself. This is, in fact, only saying that habits arise out of acts, and that character is inseparable from our moral nature. Not only do our features and make remain the same day after day, but we speak in the same tone, adopt the same phrases and turns of thought, fall into the same expressions of countenance, and walk with the same gait as yesterday. And, besides, we have an instinctive love of order and arrangement; we think and act by rule, not only unconsciously, but of set purpose. Method approves itself to us, and aids us in various ways, and to a certain point is pleasant, and in some respects absolutely necessary. Even sceptics cannot proceed without elementary principles, though they would fain dispense with every yoke and bond. Even the uneducated have their own rude modes of classifying, not the less really such, because fantastic or absurd; children too, amid their awe at all that meets them, yet in their own thoughts unconsciously subject these wonders to a law. Poets, while they disown philosophy, frame an ideal system of their own; and naturalists invent, if they do not find, orders and genera, to assist the memory. Latitudinarians, again, while they profess charity towards all doctrines, nevertheless count it heresy to oppose the principle of latitude. Those who condemn persecution for religious opinions, in self-defence, persecute those who advocate it. Few of those who maintain that the exercise of private judgment upon Scripture leads to the attainment of Gospel truth, can tolerate the Socinian and Pelagian, who in their own inquiries have taken pains to conform to this rule. Thus, what is invidiously called dogmatism and system, in one shape or other, in one degree or another, is, I may say, necessary to the human mind; we cannot reason, feel, or act, without it; it forms the stamina of thought, which, when it is removed, languishes, and droops. Sooner than dispense with principles, the mind will take them at the hand of others, will put up with such as are faulty or uncertain;—and thus much Wisdom, Bigotry, and Faith, have in common. Principle is the life of them all; but Wisdom is the application of adequate principles to the state of things as we find them, Bigotry is the application of inadequate or narrow principles, while Faith is the maintenance of principles, without caring to apply or adjust them. Thus they differ; and this distinction will serve to enable us to contrast Bigotry and Faith with Wisdom, as I proposed.

Now, certainly, Faith may be confused with Bigotry, dogmatism, positiveness, and kindred habits of mind, on several plausible grounds; for, what is Faith but a reaching forth after truth amid darkness, upon the warrant of certain antecedent notions or spontaneous feelings? It is a presumption about matters of fact, upon principle rather than on knowledge; and what is Bigotry also but this? And, further still, its grounds being thus conjectural, what does it issue in? in the absolute acceptance of a certain message or doctrine as divine; that is, it starts from probabilities, yet it ends in peremptory statements, if so be, mysterious, or at least beyond experience. It believes an informant amid doubt, yet accepts his information without doubt. Such is the *primâ facie* resemblance between two habits of mind, which nevertheless are as little to be confused as the Apostles with their Jewish persecutors, as a few words may suffice to show.

Now, in the first place, though Faith be a presumption of facts under defective knowledge, yet, be it observed, it is altogether a practical principle. It judges and decides because it cannot help doing so, for the sake of the man himself, who exercises it, not in the way of opinion, not as aiming at abstract truth, not as teaching some theory or view. It is the act of a mind feeling that it is its duty any how, under its particular circumstances, to judge and to act, whether its light be greater or less, and wishing to make the most of that light and acting for the best. Its knowledge, then, though defective, is not insufficient for the purpose for which it uses it, for this plain reason, because (such is God's will) it has no more. The servant who hid his Lord's money was punished; and we, since we did not make our circumstances, but were placed in them, shall be judged, not by them, but by our use of them. A view of duty, such as this, may lead us to wrong acts, but not to act wrongly. Christians have sometimes inflicted death from a zeal not according to knowledge; and sometimes they have been eager for the toleration of heresy from an ill-instructed charity. Under such circumstances a man's error may be more acceptable to God than his truth; for his truth, it may be, but evidences clearness of intellect, whereas his error proceeds from conscientiousness; though whence it proceeds, and what it evidences, in a particular case, must be left to the Searcher of hearts.

Faith, then, though a presumption, has this peculiarity, that it is exercised under a sense of personal responsibility. It is when our presumptions take a wide range, when they affect to be systematical and philosophical, when they are indulged in matters of speculation, not of conduct, not in reference to self but to others, then it is that they deserve the name of bigotry and dogmatism. For in such a case we make a wrong use of such light as is given us, and mistake what is "a lantern unto our feet" for the sun in the heavens.

Again, it is true that Faith as well as Bigotry maintains dogmatic statements which go beyond its knowledge. It uses words, phrases, propositions, it accepts doctrines and practices, which it but partially understands, or not at all. Now, so far indeed as these statements do not relate to matters of this world, but to heavenly things, of course they are no evidence of Bigotry. As the widest experience of life would not tend to remove the mysteriousness of the doctrine of the Holy Trinity, so even the narrowest does not deprive us of the right of asserting it. Much knowledge and little knowledge leave us very much as we were, in a matter of this kind. But the case is very different when positions are in question of a social or moral character, which claim to be rules or maxims for political combination or conduct, for the well-being of the world, or for the guidance of public opinion. Yet many such positions Faith certainly does accept; and thus it seems to place the persons who act upon it in the very position of the bigoted, theoretical, and unreal; who use words beyond their depth, or avow sentiments to which they have no right, or enunciate general principles on defective knowledge. Questions, for instance, about the theory of government, national duties, the establishment of Religion, its relations to the State, the treatment of the poor, and the nature of the Christian Church: these and other such, may, it cannot be denied, be peremptorily settled, on religious grounds, by persons whose qualifications are manifestly unequal to so great an undertaking, who have not the knowledge, penetration, subtlety, calmness, or experience, which are a claim upon our attention, and who in consequence are, at first sight, to say the least, very like bigots and partisans.

Now that Faith may run into Bigotry, or may be mixed with Bigotry in matter of fact in this instance or that, of course I do not deny; at the same time

the two habits of mind, whatever be their resemblance, differ in their dogmatism, in this:—Bigotry
professes to understand what it maintains, though it
does not; it argues and infers, it disowns Faith, and
makes a show of Reason instead of it.   It persists,
not in abandoning argument, but in arguing only in
one way.   It takes up, not a religious, but a philosophical position; it lays claim to Wisdom, whereas
Faith from the first makes men willing, with the
Apostle, to be fools for Christ's sake.   Faith sets out
with putting reasoning aside as out of place, and pro-
poses instead simple obedience to a revealed command.   Its disciples represent that they are neither
statesmen nor philosophers; that they are not developing principles or evolving systems; that their
ultimate end is not persuasion, popularity, or success;
that they are but doing God's will, and desiring His
glory.   They profess a sincere belief that certain
views which engage their minds come from God;
that they know well that they are beyond them; that
they are not able to enter into them, or to apply them
as others may do; that, understanding them but partially themselves, they are not sanguine about im-
pressing them on others; that a divine blessing alone
can carry them forward; that they look for it; that
they feel that God will maintain His own cause; that
that belongs to Him, not to them[1]; that if their cause
is God's cause, it will be blessed, in His time and

---

[1] Dan. iii. 17, 18.

way; that if it be not, it will come to nought; that
they securely wait the issue; that they leave it to
the generation to come; that they can bear to seem
to fail, but cannot bear to be " disobedient to a
heavenly vision;" that they think that God has taught
them and put a word in their mouths; that they
speak to acquit their own souls; that they protest, in
order to be on the side of God's host, of the glorious
company of the Apostles, the goodly fellowship of the
Prophets, the noble army of Martyrs, in order to be
separate from the congregation of His enemies.
" Blessed is the man that hath not walked in the
counsel of the ungodly, nor stood in the way of sinners, and hath not sat in the seat of the scornful."
They desire to gain this blessedness; and though
they have not the capacity of mind to embrace, nor
the keenness to penetrate and analyze the contents
of this vast world, nor the comprehensive faculty
which resolves all things into their true principles,
and connects them in one system, though they can
neither answer objections made to their doctrines, nor
say for certain whither they are leading them, yet
profess them they can and must. Embrace them
they can, and go out, not knowing whither they go.
Faith, at least, they may have; Wisdom, if so be,
they have not; but Faith fits them to be the instruments and organs, the voice and the hands and the
feet of Him who is invisible, the Divine Wisdom in
the Church, —who knows what they know not, understands their words, for they are His own, and directs

2

their efforts to His own issues, though they see them
not, because they dutifully place themselves upon
His path. This is what they will be found to profess;
and their state is that of the multitude of Christians
in every age, nay even in the Apostolic, when, for all
the supernatural illumination of such as St. Paul,
"God chose the foolish things of the world to confound the wise, and the weak things of the world to
confound the things which were mighty, and base
things of the world, and things which were despised, yea
and things which were not, to bring to nought things
that were, that no flesh should glory in His presence."

Such a view of things is not of a nature to be affected by what is external to it. It did not grow out
of knowledge, and an increase or loss of knowledge
cannot touch it. The revolution of kingdoms, the
rise or the fall of parties, the growth of society, the
discoveries of science, leave it as they found it. On
God's word does it depend; that word alone can alter
it. And thus we are introduced to a distinct peculiarity of Faith; for considering that Almighty God
often speaks, nay is ever speaking in one way or
another, if we would watch for His voice, Faith, while
it is so stable, is necessarily a principle of mental
growth also, in an especial way; according, that is, as
God sees fit to employ it. "I will stand upon my
watch," says the prophet, "and set me upon the
tower, and will watch to see what He will say unto
me;" and, though since Christ came, no new revelation has been given, yet much even in the latter

days has been added in the way of explaining and ap-
plying what was given, once for all. As the world
around varies, so varies also, not the principles of the
doctrine of Christ, but the outward shape and colour
which they assume. And as Wisdom only can apply or
dispense the Truth in a change of circumstances, so
Faith alone is able to accept it as one and the same
under all its forms. And thus Faith is ever the
means of learning something new, and in this respect
differs from Bigotry, which has no element of advance
in it, and is under a practical persuasion that it has
nothing to learn. To the narrow-minded and the
bigoted the history of the Church for eighteen centuries is unintelligible and useless ; but where there
is Faith, it is full of sacred principles, ever the same
in substance, ever varying in accidentals, and is a
continual lesson of " the manifold Wisdom of God."

Moreover, though Faith has not the gift of tracing
out and connecting one thing with another, which
Wisdom has, and Bigotry professes to have, but is an
isolated act of Reason upon any matter in hand, as it
comes ; yet on this very account it has as wide a
range as Wisdom, and a far wider one than can belong
to any narrow principle or partial theory, and is able
to take discursive views, though not systematic.
There is no subject which Faith working by Love may
not include in its province, on which it may not have
a judgment, and to which it may not do justice, though
it views each point by itself, and not as portions of
a whole. Hence, unable as Faith is to analyze its

grounds, or to show the consistency of one of its judgments with another, yet every one of these has its
own place, and corresponds to some doctrine or precept in the philosophical system of the Gospel, for
they are all the instincts of a pure mind, which steps
forward truly and boldly, and is never at fault. Whatever be the subject-matter and the point in question,
sacred or profane, Faith has a true view of it, and
Wisdom can have no more; nor does it become truer
because it is held in connexion with other opinions,
or less true because it is not. And thus, whereas
Faith is the characteristic gift of all Christians, a
peasant may take the same view of human affairs in
detail as a philosopher; and we are often perplexed
whether to say that such persons are intellectually
gifted or not. They have clear and distinct opinions;
they know what they are saying; they have something
to say about any subject; they do not confuse points
of primary with those of secondary importance; they
never contradict themselves: on the other hand they
are not aware that there is anything extraordinary
about their judgment; they do not connect any two
judgments together; they do not recognize any common principles running through them; they forget the
opinions they have expressed with the occasion; they
cannot defend themselves; they are easily confused
and silenced; and, if they set themselves to reason, they
use arguments which appear to be faulty, as being but
types and shadows of those which they really feel,

and attempts to analyze that vast system of thought
which is their life, but not their instrument.

It is the peculiarity, then, of Faith, that it forms
its judgment under a sense of duty and responsibility,
with a view to personal conduct, according to revealed
directions, with a confession of ignorance, with a
carelessness about consequences, in a teachable and
humble spirit, yet upon a range of subjects which
Philosophy itself cannot surpass. In all these respects it is contrasted with Bigotry. Men of narrow
minds, far from confessing ignorance and maintaining
Truth mainly as a duty, profess, as I observed just
now, to understand the subjects which they take up
and the principles which they apply to them. They
do not see difficulties. They consider that they hold
their doctrines, whatever they are, at least as much
upon Reason as upon Faith; and they expect to be
able to argue others into a belief of them, and are
impatient when they cannot. They consider that the
premisses with which they start just prove the conclusions which they draw, and nothing else. They
think that their own views are exactly fitted to solve
all the facts which are to be accounted for, to satisfy
all objections, and to moderate and arbitrate between
all parties. They conceive that they profess just *the*
truth which makes all things easy. They have their
one idea or their favourite notion, which occurs to
them on every occasion. They have their one or two
topics, which they are continually obtruding, with a

sort of pedantry, being unable to discuss, in a natural unconstrained way, or to let their thoughts take their course, in the confidence that they will come safe home at the last.   Perhaps they have discovered, as they think, the leading idea, or simple view, or sum and substance of the Gospel ; and they insist upon this or that isolated tenet, selected by themselves or by others not better qualified, to the disparagement of the rest of the revealed scheme.   They have, moreover, clear and decisive explanations always ready of the sacred mysteries of Faith; they may deny those mysteries or retain them, but in either case they think their own to be the rational view and the natural explanation of them, and all minds feeble or warped or disordered which do not acknowledge this. They profess that the inspired writers were precisely of their particular creed, be it a creed of to-day, or yesterday, or of a hundred years since ; and they do not shrink from appealing to the common sense of mankind at large to decide this point.   Then their proof of doctrines is as meagre as their statement of them.   They are ready with the very places of Scripture,—one, two, or three,—where it is to be found ; they profess to say just what each passage and verse means, what it cannot mean, and what it must mean. To see in it less than they see is, in their judgment, to explain away ; to see more, is to gloss over.   To proceed to other parts of Scripture than those which they happen to select, is, they think, superfluous, since they have already adduced the very arguments suffi-

cient for a clear proof; and if so, why go beyond
them? And again, they have their own terms and
names for every thing; and these must not be touched
any more than the things which they stand for. Words
of party or politics, of recent date and unsatisfactory
origin, are as much a portion of the Truth in their
eyes, as if they were the voice of Scripture or of Holy
Church. And they have their forms, ordinances, and
usages, which are as sacred to them as the very Sacraments given us from heaven.

Narrow minds have no power of throwing themselves into the minds of others. They have stiffened
in one position, as limbs of the body subjected to con-
finement, or as our organs of speech, which after a
while cannot learn new tones and inflections. They
have already parcelled out to their own satisfaction
the whole world of knowledge; they have drawn their
lines, and formed their classes, and given to each opinion, argument, principle, and party, its own locality;
they profess to know where to find every thing; and
they cannot learn any other disposition. They are
vexed at new principles of arrangement, and grow
giddy amid cross divisions; and, even if they make the
effort, cannot master them. They think that any one
truth excludes another which is distinct from it, and
that every opinion is contrary to their own opinions
which is not included in them. They cannot separate
words from their own ideas, and ideas from their own
associations; and if they attain any new view of a
subject, it is but for a moment. They catch it one

moment, and let it go the next; and then impute to subtlety in it, or obscurity in its expression, what really arises from their own want of elasticity or vigour. And when they attempt to describe it in their own language, their nearest approximation to it is a mistake; not from any purpose to be unjust, but because they are expressing the ideas of another mind, as it were, in translation.

It is scarcely necessary to observe upon the misconceptions which such persons form of foreign habits of thought, or again of ancient faith or philosophy; and the more so, because they are unsuspicious of their own deficiency. Thus we hear the Greek Fathers, for instance, sometimes called Arminians, and St. Augustine Calvinistic; and that not analogously, but as if each party really answered to the title given it. And again an inquiry is made whether Christians in those early days held this or that point of doctrine, which may be in repute in particular sects or schools now; as, for instance, whether they upheld the union of Church and State, or the doctrine of assurance. It is plain that to answer in the affirmative or negative would be to misrepresent them; yet the persons in question do not contemplate more than such an absolute alternative.

Nor is it only in censure and opposition that narrowness of view is shown; it lies quite as often in approval and partisanship. None are so easily deceived by others as they who are pre-occupied with their own notions. They are soon persuaded that another agrees with them, if he disagrees with their opponents. They resolve his ideas into their own, and, whatever words he may use to clear his meaning, even the most distinct and forcible, these fail to convey to them any new view, or to open to them his mind.

Again, if those principles are narrow which claim to interpret and subject the whole world of knowledge, without being adequate to the task, one of the most striking characteristics of such principles will be the helplessness which they exhibit, when new materials or fields of thought are opened upon them. True philosophy admits of being carried out to any extent; it is its very test that no knowledge can be submitted to it with which it is not commensurate, and which it cannot annex to its territory. But the theory of the narrow or bigoted has already run out within short limits, and a vast and anxious region lies beyond, unoccupied and in rebellion. Their " bed is shorter than that a man can stretch himself on it; and the covering narrower, than that he can wrap himself in it." And then what is to be done with these unreclaimed wastes?—the exploring of them must in consequence be forbidden, or even their existence denied. Thus, in the present day, there are new sciences, especially physical, which we all look at with anxiety, feeling that our views, as we at present hold them, are unequal to them, yet feeling also that no truth can really exist external to Christianity. Another striking proof of narrowness of mind among us, may be drawn from the alteration of feeling with which we often regard members of this or that communion, before we know them and after. If our theory and our view of facts agreed together, they could not lead to opposite impressions about the same matters. And another instance occurs daily: true Catholicity is commensurate with the wants of the human mind; but persons are often to be found who are surprised that they cannot persuade all men to follow them, and cannot destroy dissent, by preaching a portion of the Divine system, instead of the whole of it.

Under these circumstances, it is not wonderful that persons of narrow views are often perplexed, and sometimes startled and unsettled, by the difficulties of their position. What they did not know, or what they knew but had not weighed, suddenly presses upon their notice. Then they become impatient that they cannot make their proofs clear, and try to make a forcible riddance of objections. They look about for new arguments, and put violence on Scripture or on history. They show a secret misgiving about the truth of their principles, by shrinking from the appearance of defeat, or from occasional doubt within. They become alarmists, and they forget that the issue of all things, and the success of their own cause, (if it be what they think it,) is sealed and secured by Divine promise; and sometimes, in this conflict between broad fact and narrow principle, the hard material breaks their tools; they are obliged to give up their principles. A state of uncertainty and distress follows, and, in the end, perhaps, bigotry is supplanted by general scepticism. They who thought their own ideas could measure all things, end in thinking that even a Divine Oracle is unequal to the task.

In these remarks, it will be observed that I have been contrasting Faith and Bigotry as habits of mind entirely distinct from each other. They are so; but it must not be forgotten, as indeed I have already observed, that, though distinct in themselves, they may and do exist together in the same person. No one so imbued with a loving Faith but has somewhat, perhaps, of Bigotry to unlearn; no one so narrow-minded, and full of self, but is influenced, it is to be hoped, in his degree, by the spirit of Faith.

Let us ever make it our prayer and our endeavour, that we may know the whole counsel of God, and grow unto the measure of the stature of the fulness of Christ; that all prejudice, and self-confidence, and hollowness, and unreality, and positiveness, and partisanship, may be put away from us under the light of Wisdom, and the fire of Faith and Love; till we see things as God sees them, with the judgment of His Spirit, and according to the mind of Christ.

SERMON XIV.

THE THEORY OF DEVELOPMENTS IN RELIGIOUS DOCTRINE.

Preached on the Purification, 1843.

LUKE ii. 19.

" But Mary kept all these things, and pondered them in her
heart."

LITTLE is told us in Scripture concerning the Blessed
Virgin, but there is one grace of which the Evangelists make her the pattern, in a few simple sentences,—of Faith.   Zacharias questioned the Angel's
message, but " Mary said, Behold the handmaid of
the Lord; be it unto me according to thy word."
Accordingly Elisabeth, speaking with an apparent
allusion to the contrast thus exhibited between her
own highly-favoured husband, righteous Zacharias,
and the still more highly-favoured Mary, said, on
receiving her salutation, " Blessed art thou among
women, and blessed is the fruit of thy womb; Blessed
is she that believed, for there shall be a performance
of those things which were told her from the Lord."

But Mary's faith did not end in a mere acquiescence in Divine providences and revelations: as the text informs us, she "pondered" them. When the shepherds came, and told of the vision of Angels which they had seen at the time of the Nativity, and how one of them announced that the Infant in her arms was "the Saviour, which is Christ the Lord," while others did but wonder, "Mary kept all these things, and pondered them in her heart." Again, when her Son and Saviour had come to the age of twelve years, and had left her for awhile for His Father's service, and had been found, to her surprise, in the Temple, amid the doctors, both hearing them and asking them questions, and had, on her addressing Him, vouchsafed to justify His conduct, we are told, "His mother kept all these sayings in her heart." And accordingly, at the marriage-feast in Cana, her faith anticipated His first miracle, and she said to the servants, "Whatsoever He saith unto you do it."

Thus St. Mary is our pattern of Faith, both in the reception and in the study of Divine Truth. She does not think it enough to accept, she dwells upon it; not enough to possess, she uses it; not enough to assent, she develops it; not enough to submit the Reason, she reasons upon it; not indeed reasoning first, and believing afterwards, with Zacharias, yet first believing without reasoning, next from love and reverence, reasoning after believing. And thus she symbolizes to us, not only the faith of the unlearned,

but of the doctors of the Church also, who have to
investigate, and weigh, and define, as well as to profess the Gospel; to draw the line between truth and
heresy; to anticipate or remedy the various aber-
rations of wrong reason; to combat pride and reck-
lessness with their own arms; and thus to triumph
over the sophist and the innovator.

If, then, on a Day dedicated to such high contem-
plations as the Feast which we are now celebrating,
it is allowable to occupy the thoughts with a subject
not of a devotional or practical nature, it will be
some relief of the omission to select one in which
St. Mary at least will be our example,—the use of
Reason in investigating the doctrines of Faith; a subject, indeed, far fitter for a volume than for the most
extended notice which can here be given to it; but
one which cannot be passed over altogether in silence,
in any attempt at determining the relation of Faith
to Reason.

The overthrow of the wisdom of the world was one of
the earliest, as well as the noblest of the triumphs of the
Church; after the pattern of her Divine Master, who
took His place among the doctors before He preached
His new Kingdom, or opposed Himself to the world's
power.   St. Paul, the learned Pharisee, was the first
fruits of that gifted company, in whom the pride of
science is seen prostrated before the foolishness of
preaching.   From his day to this the Cross has
enlisted under its banner all those great endowments
of mind, which in former times had been expended

on vanities, or dissipated in doubt and speculation. Nor was it long before the schools of heathenism took the alarm, and manifested an unavailing jealousy of the new doctrine, which was robbing them of their most hopeful disciples. They had hitherto taken for granted that the natural home of the Intellect was the Garden or the Porch ; and it reversed their very first principles to be called on to confess, what yet they could not deny, that a Superstition, as they considered it, was attracting to itself all the energy, the keenness, the originality, and the eloquence of the age. But these aggressions upon heathenism were only the beginning of the Church's conquests; in the course of time the whole mind of the world, as I may say, was absorbed into the philosophy of the Cross, as the element in which it lived, and the form upon which it was moulded. And how many centuries did this endure, and what vast ruins still remain of its dominion ! In the capitals of Christendom the high cathedral and the perpetual choir still witness to the victory of Faith over the world's power. To see its triumph over the world's wisdom, we must enter those solemn cemeteries in which are stored the relics and the monuments of ancient Faith —our libraries. Look along their shelves, and every name you read there is, in one sense or other, a trophy set up in record of the victories of Faith. How many long lives, what high aims, what single-minded devotion, what intense contemplation, what fervent prayer, what deep erudition, what untiring

diligence, what toilsome conflicts has it taken to
establish its supremacy! This has been the object
which has given meaning to the life of Saints, and
which is the subject-matter of their history. For
this they have given up the comforts of earth and the
charities of home, and surrendered themselves to an
austere rule, nay, even to confessorship and persecution, if so be they could make some small offering, or
do some casual service, or provide some additional safeguard, towards the great work which was in progress.
This has been the origin of controversies, long and
various, yes, and the occasion of much infirmity, the
test of much hidden perverseness, and the subject of
much bitterness and tumult. The world has been
moved in consequence of it, populations excited,
leagues and alliances formed, kingdoms lost and won :
and even zeal, when excessive, evinced a sense of its
preciousness; nay, even rebellions in some sort did
homage to it, as insurgents imply the actual sovereignty of the power which they are assailing. Meanwhile the work went on, and at length a large fabric
of divinity was reared, irregular in its structure, and
diverse in its style, as beseemed the slow growth of
centuries; nay, anomalous in its details, from the
peculiarities of individuals, or the interference of
strangers, but still, on the whole, the development of
an idea, and like itself, and unlike anything else, its
most widely-separated parts having relations with each
other, and betokening a common origin.

Let us quit this survey of the general system, and

descend to the history of the formation of any Catholic dogma. What a remarkable sight it is, as
almost all unprejudiced persons will admit, to trace
the course of the controversy, from its first disorders
to its exact and determinate issue. Full of deep
interest, to see how the great idea takes hold of a
thousand minds by its living force, and will not be
ruled or stinted, but is " like a burning fire," as the
Prophet speaks, " shut up" within them, till they
are " weary of forbearing, and cannot stay," and
grows in them, and at length is born through them,
perhaps in a long course of years, and even successive
generations; so that the doctrine may rather be said to
employ the minds of Christians, than to occupy them.
Wonderful it is to see with what effort, hesitation,
suspense, interruption,—with how many swayings to
the right and to the left,—how many reverses, yet
with what certainty of advance, with what precision in its march, and with what ultimate completeness, it has been evolved; till the whole truth "self-
balanced on its centre hung," part answering to part,
one, absolute, integral, indissoluble, while the world
lasts! Wonderful, to see how heresy has but thrown
that idea into fresh forms, and drawn out from it
farther developments, with an exuberance which
exceeded all questioning, and a harmony which baffled all criticism, like Him, its Divine Author, who,
when put on trial by the Evil One, was but fortified
by the assault, and is ever justified in His sayings,
and overcomes when He is judged.

And this world of thought is the expansion of a
few words, uttered, as if casually, by the fishermen
of Galilee.   Here is another topic which belongs
more especially to that part of the subject to which
I propose to confine myself.   Reason has not only
submitted, it has ministered to Faith ; it has illustrated its documents ; it has raised illiterate peasants
into philosophers and divines; it has elicited a meaning from their words which their immediate hearers
little suspected.   Stranger surely is it that St. John
should be a theologian, than that St. Peter should
be a prince.   This is a phenomenon proper to the
Gospel, and a note of divinity.   Its half sentences,
its overflowings of language, admit of development[1] ;

[1] " Practical Christianity, or that faith and behaviour which
render a man a Christian, is a plain and obvious thing; like
the common rules of conduct, with respect to our ordinary temporal affairs.   The more distinct and particular knowledge of
those things, the study of which the Apostle calls ' going on unto
perfection,' and of the prophetic parts of Revelation, like many
parts of natural and even civil knowledge, may require very
exact thought and careful consideration.   The hindrances, too,
of natural and of supernatural light and knowledge, have been of
the same kind.   And as it is owned the whole scheme of Scripture
is not yet understood ; so, if it even comes to be understood, before ' the restitution of all things,' and without miraculous interposition, it must be in the same way as natural knowledge is come
at,—by the continuance and progress of learning and of liberty, and
by particular persons attending to, comparing, and pursuing, intimations scattered up and down it, which are overlooked and disre-
garded by the generality of the world : for this is the way in
which all improvements are made ; by thoughtful men's tracing

they have a life in them which shows itself in progress; a truth, which has the token of consistency; a reality, which is fruitful in resources; a depth, which extends into mystery: for they are representations of what is real and has a definite location, and necessary bearings, and a meaning in the great system of things, and a harmony in what it is, and a compatibility in what it involves. What form of Paganism can furnish a parallel? What philosopher has left his words to posterity as a talent which could be put to usury, as a mine which could be wrought? Here, too, is the badge of heresy; its dogmas are unfruitful; it has no theology; so far forth as it is heresy, it has none. Deduct its remnant of Catholic theology, and what remains? Polemics, explanations,

out obscure hints, as it were, dropped us by nature accidentally, or which seem to come into our minds by chance. Nor is it at all incredible, that a book, which has been so long in the possession of mankind, should contain many truths as yet undiscovered; for all the same phenomena, and the same faculties of investigation, from which such great discoveries in natural knowledge have been made in the present and last age, were equally in the possession of mankind several thousand years before. And possibly it might be intended, that events, as they come to pass, should open and ascertain the meaning of several parts of Scripture."—*Butler's Analogy*, part 2, ch. 3.

This view of Butler's differs from the remark in the text so far as this, that Butler is speaking of the *discovery* of *new* truths in passages of Scripture, and the text speaks of a *further insight* into the *primitive* and *received* sense of Scripture passages, gained by meditating upon them, and bringing out their one idea more completely.

protests. It turns to Biblical Criticism, or to the Evidences of Religion, for want of a province. Its formulæ end in themselves, without development, because they are words; they are barren, because they are dead. If they had life, they would increase and multiply; or, if they live, and bear fruit, it is but as " sin, when it is finished, bringeth forth death." It develops into dissolution; but it creates nothing, it tends to no system, its resultant dogma is but the denial of all dogmas, any theology, under the Gospel. No wonder it denies what it cannot attain.

Heresy denies to the Church what is wanting in itself. Here, then, we are brought to the subject to which I wish to give attention. It need not surely formally be proved that this disparagement of doctrinal statements, and in particular of those relating to the Holy Trinity and the Incarnation, is especially prevalent in our times. There is a suspicion widely abroad,—felt, too, perhaps, by many who are unwilling to confess it,—that the development of ideas and formation of dogmas is a mere abuse of Reason, which, when it attempted such sacred subjects, went beyond its powers, and could do nothing more than multiply words without meaning, and deductions which come to nothing. The conclusion follows, that such an attempt does but lead to mischievous controversy, from the discordance of doctrinal opinions, which is its immediate consequence; that there is, in truth, no necessary or proper connexion between inward religious belief and scientific expositions; and that charity, as well as good sense, is best consulted by reducing creeds to the number of private opinions, which, if individuals will hold for themselves, at least they have no right to impose upon others.

It is my purpose, then, in what follows, to investigate the connexion between Faith and Dogmatic Confession, as far as relates to the sacred doctrines, which were just now mentioned, and to show the office of the Reason in reference to it : and, in doing so, I shall make as little allusion as may be to erroneous views on the subject, which have been mentioned only for the sake of perspicuity ; following rather the course which the discussion may take, and pursuing those issues on which it naturally opens. Nor am I here in any way concerned with the question, who is the legitimate framer and judge of these dogmatic inferences under the Gospel, or if there be any. Whether the Church is infallible, or the individual, or the first ages, or none of these, is not the point here, but the theory of developments itself.

Theological dogmas are propositions expressive of the judgments which the mind forms, or the impressions which it receives, of Revealed Truth. Revelation sets before it certain supernatural facts and actions, beings and principles ; these make a certain impression or image upon it ; and this impression spontaneously, or even necessarily, becomes the subject of reflection on the part of the mind itself, which proceeds to investigate it, and to draw it forth in suc-

cessive and distinct sentences. Thus the Catholic
doctrine of Original Sin, or of Sin after Baptism, or
of the Eucharist, or of Justification, is but the expression of the inward belief of Catholics on these several
points, formed upon an analysis of that belief[2]. Such,
too, are the high doctrines with which I am especially
concerned.

Now, here I observe, first of all, that, naturally as
the inward idea of divine truth, such as has been
described, passes into explicit form by the activity
of our reflective powers, still such an actual delineation is not essential to its genuineness and perfection.
A peasant may have such a true impression, yet be
unable to give any intelligible account of it, as will
easily be understood. But what is remarkable at
first sight is this, that there is good reason for saying
that the impression made upon the mind need not
even be recognized by the parties possessing it. It
is no proof that persons are not possessed, because
they are not conscious, of an idea. Nothing is of
more frequent occurrence, whether in things sensible
or intellectual, than the existence of such unperceived
impressions. What do we mean when we say, that
certain persons do not know themselves, but that
they are ruled by views, feelings, prejudices, objects

[2] The controversy between our own Church and the Church of
Rome lies, it is presumed, *in the matter of fact*, whether such
and such developments are true, (e. g. Purgatory a true development of the doctrine of sin after baptism,) not in the *principle*
of development itself.

which they do not recognize? How common is it
to be exhilarated or depressed, we do not recollect
why, though we are aware that something has been
told us, or has happened, good or bad, which accounts for our feeling, could we recal it! What is
memory itself, but a vast magazine of such dormant,
but present and excitable ideas? Or consider, when
persons would trace the history of their own opinions
in past years, how baffled they are in the attempt to
fix the date of this or that conviction, their system
of thought having been all the while in continual,
gradual, tranquil expansion ; so that it were as easy
to follow the growth of the fruit of the earth, " first
the blade, then the ear, after that the full corn in
the ear," as to chronicle changes, which involved no
abrupt revolution, or reaction, or fickleness of mind,
but have been the birth of an idea, the development, in
explicit form, of what was already latent within it. Or,
again, critical disquisitions are often written upon the
idea which this or that poet might have in his mind
in certain of his compositions and characters; and
we call such analysis the philosophy of poetry, not
implying thereby of necessity that the author wrote
upon a theory in his actual delineation, or knew
what he was doing ; but that, in matter of fact, he
was possessed, ruled, guided by an unconscious idea.
Moreover, it is a question whether that strange and
painful feeling of unreality, which religious men experience from time to time, when nothing seems
true, or good, or right, or profitable, when Faith

seems a name, and duty a mockery, and all endeavours to do right, absurd and hopeless, and all things forlorn and dreary, as if religion were wiped out from the world, may not be the direct effect of the temporary obscuration of some master vision, which unconsciously supplies the mind with spiritual life and peace.

Or, to take another class of instances which are to the point so far as this, that at least they are real impressions, even though they be not influential. How common is what is called vacant vision, when objects meet the eye, without any effort of the judgment to measure or locate them; and that absence of mind, which recollects minutes afterwards the occurrence of some sound, the striking of the hour, or the question of a companion, which passed unheeded at the time it took place! How, again, happens it, in dreams, that we suddenly pass from one state of feeling, or one assemblage of circumstances to another, without any surprise at the incongruity, except that, while we are impressed first in this way, then in that, we take no active cognizance of the impression? And this, perhaps, is the life of inferior animals, a sort of continuous dream, impressions without reflections; such, too, seems to be the first life of infants; nay, in heaven itself, such may be the high existence of some exalted orders of blessed spirits, as the Seraphim, who are said to be, not knowledge, but all love.

Now, it is important to insist on this circumstance,

because it suggests the reality and permanence of inward knowledge, as distinct from explicit confession. The absence, or partial absence, or incompleteness of dogmatic statements, is no proof of the absence of impressions or implicit judgments, in the mind of the Church. Even centuries might pass without the formal expression of a truth, which had been all along the secret life of millions of faithful souls. Thus, not till the thirteenth century was there any direct and distinct avowal, on the part of the Church, of the numerical Unity of the Divine Nature, which the language of some of the principal Greek fathers, *prima facie*, though not really, denies. Again, the doctrine of the Double Procession was no Catholic dogma in the first ages, though it was more or less clearly stated by individual Fathers; yet, if it is now to be received, as surely it must be, as part of the Creed, it was really held everywhere from the beginning, and therefore, in a measure, held as a mere religious impression, and perhaps an unconscious one.

But, further, if the ideas may be latent in the Christian mind, by which it is animated and framed, it is less wonderful that they should be difficult to elicit and define; and of this difficulty we have abundant proof in the history whether of the Church, or of individuals. Surely it is not at all wonderful, that, when individuals attempt to analyze their own belief, they should find the task arduous in the extreme, if not altogether beyond them; or, again, a work of many years; or, again, that they should shrink from the true developments, if offered to them, as foreign to their thoughts. This may be illustrated in a variety of ways.

It will often happen, perhaps from the nature of things, that it is impossible to master and express an idea in a short space of time. As to individuals, sometimes they find they cannot do so at all; at length, perhaps, they recognize, in some writer they meet, with the very account of their own thoughts, which they desiderate; and then they say, that " here is what they have felt all along, and wanted to say, but could not," or " what they have ever maintained, only better expressed." Again, how many men are burdened with an idea, which haunts them through a great part of their lives, and of which only at length, with great trouble, do they dispossess themselves! I suppose most of us have felt at times the irritation, and that for a long period, of thoughts and views which we felt, and felt to be true, only dimly showing themselves, or flitting before us; which at length we understood must not be forced, but must have their way, and would, if it were so ordered, come to light in their own time. The life of some men, and those not the least eminent among divines and philosophers, has centred in the development of one idea; nay, perhaps, has been too short for the process. Again, how frequently it happens, that, on first hearing a doctrine propounded, a man hesitates, first acknowledges, then disowns it ; then says that he has always held it, but finds fault with the mode in which it is presented to him, accusing it of paradox or over-refinement; that is, he cannot at the moment analyze his own opinions, and does not know whether he holds the doctrine or not, from the difficulty of mastering his thoughts.

Another characteristic, as I have said, of dogmatic statements, is the difficulty of recognizing them, even when attained, as the true representation of our meaning. This happens for many reasons; sometimes, from the faint hold we have of the impression itself, whether its nature be good or bad, so that we shrink from principles in substance, which we acknowledge in influence. Many a man, for instance, is acting on utilitarian principles, who is shocked at them in set treatises, and disowns them. Again, in sacred subjects, the very circumstance that a dogma professes to be a direct contemplation, and, if so be, a definition of what is infinite and eternal, is painful to serious minds. Moreover, from the hypothesis, it is the representation of an idea in a medium not native to it, not as originally conceived, but, as it were, in projection; no wonder, then, that, though there be an intimate correspondence, part by part, between the impression and the dogma, yet there should be an harshness in the outline of the latter; as, for instance, a want of harmonious proportion; and yet this is unavoidable, from the infirmities of our intellectual powers.

Again, another similar peculiarity in developments in general, is the great remoteness of the separate results of a common idea, between which at first sight there seems to be no connexion.   Thus it often happens that party spirit is imputed to persons who merely agree with one another in certain points of opinion and conduct, which are thought too minute, divergent, and various, in the large field of religious doctrine and discipline, to proceed from any but an external influence and a positive rule; whereas an insight into the wonderfully expansive power and penetrating virtue of theological or philosophical ideas would have shown, that what is apparently arbitrary in rival or in kindred schools of thought, is after all rigidly determined by the original hypothesis.   The remark has been made, for instance, that rarely have persons maintained the sleep of the soul before the Resurrection, without falling into more grievous errors; again, those who deny the Lutheran doctrine of Justification, commonly have tendencies towards a ceremonial religion; again, it is a serious fact that Protestantism has at various times unexpectedly developed into an allowance or vindication of polygamy; and heretics in general, however opposed in tenets, are found to have an inexplicable sympathy for each other, and never wake up from their ordinary torpor, but to exchange courtesies and meditate coalitions.   One other remark is in point here, and relates to the length to which statements run, though before the attempt we fancied our idea could be expressed in one or two sentences. Explanations grow under our hands, in spite of our

effort at compression. Such, too, is the contrast between conversing and corresponding. We speak our
meaning with little trouble ; our voice, manner, and
half words completing it for us ; but in writing, when
details must be drawn out, and misapprehensions anticipated, we seem never to be rid of the responsibility of our task. This being the case, it is surprising
that the Creeds are so short, not surprising that they
need a comment.

The difficulty, then, and hazard of developing doctrines implicitly received, must be fully allowed ; and
this is often made a ground for inferring that they
have no proper developments at all ; that there is no
natural connexion between certain dogmas and certain impressions ; and that theological science is a
matter of time, and place, and accident, though inward
belief is ever and everywhere one and the same. But
surely the instinct of every Christian revolts from such
a position ; for the very first impulse of his faith is to
try to express itself about the great sight which is
vouchsafed to it ; and this seems to argue that a
science there is, whether that faith is equal to its
discovery or no. And, indeed, what science is open
to every chance inquirer ? which is not recondite in
its principles ? which requires not special gifts of mind
for its just formation ? All subject-matters admit of
true theories and false, and the false are no prejudice
to the true. Why should this class of ideas be different from all other ? Principles of philosophy,
physics, ethics, politics, taste, admit both of implicit

reception and explicit statement; why should not
the ideas, which are the secret life of the Christian,
be recognized also as fixed and definite in themselves, and as capable of scientific analysis? Why
should not there be that real connexion between
science and its subject-matter in religion, which exists
in other departments of thought? No one would
deny that the philosophy of Zeno or Pythagoras was
the exponent of a certain mode of viewing things;
or would affirm that Platonist and Epicurean acted
on one and the same idea of nature, life, and duty,
and meant the same thing, though they verbally dif-
fered, all because a Plato or an Epicurus was needed
to detect the abstruse elements of thought out of
which each philosophy was eventually constructed.
A man surely may be a Peripatetic or an Academic
in his feelings, views, aims, and acts, who never heard
the names. Granting, then, extreme cases, when
individuals who would analyze their views of religion
are thrown entirely upon their own reason, and find
that reason unequal to the task, this will be no argument against a general, natural, and ordinary correspondence between the dogma and the inward idea.
Surely, if Almighty God is ever one and the same,
and is revealed to us as one and the same, the true
inward impression of Him, made on the recipient of
the revelation, must be one and the same; and, since
human nature proceeds upon fixed laws, the statement of that impression must be one and the same,
so that we may as well say that there are two Gods

as two Creeds. And considering the strong feelings and energetic acts and severe sufferings which age after age have been involved in the maintenance of the Catholic dogmas, it is surely a very shallow philosophy to account such maintenance a mere contest about words, and a very abject philosophy to attribute it to mere party spirit, or to personal rivalry, or to ambition, or to covetousness.

Reasonable, however, as is this view of doctrinal developments in general, it cannot be denied that those which relate to the Objects of Faith, of which I am particularly speaking, have a character of their own, and must be considered separately. Let us, then, consider how the case stands, as regards the sacred doctrines of the Trinity and the Incarnation.

The Apostle said to the Athenians, " Whom ye ignorantly worship, Him declare I unto you;" and the mind which is habituated to the thought of God, of Christ, of the Holy Spirit, naturally turns, as I have said, with a devout curiosity to the contemplation of the Object of its adoration, and begins to form statements concerning it before it knows whither, or how far, it will be carried. One proposition necessarily leads to another, and a second to a third; then some limitation is required; and the combination of these opposites occasions some fresh evolutions from the original idea, which indeed can never be said to be entirely exhausted. This process is its development, and results in a series, or rather body of dogmatic statements, till what was an impression on the Imagination has become a system or creed in the Reason.

Now such impressions are obviously individual and complete above other theological ideas, because they are the impressions of Objects. Ideas and their developments are commonly not identical, the development being but the carrying out of the idea into its consequences. Thus the doctrine of Penance may be called a development of the doctrine of Baptism, yet still is a distinct doctrine ; whereas the developments in the doctrines of the Holy Trinity and the Incarnation are mere portions of the original impression, and modes of representing it. As God is one, so the impression which He gives us of Himself is one ; it is not a thing of parts ; it is not a system ; nor is it anything imperfect, and needing a counterpart. It is the vision of an object. When we pray, we pray, not to an assemblage of notions, or to a creed, but to One Individual Being ; and when we speak of Him we speak of a Person, not of a Law or a Manifestation. This being the case, all our attempts to delineate our impression of Him go to bring out one idea, not two or three or four ; not a philosophy, but an individual idea in its separate aspects.

This may be fitly compared to the impressions made on us by the senses. Material objects are real, whole, and individual ; and the impressions which they make on the mind by means of the senses, are of a corresponding nature, complex and manifold in

their relations and bearings, but considered in themselves integral and one. And in like manner the
ideas which we are granted of Divine Objects under
the Gospel, from the nature of the case and because
they are ideas, answer to the Originals so far as this,
that they are whole, indivisible, substantial, and may
be called real, as being images of what is real. Objects which are conveyed to us through the senses,
stand out in our minds, as I may say, with dimensions
and aspects and influences various, and all of these
consistent with one another, and many of them beyond our memory or even knowledge, while we contemplate the objects themselves; thus forcing on us
a persuasion of their reality from the spontaneous
congruity and coincidence of these accompaniments,
as if they could not be creations of our minds, but
were the images of external and independent beings.
This of course will take place in the case of the
sacred ideas which are the objects of our faith. Religious men, according to their measure, have an idea
or vision of the Blessed Trinity in Unity, of the Son
incarnate and of His Presence, not as a number of
qualities, attributes, and actions, not as the subject of
a number of propositions, but as one and individual,
and independent of words, as an impression conveyed
through the senses.

Particular propositions, then, which are used to
express portions of the great idea vouchsafed to us,
can never really be confused with the idea itself, which
all such propositions taken together can but reach, and

cannot exceed.   As definitions are not intended to
go beyond their subject, but to be adequate to it, so
the dogmatic statements used in our confessions of
the Divine Nature, however multiplied, cannot say
more than is implied in the original idea, considered
in its completeness, without the risk of heresy.
Creeds and dogmas live in the one idea which they
are designed to express, and which alone is substan-
tive; and are necessary only because the human mind
cannot reflect upon it, except piecemeal, cannot use
it in its oneness and entireness, or without resolving
it into a series of aspects and relations.   And in
matter of fact these expressions are never equivalent
to it; we are able, indeed, to define the creations of
our own minds, for they are what we make them and
nothing else; but it were as easy to create what is
real as to define it; and thus the Catholic dogmas
are, after all, but symbols of a Divine fact, which,
far from being compassed by those very propositions,
would not be exhausted, not fathomed, by a thousand.

Now of such sacred ideas and their attendant expressions, I observe:—

1. First, that an impression of this intimate kind
seems to be what Scripture means by "knowledge."
"This is life eternal," says our Saviour, "that they
might know Thee the only True God, and Jesus
Christ whom Thou hast sent."   In like manner St.
Paul speaks of willingly losing all things, "for the
excellency of the knowledge of Christ Jesus;" and
St. Peter of "the knowledge of Him who hath

called us to glory and virtue[3]." Knowledge is
the possession of those living ideas of sacred things,
from which alone change of heart or conduct can
proceed. This awful vision is what Scripture seems
to designate by the phrases "Christ in us," "Christ
dwelling in us by faith," "Christ formed in us,"
and "Christ manifesting Himself unto us." And
though it is faint and doubtful in some minds, and
distinct in others, as some remote object in the twilight or in the day, this arises from the circumstances
of the particular mind, and does not interfere with
the perfection of the gift itself.

2. This leads me next, however, to observe, that
these religious impressions differ from those of material objects, in the mode in which they are made.
The senses are direct, immediate, and ordinary informants, and act spontaneously without any will or
effort on our part; but no such faculties have been
given us, as far as we know, for realizing the Objects
of Faith. It is true that inspiration may be a gift
of this kind to those who have been favoured with
it; nor would it be safe to deny to the illuminating
grace of Baptism a power, at least of putting the
mind into a capacity for receiving impressions; but
the former of these is not ordinary, and both are
supernatural. The secondary and intelligible means
by which we receive the impression of Divine Verities, are such as the habitual and devout perusal of

---

[3] John xvii. 3.   Phil. iii. 8.   2 Pet. i. 3.

2

Scripture, which gradually acts upon the mind ; again, the gradual influence of intercourse with those who are in themselves in possession of the sacred ideas ; again, the study of Dogmatic Theology, which is our present subject ; again, a continual round of devotion ; or again, sometimes, in minds both fitly disposed and apprehensive, the almost instantaneous operation of a keen faith. This obvious distinction follows between sensible and religious ideas, that we put the latter into language in order to fix, teach, and transmit them, but not the former. No one defines a material object by way of conveying to us what we know so much better by the senses, but we form creeds as a chief mode of perpetuating the impression.

3. Further, I observe, that though the Christian mind reasons out a series of dogmatic statements, one from another, this it has ever done, and always must do, not from those statements taken in themselves, as logical propositions, but as illustrated and (as I may say) inhabited by that sacred impression which is prior to them, which acts as a regulating principle, ever present, upon the reasoning, and without which no one has any warrant to reason at all. Such sentences as "the Word was God" or "the Only-begotten Son who is in the bosom of the Father," or "the Word was made flesh," or "the Holy Ghost which proceedeth from the Father," are not a mere letter which we may handle by the rules of art at our own will, but august tokens of most simple, ineffable, adorable facts, embraced, enshrined, accord-

ing to its measure, in the believing mind. For though the development of an idea is a deduction of proposition from proposition, these propositions are ever formed in and round the idea itself (so to speak), and are in fact one and all only aspects of it. Moreover, this will account both for the mode of arguing from particular texts or single words of Scripture, practised by the early Fathers, and for their fearless decision in practising it; for the great Object of Faith on which they lived both enabled them to appropriate to itself particular passages of Scripture, and became a safeguard against heretical deductions from them. Also, it will account for the charge of weak reasoning, commonly brought against those Fathers; for never do we seem so illogical to others, as when we are arguing under the continual influence of impressions to which they are insensible.

4. Again, it must of course be remembered, as I have just implied, though as being an historical matter it hardly concerns us here, that Revelation itself has provided in Scripture the main outlines and also large details of the dogmatic system. Inspiration has superseded the exercise of human Reason in great measure, and left it but the comparatively easy task of finishing the sacred work. The question, indeed, at first sight occurs, why such inspired statements are not enough without further developments; but in truth, when Reason has once been put on the investigation, it cannot stop till it has finished it; one dogma creates another, by the same right by

which it was itself created; the Scripture statements are sanctions as well as informants in the inquiry; they begin and they do not exhaust.

5. Scripture, I say, begins a series of developments which it does not finish; that is to say, in other words, it is a mistake to look for every separate proposition of the Catholic doctrine in Scripture. This is plain from what has gone before. For instance, the Athanasian Creed professes to lay down the right faith, which we must hold on its most sacred subjects, in order to be saved. This must mean that there is one view concerning the Holy Trinity, or concerning the Incarnation, which is true, and distinct from all others; one definite, consistent, entire view, which cannot be mistaken, not contained in any certain number of propositions, but held as a view by the believing mind, and not held, but denied, by Arians, Sabellians, Tritheists, Nestorians, Monophysites, Socinians, and other heretics. That idea is not enlarged, if propositions are added, nor impaired if they are withdrawn: if they are added, this is with a view of conveying that one integral view, not of amplifying it. That view does not depend on such propositions; it does not consist in them; they are but specimens and indications of it. And they may be multiplied without limit. They are necessary, but not needful to it, being but portions or aspects of that previous impression which has now come under the cognizance of Reason and the terminology of science. The question, then, is not whether this or that pro-

position of the Catholic doctrine is *in terminis* in Scripture, unless we would be slaves to the letter, but whether that one view of the Mystery, of which they are all the exponents, be not there; a view which would be some other view, and not itself, if any one of such propositions, if any one of a number of similar propositions, were not true. Those propositions imply each other, as being parts of one whole; so that to deny one is to deny all, and to invalidate one is to deface and destroy the view itself. One thing alone has to be proved from Scripture, the Catholic idea, and in it they all are included. To object, then, to the number of propositions, upon which an anathema is placed, were altogether to mistake their use; for their multiplication is not intended to enforce many things, but to express one,—to form within us that one impression concerning Almighty God, as the ruling principle of our minds, and that, whether we can fully recognize our own possession of it or no. And surely it is no paradox to say that such ruling ideas may exert a most powerful influence, at least in their various aspects, on our moral character, and on the whole man : as no one would deny in the case of belief or disbelief of a Supreme Being.

6. And here we see the ordinary mistake of doctrinal innovators, viz. to go away with this or that proposition of the Creed, instead of embracing the one idea which all of them together are meant to convey; it being almost a definition of heresy, that it fastens on some one statement as if the whole

truth, to the denial of all others, and as the basis of
a new faith; erring rather in what it rejects, than in
what it maintains: though, in truth, if the mind deliberately rejects any portion of the doctrine, this is a
proof that it does not really hold even that very
statement for the sake of which it rejects the others.
Realizing is the very life of true developments; it
is peculiar to the Church, and the justification of its
definitions.

Enough has now been said on the distinction, yet
connexion, between the implicit knowledge and the
explicit confession of the Divine Objects of Faith, as
they are revealed to us under the Gospel. An objection, however, remains, which cannot be satisfactorily treated in a few words. And what is worse
than prolixity, the discussion may bear with it some
appearance of unnecessary or even wanton refinement;
unless, indeed, it is thrown into the form of controversy, a worse evil. Let it suffice to say, that my
wish is, not to discover difficulties in any subject, but
to solve them.

It may be asked, then, whether the mistake of
words and names for things is not incurred by ortho-
dox as well as heretics, in dogmatizing at all about
the " secret things which belong unto the Lord our
God," inasmuch as the idea of a supernatural object
must itself be supernatural, and since no such ideas
are claimed by ordinary Christians, no knowledge of
Divine Verities is possible to them. How should any

thing of this world convey ideas which are beyond and above this world? How can teaching and intercourse, how can human words, how can earthly images, convey to the mind an idea of the Invisible? They cannot rise above themselves. They can suggest no idea but what is resolvable into ideas natural and earthly. The words " Person," " Substance," " Consubstantial," " Generation," " Procession," " Incarnation," " Taking of the manhood into God," and the like, have either a very abject and human meaning, or none at all. In other words, there is no such inward view of these doctrines, distinct from the dogmatic language used to express them, as was just now supposed. The metaphors by which they are signified are not mere symbols of ideas which exist independently of them, but their meaning is coincident and identical with the ideas. When, indeed, we have knowledge of a thing from other sources, then the metaphors we may apply to it are but accidental appendages to that knowledge; whereas our ideas of Divine things are just co-extensive with the figures by which we express them, neither more nor less, and without them are not; and when we draw inferences from those figures, we are not illustrating one existing idea, but drawing mere logical inferences. We speak, indeed, of material objects freely, because our senses reveal them to us apart from our words; but as to these ideas about heavenly things, we learn them from words, yet (it seems) we are to say what we conceive of them without words, as if words could convey

what they do not contain.   It follows that our
anathemas, our controversies, our struggles, our sufferings, are merely about the poor ideas conveyed to
us in certain figures of speech.

Some obvious remarks suggest themselves in
answer to this representation.   First, it is difficult to
determine what divine grace may not do for us, if
not in immediately implanting new ideas, yet in re-
fining and elevating those which we gain through
natural informants.   If, as we all acknowledge, grace
renews our moral feelings, yet through outward means,
if it opens upon us new ideas about virtue and goodness and heroism and heavenly peace, it does not
appear why, in a certain sense, it may not impart
ideas concerning the nature of God.   Again, the
various terms and figures which are used in the doctrine of the Holy Trinity or of the Incarnation, surely
may by their combination create ideas which will be
altogether new, though they are still of an earthly
character.   And further, when it is said that such
figures convey no knowledge of the Divine Nature
itself, but only of those figures, it should be considered whether our senses can be proved to suggest
any real idea of matter.   All that we know, strictly
speaking, is the existence of the impressions they
make on us; and yet we scruple not to speak as if
they conveyed to us the knowledge of material substances.   Let, then, the Catholic dogmas, as such, be
freely admitted to convey no true idea of Almighty
God, but only an earthly one, gained from earthly

figures, provided it be allowed, on the other hand, that the senses do not convey to us any true idea of matter, but only an idea commensurate with sensible impressions.

Nor is there any reason why this should not be fully granted. Still there may be a certain correspondence between the idea, though earthly, and its heavenly archetype, such, that that idea belongs to the archetype, in a sense in which no other earthly idea belongs to it, as being the nearest approach to it which our present state allows. Indeed Scripture itself intimates the earthly nature of our present ideas of Sacred Objects, when it speaks of our now " seeing in a glass *darkly*, ἐν αἰνίγματι, but then face to face ;" and it has ever been the doctrine of divines that the beatific vision, or true sight of Almighty God, is reserved for the world to come. Meanwhile we are allowed such an approximation to the truth as earthly images and figures may supply to us.

It must not be supposed that this is the only case in which we are obliged to receive information needful to us, through the medium of our existing ideas, and consequently with but a vague apprehension of its subject-matter. Children, who are made our pattern in Scripture, are taught, by an accommodation, on the part of their teachers, to their immature faculties and their scanty vocabulary. To answer their questions in the language which we should use towards grown men, would be simply to mislead them, if they could construe it at all. We must dispense

and "divide" the word of truth, if we would not
have it changed, as far as they are concerned, into a
word of falsehood; for what is short of truth in the
letter may be to them the most perfect truth, that
is, the nearest approach to truth, compatible with
their condition[4]. The case is the same as regards
those who have any natural defect or deprivation,
which cuts them off from the circle of ideas common
to mankind in general. To speak to a blind man of
light and colours, in terms proper to those phenomena,
would be to mock him; we must use other media of
information accommodated to his circumstances, according to the well-known instance in which his own
account of scarlet was to liken it to the sound of a
trumpet. And so again, as regards savages, or the
ignorant, or weak, or narrow-minded, our representations and arguments must take a certain form, if they
are to gain admission into their minds at all, and to
reach them. Again, what impediments do the diversities of language place in the way of communicating

[4] Hence it is not more than an hyperbole to say that, in certain cases, a lie is the nearest approach to truth. This seems the
meaning, for instance, of St. Clement, when he says, "He [the
Christian] both thinks and speaks the truth, unless when at any
time, in the way of treatment, as a physician towards his patients,
so for the welfare of the sick he will be false, or will tell a falsehood, as the Sophists speak. For instance, the noble Apostle
circumcised Timothy, yet cried out and wrote, Circumcision
availed not," &c.—Strom. vii. 9. We are told that "God is not
the son of man, that He should repent;" yet "it repented the
Lord that He had made man."

ideas! Language is a sort of analysis of thought; and, since ideas are infinite, and infinitely combined, and infinitely modified, whereas language is a method definite and limited, and confined to an arbitrary selection of a certain number of these innumerable materials, it were idle to expect that the courses of thought marked out in one language should, except in their great outlines and main centres, correspond to those of another. Multitudes of ideas expressed in the one do not even enter into the other, and can only be conveyed by some economy or accommodation, by circumlocutions, phrases, limiting words, figures, or some bold and happy expedient. And sometimes, from the continual demand, foreign words become naturalized. Again, the difficulty is extreme, as all persons know, of leading certain individuals (to use a familiar phrase) to understand one another; their habits of thought turning apparently on points of mutual repulsion. Now this is always in a measure traceable to moral diversities between the parties; still, in many cases, it arises mainly from difference in the principle on which they have divided and subdivided that world of ideas, which comes before them both. They seem ever to be dodging each other, and need a common measure or economy to mediate between them.

Fables, again, are economies or accommodations, being truths and principles cast into that form in which they will be most vividly recognized; as in the well-known instance attributed to Menenius

Agrippa. Again, mythical representations, at least in their better form, may be considered facts or narratives, untrue, but like the truth, intended to bring out the action of some principle, point of character, and the like. For instance, the tradition that St. Ignatius was the child whom our Lord took in His arms, may be unfounded ; but it realizes to us His special relation to Christ and His Apostles, with a keenness peculiar to itself. The same remark may be made upon certain narratives of martyrdoms, or of the details of such narratives, or of certain alleged miracles, or heroic acts, or speeches, all which are the spontaneous produce of religious feeling under imperfect knowledge. If the alleged facts did not occur, they ought to have occurred (if I may so speak) ; they are such as might have occurred, and would have occurred, under circumstances ; and they belong to the parties to whom they are attributed, potentially, if not actually ; or the like of them did occur ; or occur to others similarly circumstanced, though not to those very persons. Many a theory or view of things, on which an institution is founded, or a party held together, is of the same kind. Many an argument, used by zealous and earnest men, has this economical character, being not the very ground on which they act, (for they continue in the same course, though it be refuted,) yet, in a certain sense, a representation of it, a proximate description of their feelings in the shape of argument, on which they can rest, to which they can recur when perplexed, and appeal when

2

questioned. Now, in this reference to accommodation or economy in human affairs, I do not meddle
with the question of casuistry, viz. which of such
artifices, as they may be called, are innocent, or where
the line is to be drawn. That some are immoral,
common sense tells us; but it is enough for my purpose, if some are necessary, as the same common
sense will allow; and then the very necessity of the
use will account for the abuse and perversion.

Even among men, then, constituted, as they are,
alike, various distinct instruments, keys, or *calculi* of
thought, obtain, on which their ideas and arguments
shape themselves respectively, and which we must
use, if we would reach them. The cogitative method,
as it may be called, of one man is notoriously very
different from that of another; of the lawyer from
that of the soldier, of the rich from that of the poor.
The territory of thought is portioned out in a hundred different ways. Abstractions, generalizations,
definitions, propositions, all are framed on distinct
standards; and if this is found in matters of this
world between man and man, surely much more
must it exist between the ideas of men, and the
thoughts, ways, and works of God.

One of the obvious instances of this contrariety is
seen in the classifications we make of the subjects of
the animal or vegetable kingdoms. Here a very intelligible order has been observed by the Creator
Himself; still one of which we have not, after all,
the key. We are obliged to frame one of our own;

and when we apply it, we find that it will not exactly answer the Divine idea of arrangement, as it discovers itself to us; there being phenomena which we cannot locate, or which, upon our system of division, are anomalies in the general harmony of the Creation.

Mathematical science will afford us a more extended illustration of this distinction between supernatural and eternal laws, and our attempts to represent them, that is, our economies.   Various methods or *calculi* have been adopted to embody those immutable principles and dispositions of which the science treats, which are really independent of any, yet cannot be contemplated or pursued without one or other of them.   The first of these instruments of investigation employs the medium of extension; the second, that of number; the third, that of motion; the fourth proceeds on a more subtle hypothesis, that of increase. These methods are very distinct from each other, at least the geometrical and the differential; yet they are, one and all, analyses, more or less perfect, of those same necessary truths, for which we have not a name, of which we have no idea, except in the terms of such economical representations. They are all developments of one and the same range of ideas; they are all instruments of discovery as to those ideas.   They stand for real things, and we can reason with them, though they be but symbols, as if they were the things themselves, for which they stand.   Yet none of them carries out the lines of truth to their limits: first one stops in the analysis, then another; like some calculating tables, which answer for a thousand times, and miss in the thousand and first. While they answer, we can use them just as if they were the realities which they represent, and without thinking of those realities; but at length our instrument of discovery issues in some great impossibility or contradiction, or, what we call in religion, a mystery. It has run its length; and by its failure shows that all along it has been but an expedient for practical purposes, not a true analysis or adequate image of those recondite laws which are investigated by means of it. It has never fathomed their depth, because it now fails to measure their course. At the same time, no one, because it cannot do everything, would refuse to use it within the range in which it will act; no one would say that it was a system of empty symbols, though it be but a shadow of the unseen. Though we use it with caution, still we use it, as being the nearest approximation to the truth which our condition admits.

Let us take another instance, of an outward and earthly form, or economy, under which great wonders unknown seem to be typified; I mean musical sounds, as they are exhibited most perfectly in instrumental harmony. There are seven notes in the scale; make them fourteen; yet what a slender outfit for so vast an enterprise! What science brings so much out of so little? Out of what poor elements does some great master in it create his new world! Shall we say that all this exuberant inventiveness is a mere inge-

nuity or trick of art, like some game or fashion of
the day, without reality, without meaning? We
may do so; and then, perhaps, we shall also account
the science of theology to be a matter of words; yet,
as there is a divinity in the theology of the Church,
which those who feel cannot communicate, so is there
also in the wonderful creation of sublimity and beauty
of which I am speaking. To many men the very names
which the science employs are utterly incomprehensible. To speak of an idea or a subject seems to be
fanciful or trifling, and of the views which it opens
upon us to be childish extravagance; yet is it possible
that that inexhaustible evolution and disposition of
notes, so rich yet so simple, so intricate yet so regulated, so various yet so majestic, should be a mere
sound, which is gone and perishes? Can it be that
those mysterious stirrings of heart, and keen emotions,
and strange yearnings after we know not what, and
awful impressions from we know not whence, should
be wrought in us by what is unsubstantial, and comes
and goes, and begins and ends in itself? It is not so;
it cannot be. No; they have escaped from some
higher sphere; they are the outpourings of eternal harmony in the medium of created sound; they are echoes
from our Home; they are the voice of Angels, or the
Magnificat of Saints, or the living laws of Divine
Governance, or the Divine Attributes; something
are they besides themselves, which we cannot compass, which we cannot utter,—though mortal man,

and he perhaps not otherwise distinguished above his fellows, has the gift of eliciting them.

So much on the subject of musical sound; but what if the whole series of impressions, made on us through the senses, be, as I have already hinted, but a Divine economy suited to our need, and the token of realities distinct from them, and such as might be revealed to us, nay, more perfectly, by other senses, as different from our existing ones as they from each other? What if the properties of matter, as we conceive of them, are merely relative to us, so that facts and events, which seem impossible when stated concerning it in terms of those impressions, are only impossible in those terms, not in themselves, —impossible only because of the imperfection of the idea, which, in consequence of those impressions, we have conceived of material substances? If so, it would follow that the laws of physics, as we consider them, are themselves but generalizations of economical exhibitions, inferences from figure and shadow, and not more real than the phenomena from which they are drawn. Scripture, for instance, says that the sun moves and the earth is stationary; and science, that the earth moves, and the sun is comparatively at rest. How can we determine which of these opposite statements is the very truth, till we know what motion is? If our idea of motion be but an accidental result of our present senses, neither proposition is true, and both are true; neither true philosophically, both true for certain practical purposes in the system in which they are respectively found; and physical science will have no better meaning when it says that the earth moves, than plane astronomy when it says that the earth is still.

And should any one fear lest thoughts such as these should tend to a dreary and hopeless scepticism, let him take into account the Being and Providence of God, the Merciful and True; and he will at once be relieved of his anxiety. All is dreary till we believe, what our hearts tell us, that we are subjects of His Governance; nothing is dreary, all inspires hope and trust, directly we understand that we are under His hand, and that whatever comes to us is from Him, as a method of discipline and guidance. What is it to us whether the knowledge He gives us be greater or less, if it be He who gives it? What is it to us whether it be exact or vague, if He bids us trust it? What have we to care whether we are or are not given to divide substance from shadow, if He is training us heavenwards by means of either? Why should we vex ourselves to find whether our deductions are philosophical or no, provided they are religious? If our senses supply the media by which we are put on trial, by which we are all brought together, and hold intercourse with each other, and are disciplined and are taught, and enabled to benefit others, it is enough. We have an instinct within us, impelling us, we have external necessity forcing us, to trust our senses, and we may leave the question of their substantial truth for another world, " till the day break, and the shadows flee away." And what is true of reliance on our senses, is true of all the information which it has pleased God to vouchsafe to us, whether in nature or in grace.

Instances, then, such as these, will be found both to sober and to encourage us in our theological studies,—to impress us with a profound sense of our ignorance of Divine Verities, when we know most; yet to hinder us from relinquishing their contemplation, though we know so little. On the one hand, it would appear that even the most subtle questions of the schools may have a real meaning, as the most intricate formulæ in analytics; and, since we cannot tell how far our instrument of thought reaches in the process of investigation, and at what point it fails us, no questions may safely be despised. " Whether God was anywhere before creation?" "whether He knows all creatures in Himself?" "whether the blessed see all things possible and future in Him?" " whether relation is the form of the Divine Persons?" " in what sense the Holy Spirit is Divine Love?" these, and a multitude of others, far more minute and remote, are all sacred from their subject.

On the other hand, it must be recollected that not even the Catholic reasonings and conclusions, as contained in Confessions, and most thoroughly received by us, are worthy of the Divine Verities which they represent, but are the truth only in as full a measure as our minds can admit it; the truth as far as they go, and under the conditions of thought which human feebleness imposes. It is true that God is without beginning, if eternity may worthily be considered to imply succession; in every place, if He who is a Spirit can have relations with space. It is right to speak of His Being and Attributes, if He be not rather super-essential; it is true to say that He is wise or power-ful, if we may consider Him as other than the most simple Unity. He is truly Three, if He is truly One; He is truly One, if the idea of Him falls under earthly number. He has a triple Personality, in the sense in which the Infinite can be understood to have Person-ality at all. If we know anything of Him,—if we may speak of Him in any way,—if we may emerge from Atheism or Pantheism into religious faith,—if we would have any saving hope, any life of truth and holiness within us,—this only do we know, with this only confession, we must begin and end our worship—that the Father is the One God, the Son the One God, and the Holy Ghost the One God; and that the Father is not the Son, the Son not the Holy Ghost, and the Holy Ghost not the Father.

The fault, then, which we must guard against in receiving such Divine intimations, is the ambition of being wiser than what is written; of employing the Reason, not in carrying out what is told us, but in impugning it; not in support, but in prejudice of Faith. Brilliant as are such exhibitions of its powers, they bear no fruit. Reason can but ascertain the profound difficulties of our condition, it cannot remove them; it has no work, it makes no beginning, it does but continually fall back, till it is content to be a little child, and to follow where Faith guides it.

What remains, then, but to make our prayer to the Gracious and Merciful God, the Father of Lights, that in all our exercises of Reason, His gift, we may thus use it, as He would have us, in the obedience of Faith, with a view to His glory, with an aim at His Truth, in dutiful submission to His will, for the comfort of His elect, for the edification of Holy Jerusalem, His Church, and in recollection of His own solemn warning, " Every idle word that men shall speak, they shall give account thereof in the day of judgment; for by thy words thou shalt be justified, and by thy words thou shalt be condemned."

THE END.